IS IT SAFE?

PROTECTING YOUR COMPUTER, YOUR BUSINESS, AND YOURSELF ONLINE

Michael Miller

800 East 96th Street, Indianapolis, Indiana 46240 USA

Is It Safe? Protecting Your Computer, Your Business, and Yourself Online

Copyright © 2008 by Que Publishing

All rights reserved. No part of this book shall be reproduced, stored in a retrieval system, or transmitted by any means, electronic, mechanical, photocopying, recording, or otherwise, without written permission from the publisher. No patent liability is assumed with respect to the use of the information contained herein. Although every precaution has been taken in the preparation of this book, the publisher and author assume no responsibility for errors or omissions. Nor is any liability assumed for damages resulting from the use of the information contained herein.

ISBN-13: 978-0-7897-3782-3
ISBN-10: 0-7897-3782-5

Library of Congress Cataloging-in-Publication Data:

Miller, Michael, 1958-

    Is it safe : protecting your computer, your business, and yourself

online / Michael Miller.

        p. cm.

    ISBN-13: 978-0-7897-3782-3

    ISBN-10: 0-7897-3782-5

    1. Computer security. 2. Computer networks--Security measures. I.

Title.

    QA76.9.A25M5822 2008

    005.8--dc22

2008019947

Printed in the United States of America

First Printing: June 2008

Trademarks

All terms mentioned in this book that are known to be trademarks or service marks have been appropriately capitalized. Que Publishing cannot attest to the accuracy of this information. Use of a term in this book should not be regarded as affecting the validity of any trademark or service mark.

Warning and Disclaimer

Bulk Sales

Que Publishing offers excellent discounts on this book when ordered in quantity for bulk purchases or special sales. For more information, please contact

    U.S. Corporate and Government Sales   1-800-382-3419   corpsales@pearsontechgroup.com
For sales outside of the U.S., please contact   International Sales   international@pearson.com

This Book Is Safari Enabled

 The Safari® Enabled icon on the cover of your favorite technology book means the book is available through Safari Bookshelf. When you buy this book, you get free access to the online edition for 45 days.

Safari Bookshelf is an electronic reference library that lets you easily search thousands of technical books, find code samples, download chapters, and access technical information whenever and wherever you need it.

To gain 45-day Safari Enabled access to this book:

- Go to http://www.informit.com/onlineedition
- Complete the brief registration form
- Enter the coupon code WLFU-SXQG-LBIB-RAGH-WCS2

If you have difficulty registering on Safari Bookshelf or accessing the online edition, please email customer-service@safaribooksonline.com.

Associate Publisher
Greg Wiegand

Acquisitions Editor
Rick Kughen

Development Editor
Rick Kughen

Managing Editor
Patrick Kanouse

Senior Project Editor
San Dee Phillips

Copy Editor
Margo Catts

Indexer
Ken Johnson

Proofreader
Molly Proue

Technical Editor
Karen Weinstein

Publishing Coordinator
Cindy Teeters

Cover and Interior Designer
Anne Jones

Composition
Mark Shirar

Contents at a Glance

Contents

About the Author

Michael Miller is a successful and prolific author. He is known for his casual, easy-to-read writing style and his ability to explain a wide variety of complex topics to an everyday audience.

Mr. Miller has written more than 80 nonfiction books over the past two decades, with more than a million copies in print. His books for Que include *Absolute Beginner's Guide to Computer Basics*, *How Microsoft Windows Vista Works*, *Your First Notebook PC*, *Making a Living from Your eBay Business*, and *Googlepedia: The Ultimate Google Resource*.

You can email Mr. Miller directly at safe@molehillgroup.com. His website is located at www.molehillgroup.com.

Dedication

To Sherry. Of course it's safe.

Acknowledgments

Thanks to the usual suspects at Que, including but not limited to Greg Wiegand, Rick Kughen, San Dee Phillips, Margo Catts, Mark Shirar, and technical editor Karen Weinstein.

We Want to Hear from You!

As the reader of this book, you are our most important critic and commentator. We value your opinion and want to know what we're doing right, what we could do better, what areas you'd like to see us publish in, and any other words of wisdom you're willing to pass our way.

As an associate publisher for Que Publishing, I welcome your comments. You can email or write me directly to let me know what you did or didn't like about this book—as well as what we can do to make our books better.

Please note that I cannot help you with technical problems related to the topic of this book. We do have a User Services group, however, where I will forward specific technical questions related to the book.

When you write, please be sure to include this book's title and author as well as your name, email address, and phone number. I will carefully review your comments and share them with the author and editors who worked on the book.

Email: feedback@quepublishing.com

Mail: Greg Wiegand
       Associate Publisher
       Que Publishing
       800 East 96th Street
       Indianapolis, IN 46240 USA

Reader Services

Visit our website and register this book at informit.com/register for convenient access to any updates, downloads, or errata that might be available for this book.

Introduction

Is it safe?

You listen a lot to talk radio, and have been hearing ads for services that promise to protect you from the threat of identity theft. You're pretty sure that a friend of a friend had her identity stolen a while back, and you're worried that someone could steal your Social Security number, bank account information, and other important data.

Is it safe?

Your company deals with a large customer base via its website. Behind the scenes, you have several key databases that store both customer and employee information. You've been reading about a rash of data thefts at similar companies, and your company's management team wants to know what you're doing to address threats to your electronic data.

Is it safe?

It's holiday time, and you've been doing your shopping online. You've found some great deals at a number of online retailers, and even identified some eBay auction items that would make great gifts. But you're concerned about giving out your credit card number online, and not sure how you feel about the whole online auction thing.

Is it safe?

You receive a ton of email messages every day. Some are legitimate messages from friends and colleagues, but a lot of it is unwanted spam. And then there's this one message, from someone promising that he can reduce your credit card debt, or maybe guaranteeing you a high-paying income from a work-from-home business. You're interested in these offers, but are concerned about their legitimacy.

Is it safe?

Last week you watched one of those "To Catch a Predator" shows, where a middle-aged pervert was entrapped trying to arrange a tryst with an underaged computer user. And just yesterday, your local paper ran an article about sex offenders preying on children via MySpace and Facebook. You want your children to benefit from the Internet, and use it to communicate with their friends, but you're worried about cyberstalkers and online predators.

Is it safe?

Your computer hasn't been acting right lately. Someone at work thinks you might have a computer virus, or maybe your teenaged son has downloaded some spyware while downloading MP3 files. You're worried about all the nasty technological gunk that can infest your computer, especially given the websites your kids visit.

Is it safe?

A few days ago you had trouble getting to one of your favorite websites; the whole site was out of commission for several hours. One of your friends thinks the site may have the victim of an attack by computer hackers; in fact, you're worried about your own computer being attacked, especially now that you have a broadband Internet connection and wireless home network.

Is it safe?

There are lots of potential threats on the Internet, ranging from spam and email scams to computer attack and identity theft. With so many threats out there, it's easy to get paranoid about what can happen to you, your computer, your family, and your business when you go online. It's natural to think about all these potential risks and wonder to yourself, is it safe?

That's why I've written this book—*Is It Safe? Protecting Your Computer, Your Business, and Yourself Online*. I wanted to evaluate all the potential threats, let you know which ones you should and shouldn't worry about, and show you ways to minimize your risk. The Internet, after all, needn't be a scary place.

And here's the good news: For most threats, the risk is much lower than you might think. For example, despite all the sensational stories about online predators and sex offenders, the actual risk is not only low, it's lower than it used to be. And even though you hear a lot about online credit card theft, you stand a greater chance of having your credit card stolen in a local restaurant than you do on the Internet.

That's not to say, however, that your risk for any of these things is zero. Any given computer user can be a victim of any of these threats; the Internet is not and will never be 100% safe.

For that reason, you need to know what the threats are, what your individual risk is for each threat, and how to deal with the issue should you fall victim. The risk of something happening might be low, but if you're a victim, it's a major problem.

So when it comes to identity theft or email fraud or spyware or computer hackers, is it safe? The answer is, it all depends—but you can definitely make it safer. That's what this book is about.

How This Book Is Organized

With so many different threats floating about the Internet, it's easy to get overwhelmed. Don't worry; I've tried to simplify things for you, by organizing the threats into seven major categories:

- Part I, "Protecting Against Identity Theft," deals with one of the scariest threats on the Internet—having your personal identity stolen and used for criminal purposes. In this section, you'll learn about how big the risk is, how to keep your personal information personal, and what to do if you fall victim to identity theft.

- Part II, "Protecting Against Data Theft," looks at the cause of much of today's identity theft—large-scale data theft from big companies and organizations. How does a company protect its customer and employee data—and what should it do if those records are stolen? That's what we cover here.

- Part III, "Protecting Against Online Fraud," examines online shopping and auction fraud. How safe is it to buy something online—and how can you make it safer? And what about the issue of advertising click fraud—how does that affect you?

- Part IV, "Protecting Against Email Scams and Spam," looks at the many different ways consumers can be fleeced via email. It's all about avoiding con artists who promise something that sounds too good to be true—because it is. And, while we're on the topic of email, we'll examine the issue of email spam—and what you can do to reduce it.

- Part V, "Protecting Against Online Surveillance," discusses the various ways that people and organizations can spy on you online. We cover everything from cyberstalkers and online predators to how your employer and the U.S. government are keeping tabs on everything you do online—whether you like it or not.

- Part VI, "Protecting Against Computer Viruses and Spyware," examines two of the oldest and most significant scourges of computer users everywhere. You'll learn how viruses and spyware work, as well as what you can do to protect against them.

- Part VII, "Protecting Against Computer Hacks and Attacks," looks at what hackers do online—to home networks, large corporate networks, and websites. Did you know that a hacker can break into your home network and hijack your computer for use in a larger Internet attack, or to send thousands of spam messages? Obviously, we also discuss how you can protect your computer from attack, including the use of firewall software.

Taken together, the 25 chapters in this book cover just about any threat you can think of to the security of your home or work computer. I try not to sensationalize the threat; in fact, I go out of my way to put every threat in perspective. But I want you to know exactly what it is that you're up against, so that you can work to minimize your risk.

Conventions Used in This Book

I hope that this book is easy enough to figure out on its own, without requiring its own instruction manual. As you read through the pages, however, it helps to know precisely how I've presented specific types of information.

Web Page Addresses

There are a lot of Web page addresses in this book. They're noted as such:

www.molehillgroup.com

Technically, a web page address is supposed to start with http:// (as in http://www.molehillgroup.com). Because Internet Explorer and other web browsers automatically insert this piece of the address, however, you don't have to type it—and I haven't included it in any of the addresses in this book.

Software and Services

I also list a lot of software programs, website services, and the like to help you protect against specific threats. Know, however, that companies are constantly changing prices, coming out with new versions, introducing completely new products, and discontinuing older ones. With that in mind, every product and URL listed in this book is valid as of Spring 2008; chances are, however, that something will have changed by the time you read the book.

Special Elements

This book includes four special elements that provide additional information not included in the basic text. These elements are designed to supplement the text to make it your learning faster, easier, and more efficient.

> > > **N O T E**

A note is designed to provide information that is generally useful but not specifically necessary for what you're doing at the moment.

< < < **T I P**

A tip offers additional advice that might prove useful to the task at hand.

CAUTION!!!

A caution warns you of a particular situation—be alert to the warning!

{PERSONAL EXPERIENCE}

Personal experiences recall my own personal experience with the topic at hand, or a personal recommendation regarding the topic.

Let Me Know What You Think

I always love to hear from readers. If you want to contact me, feel free to email me at safe@molehillgroup.com. I can't promise that I'll answer every message, but I do promise that I'll read each one!

If you want to learn more about me and any new books I have cooking, check out my Molehill Group website at www.molehillgroup.com. Who knows—you might find some other books there that you'd like to read.

Identity Theft: How Big a Problem?

Your identity is important to you. It not only defines who you are, personally, but it distinguishes you to all the different organizations, businesses, and authorities with which you deal on an everyday basis. Lose your identity, and you become invisible to society. Even worse, if someone else steals your identity, he becomes you—and gains access to everything you own and have access to.

Having one's identity stolen is a serious concern, especially in this age of Internet shopping, banking, and transaction tracking. When you're dealing with any online entity, no one knows your friendly face; you're identified only by a series of numbers. If an identity thief steals your identifying numbers, he can masquerade as you online, without anyone knowing.

Thus we have our introduction to the first major topic of this book—identity theft. What exactly is identity theft and how big a concern is it? Those are the questions answered in this chapter.

Who Are You?

"I am not a number—I am a free man!"

Despite the protests of Patrick McGoohan's character Number Six (from the television series *The Prisoner*), all of us today are numbers—or at least are identified by numbers. To your credit card company, you are the series of numbers embossed on a plastic card. To your bank, you are a multi-digit account number. To your mortgage company, you are the numbers assigned to your home loan. And to the government, you are the Social Security number given to you at birth.

You know how important numbers are. When you call to check on your credit card balance or look into an account irregularity, the first thing you're asked for is your account number, not your name. Yes, your name is associated with the number—and, in a pinch, the account rep can try to look up your account by name—but the number is actually a better form of identification. Think about it: A 10- or 12-digit number is unique, whereas any number of individuals can have the name "John Smith" or "Martha Brown." There's no confusing you for another customer when using a unique multi-digit number; there is the chance that you could be confused with another customer who shares the same first and last name.

{PERSONAL EXPERIENCE}

I recently sold one house and bought another. In both transactions, the powers that be found legal transactions on the books for people named "Michael Miller" that could have interfered with the selling/purchasing process. The fact that no other "Michael Miller" was me exemplifies why identification by name is not as accurate as identification by number.

This identification by number is more common today than it was in the past. There was a time, believe it or not, when you could walk into your local bank and be recognized by face, no official identification necessary. Not so today, of course; even the friendliest bank teller is required by her bosses to ask for one or more pieces of identification (all numeric-based, of course) before you can cash a check or withdraw funds. It's a safety feature of our litigious society; every transaction must be checked and double-checked, just in case.

More important is the fact that more and more transactions are taking place over the Internet. When you're not there in person, the only way to identify you is by number. So you access a website and are prompted by your username or account number or card number or Social Security number or whatever; that's how you're known to the websites' computers. Again, that number eventually ties into your name, but the website uses your number, not your name, for that initial identification.

So what pieces of data form your identity? Here's a short list of the important numbers by which various businesses and organizations know you:

- Social Security number, used by the government and various financial institutions
- Driver's license number, used by insurance companies, utility companies, video rental stores, and other institutions
- Credit card number, often the same as your credit card account number, used by your credit card company
- Account number, used by the issuing institution—insurance companies, credit card companies, financial institutions, and the like
- Personal identification number (PIN), used to access your bank accounts from ATM machines

- Username and password, used to access just about every website on the Internet
- Date of birth, used by virtually every business, financial institution, and government entity, as well as many general-interest websites (to establish legal authority to view or access certain types of information, among other things)

> > > **NOTE**

In addition, you have the passwords associated with many of these numbers. For example, you may not be able to access your online banking account with just your account number; you may also be prompted to enter a numeric PIN or alpha-numeric password.

All these numbers are important, which you would know if you ever forgot or lost any of them—or had them stolen. Just try to access credit card or loan information without your account number, or to establish a new account of any type without your date of birth or driver's license number or even your Social Security number. You are nothing without your identification, and your identification is increasingly numerical.

What Is Identity Theft?

Imagine a stranger impersonating you. Depending on the stranger's intent and resolve, he could engage in anything from minor mischief (ordering an unwanted pizza delivered to your address, looking at your past order info on Amazon.com, putting a hold on your mail delivery) to major mayhem (withdrawing funds from your bank account, charging a big purchase to your credit card, filing for bankruptcy in your name). Seem unlikely? Perhaps. But it is possible—and all it takes is the appropriation of a few little numbers.

When someone steals your personal identifying information—whether that be your credit card number, Social Security number, or ATM PIN—that constitutes the crime known as *identity theft*. This phrase is a catch-all term for any crime, no matter how minor, involving the illegal use of your individual identity in any form.

> > > **NOTE**

Identity theft is, more accurately, fraud rather than theft. Even though your identity is stolen, that information is used for fraudulent activities. Hence the more proper designation as *identity fraud*.

Identity theft can be result of online negligence (responding to phishing emails or being the victim of a computer virus) or real-world theft (having your wallet stolen or credit card statements pilfered from your trash). However it's accomplished, the identity thief obtains one or more of your valuable numbers, and then uses those numbers to access things that are yours—typically, your money.

That's not to say that all identity theft crimes are financial in nature. Stolen Social Security numbers are often used by illegal immigrants to establish an official presence or obtain work;

terrorists have been known to use stolen account and driver's license numbers to create false identities in a new community. In addition, identity theft can be used as a means of blackmail (the victim is forced to pay a ransom to avoid some form of embarrassment, or to retrieve his stolen information), and in industrial espionage (to "fake" entrance into secure systems).

Although there are many different types of identity theft, experts tend to organize them into four major categories: financial ID theft, criminal ID theft, identity cloning, and business/commercial ID theft. We look at each category in its turn.

Financial Identity Theft

Financial identity theft is the type of ID theft that garners the most headlines. In a nutshell, it's the act of using another person's identity to fraudulently obtain money, goods, or services.

This type of ID theft can take many forms, but typically is the result of stolen credit card or bank account numbers. As soon as the thief is in possession of these identifying numbers, he can access your bank account or charge purchases to your credit card. In other words, the ID thief gets to spend your money.

Here are some common forms of financial identity theft:

- Stolen credit card information is used to charge large purchases to the victim's charge account, typically online (where other methods of identification, such as picture ID, are not used).

- Stolen bank account information is used to empty the victim's checking or savings account.

- Stolen personal checks are used to pay for goods and services at local establishments.

- Stolen Social Security number and other personal information is used by the criminal to obtain a loan in the victim's name; the criminal absconds with the loaned funds while the victim is held accountable for the loan amount (on which he typically defaults, thus hurting his credit rating).

Let's walk through a few examples.

The most common form of financial identity theft happens when your credit card number is stolen—typically via a physically stolen credit card. As soon as the thief has your credit card number, he either jumps online or starts dialing up various mail order merchants. His goal is typically big-purchase items, such as flat screen TVs, home theater systems, digital cameras, personal computer systems, and such. He keeps dialing or surfing and ordering, charging multiple purchases to your card but having those purchases shipped to his address. The charging continues until your card is maxed out or until your credit card company gets a whiff of something wrong; a bunch of large purchases typically flag the company as unusual purchase behavior, and the account may be frozen until the company contacts you for verification. In any case, the thief has already done his damage and is ready to move onto his next victim.

A less common but more harmful crime involves the theft of your Social Security number, most commonly pilfered by someone working at a firm that deals in secure information—your doctor's office, for example, or your insurance company. This is typically a multiple-person scam; a low-level operative is used to obtain the ID numbers, while a higher-level associate performs the more complex fraudulent activity. And the activity is complex; the goal here is a much larger fraud than can be accomplished with a mere credit card number. The high-level associate takes your Social Security number with him to a nearby bank office, along with other necessary forged documents, and uses it as a basis to open a new checking or savings account. This accomplished, the scammer returns to the bank and again uses your SSN, this time to apply for a loan—and not a small one. If everything checks out, the thief gets a big check from the bank's loan officer and is never heard from again. You find out about the fraud when either the bank or the bank's collection agency knocks on your door, or when you apply for your next loan—and find your credit rating trashed.

Criminal Identity Theft

As you can see, not all financial identity theft is online related, nor is all online ID theft financial in nature. This leads to the next form of ID theft, so-called criminal identity theft, where the criminal or terrorist uses stolen personal information to create a false identity. This false identity is then used in the commission of a crime or terrorist act.

A false ID can be used to reserve a hotel room, obtain an apartment, apply for a job, and other aspects of daily life. With the right false ID, a criminal or terrorist can seamlessly blend into the fabric of a community, becoming, in the eyes of the community, the person behind the stolen ID.

By establishing a false ID, the criminal or terrorist is free to go about his surreptitious assignment without fear of being discovered. The law might be looking for John Smith, so John Smith becomes Harry Brown; because the law isn't looking for Harry Brown, Mr. Smith/Brown can operate freely.

The false ID is also useful if the criminal or terrorist is ever noticed by authorities. Let's say that John Smith is pulled over for a minor traffic violation. If he presented ID with his real name, Mr. Smith would likely be hauled in on prior charges. By presenting fake ID under the name of Harry Brown, however, Mr. Smith skates free with the authorities being none the wiser. (The same holds true if Mr. Smith is ever arrested; the system doesn't tie the Brown ID to the Smith who is no doubt on any number of watch lists.)

This is no good for the real Harry Brown, however. If Mr. Smith is apprehended for a crime in his Harry Brown persona, it's the real Harry Brown the authorities will be looking for when Smith skips on bail. Imagine the real Harry Brown waking up to a not-so-friendly knock on his door from the local police, or discovering that his driver's license has been suspended or that there's a warrant out for his arrest. And, as you might suspect, this sort of incorrect charge is hard to expunge from the various data systems in use across the country, affecting Mr. Brown in numerous background checks in years to come.

Identity Cloning

Identity cloning is similar to criminal ID theft, but without the overt criminal nature. With ID cloning, the thief uses stolen personal information to assume the victim's identity in daily life. By impersonating the victim, the criminal is able to hide from authorities.

This type of ID theft takes many forms, but one that's increasingly common involves the stealing of online identities. The rise of social networks (Facebook, MySpace, and so on) and online virtual worlds has created a fertile new field for identity thieves. Take Facebook, for example. You work long and hard to build your Facebook network; imagine your surprise when you log on one morning and find that someone else has been making posts and comments under your name. Now, this may seem to be a minor annoyance, but a thief posing as you with a stolen ID can do ruin to your hard-earned Facebook reputation and alienate all your online friends. Your online friends have no way of knowing that they've just been insulted by a fake, not by the real you.

> > > **NOTE**

In addition, most Facebook users include a lot of personal information about themselves on their pages, including birth date, location, and the like. This information can be used to fill in the details in a larger ID theft scheme.

It's even worse if you're a well-known personality and find someone else using your name to make fake pronouncements, as happened in early 2008 to Prince Moulay Rachid, the younger brother of the King of Morocco. It seems that one Fouad Mourtada had created a Facebook page under the Prince's name, and used it to issue fake royal pronouncements. (The Moroccan royal family does not maintain any websites or blogs.) Mourtada was subsequently arrested and charged with "villainous practices," but not until after the damage was done.

Identity cloning is also commonly used by illegal immigrants—or by those sponsoring their stays in the U.S. In this instance, there is seldom intent to use the stolen ID to commit crimes; instead the impersonator merely needs the new identity to obtain work, housing, and the like. Still, it's a shocker to wake up and find that an illegal immigrant has been using your identity.

Business/Commercial Identity Theft

The final form of ID theft is business/commercial identity theft—that is, using information from another business to obtain credit for your business. This typically takes the form of loan fraud, where an individual or another business uses your company's ID to obtain their own loan or line of credit.

For example, the Regional Center for Border Health Inc., a walk-in health clinic in San Luis, Arizona, had its business identity compromised in 2006. An ID thief somehow obtained the routing number for the clinic's bank account, then went online and used the clinic's funds to pay various personal bills. Over $6,000 in funds went missing before the scam was discovered.

Although this is a less common crime than the personal forms of ID theft, it's still somewhat of a problem, especially for smaller businesses.

> > > N O T E

> Commercial identity theft is often a form of corporate data theft. Learn more in Chapter 4, "Data Theft: How Big a Problem?"

How Big Is the Identity Theft Problem?

Now you know the various forms that identity theft can take. The real question is, Is it worth worrying about? How big is the problem, really?

The answer is that the problem is big, but not so big as to be paranoid about it. Yes, it's possible that you could become a victim of identity theft, but the odds of it happening aren't as serious as alarmist news reports might have you believe.

The statistics are thus. The Federal Trade Commission (FTC) estimates that somewhere around 9 million Americans have their identities stolen each year. (The Gartner Group puts that number at 15 million, but I'll go with the government on this one.) That sounds like a big number, but it's less than 3% of the total U.S. population. It wouldn't be pleasant to be among that unfortunate 3%, but it's unlikely that you'll end up in that number.

It should also be noted that these "identity theft" numbers are heavily weighted in favor of simple credit card theft. If you dig deep into the details of the FTC's Identity Theft Clearinghouse, you find that the number of people in any given year who actually report that their identities are stolen is under 200,000. The remaining millions of victims simply had their credit cards stolen.

Based on these numbers, it might surprise you to hear authorities and experts refer to identity theft as an "epidemic." That's because the press likes to sensationalize these things to boost ratings and circulation; in addition, companies who sell ID theft research and solutions also have a financial stake in making things look worse than they actually are. So we need to be realistic about the problem; identity theft is not influenza, by any stretch of the imagination, even if it is a serious issue.

Although identity theft might not truly be an epidemic, it has been one of the fastest-growing crimes in the country. According to Harris Interactive, the incidence of identity theft increased 20% between 2001 and 2002, and 80% between 2002 and 2003. That said, it appears that 2003 was a peak year for the crime; more recent studies indicate a decrease in the total number of victims. The 2007 Identity Fraud Survey Report from Javelin Strategy and Research reports that the number of identity fraud victims in the U.S. decreased from 10.1 million in 2003 to 8.4 million in 2007. (This jibes with the FTC's rough 9 million number.)

The cost of identity theft is also decreasing. Whereas the average fraud per victim increased from $5,316 in 2003 to $6,278 in 2006, the numbers decreased in 2007, to $5,720.

> > > **N O T E**

This decrease in both the incidence and severity of identity theft appears to be due to increased awareness and diligence from the general public and the business community. People are more aware of the problem and are taking steps to confront the threat.

In other words, identity theft is a moderate problem, but one that's decreasing in both occurrence and severity. That's good news.

Of course, individuals aren't the only victims of identity theft; businesses also have to shoulder their share of the losses. Although estimates of damages vary, one study reports that identity theft costs U.S. businesses more than $50 billion each year.

> > > **N O T E**

Identity theft is not unique to the United States. In the United Kingdom, ID fraud costs the economy 1.7 billion pounds each year; in Australia, the costs are more than 1 billion Australian dollars per year.

There is also the cost, in terms of time, in repairing the damage of identity theft. The Identity Theft Resource Center conducted a series of Aftermath Studies in 2004 and determined that ID theft victims spent an average of 330 hours recovering from the crime. The recovery activity is typically spread over a period from four to six months—that is, it takes a long time to sort everything out. In fact, 11% of victims reported that they had been dealing with their cases for up to a year.

> > > **N O T E**

The amount of time it takes to deal with ID theft varies considerably from one victim to the next. Obviously, a simple stolen credit card number takes less time to rectify than having one's Social Security number stolen.

Not all the costs of ID theft are immediate. Even after a thief stops using the stolen information (which is often within a few days of the theft, especially with stolen credit cards), victims must struggle with the long-term impact of the theft. This may take the form of increased interest rates or insurance fees, a lowered credit rating, calls from collection agencies, even an inability to obtain future credit or find a new job.

The combination of short-term and long-term impact also exerts an emotional toll on victims. Experts report that the emotional impact of identity theft is similar to that felt by victims of violent crime. Victims typically report that they feel embarrassed, ashamed, and dirty; not only do they feel duped, but they've had their personal lives invaded by a stranger. This typically leads to increased stress, often in the victim's family life and personal relationships. A sobering fact: 9% of ID theft victims reported that their relationship with their spouse or partner was "on the rocks" or had ended as a result of the victimization.

Who Is Most Vulnerable to Identity Theft?

Who are the 9 million or so victims each year of identity theft? Although victims can be found from all areas and from all walks of life, the reality is that some groups are more prone to theft and scams than are others.

The elderly are particularly vulnerable to ID theft, typically in the form of both email and phone-based scams. They're more likely to respond to phishing emails, not having the built-in wariness of the young; if it looks like an official communication, it must be an official communi-cation—and it must be responded to. The same thing with phone scams; it's all too easy for a scammer to pose as a representative from their insurance company or doctor's office, ask for account numbers and other personal information, and then be given said information. It's sad, but true.

Also vulnerable are the young and naïve—including college students and recent graduates. Like the elderly, those less experienced in the ways of the world tend to trust authority—including scammers representing themselves as official representatives of a trusted organiza-tion. It takes time and experience for youth to realize that people are not always who they say they are.

Beyond that, know that many ID theft victims have some sort of previous relationship with their thieves. The Identity Theft Resource Center reports that 43% of victims believed they knew their imposter; 14% said the thief was an employee of a business who had their information.

Nationally, some regions are more prone to theft than others. Most studies report that the top states in terms of victims per capita include New York, California, Nevada (particularly Las Vegas, not surprisingly), Arizona (because of its concentration of older citizens), Washington, and Texas. The 2006 FTC report adds Florida, Georgia, and Colorado to that list, and a 2007 ID Analytics study also includes Illinois, Michigan, Oregon, and Hawaii.

The bottom line is that anyone can be a victim of identity theft—although your odds of being a victim increase as you get older.

How Do Identity Thieves Steal Your Personal Information?

Why is identity theft such a big problem? It's simple: For the ID thief, it's a relatively low-risk, high-reward endeavor. It's certainly not as dangerous as holding up a bank or breaking into an apartment; the thief never sees his victims in person, so there's no chance they'll fight back. This lack of personal confrontation contributes to the low chance of the thief ever being found out, let alone caught and brought to justice. In fact, many credit card issuers don't even prosecute those few thieves that are caught, figuring that it's less costly to write off a loss than it is to finance a court trial. In addition, it's very difficult to prosecute ID criminals outside the U.S.—where most of these thieves reside.

After the ID thief has your personal information, the rest is easy. A simple credit card number is often all it takes to order reams of expensive merchandise over the Internet. If the thief has your bank account data, he can quickly empty your accounts of any and all cash. And if it's your Social Security number that's been compromised, all manner of activities can result—up to and including establishing a completely new identity in your name, complete with job application and apartment rental.

It's this more comprehensive form of ID theft that is particularly scary. With one piece of information, the thief can apply for credit, providing a new address of her own, claiming that she (you) has moved. After the first account is opened, it can be used to open additional accounts. The more fraudulent activity that results, the more credibility the thief has; over the course of a few weeks or months, the thief can rake in some big bucks, in the process totally destroying your credit and reputation.

So how does a thief obtain your personal information? There are any number of ways—both online and offline.

Stealing Information Online

There are a number of high-tech ways to steal personal information, all facilitated by the fact that Internet communications travel over a public network. A tech-savvy ID thief can obtain access to your data by any one of several methods.

Phishing Scams

A phishing email is one that purports to be from a real website or institution; the communication looks quite official, often using the official logo of the original firm. What's fishy about the phishing email is that it asks for some sort of interaction with the recipient, most often directing you to the host website via an embedded link in the email itself.

When the recipient clicks the link to go to the referenced website, however, it's not the real website. Instead, the scammer has created a clever forgery of the referenced site; it looks like the original, but instead is hosted by the scammer. If the recipient proceeds to enter a password or personal information, that information is passed directly to the ID thief—and then used for various fraudulent activities.

> > > **N O T E**

Learn more about phishing scams in Chapter 11, "Avoiding Email Fraud and Phishing Scams."

Email Interception

That's right, it's possible for a tech-savvy scammer to intercept your private emails—including those that contain personal information. This can be done at either end of the communication, or at the ISP's incoming or outgoing mail servers.

The most common weak links in the transmission chain, however, are the email monitoring programs used by many corporations and organizations, ostensibly to keep unwanted messages from clogging their email systems. These same programs can be used to grab messages sent to or from employees, including those containing credit card numbers and other personal information.

Wi-Fi Data Sniffing

If you have a notebook PC, you've probably done some work at a public Wi-Fi hotspot. If so, know that every bit of data you receive from the Internet or send via email can be intercepted, by thieves using special "sniffer" programs. These programs enable the thief to eavesdrop on all your incoming and outgoing communications, see all the websites you visit, and intercept any form data you send to those websites. That means if you order something from an online retailer while at a public hotspot, your ordering info (including your credit card number) can be picked off by the Wi-Fi-sniffing thief.

The only sure-fire way to protect your data on a public hot spot is to log on to encrypted sites—those that start with **https:** instead of **http:**. (For example, most online shopping checkout pages are encrypted, as are most online banking sites.) Unencrypted data, however, can be intercepted.

Alternately, you can use a virtual private network (VPN) for all your public browsing. A VPN establishes a secured private network across the public Wi-Fi network by creating a "tunnel" between the two endpoints. The data sent through the tunnel (web page addresses, email, etc.) is encrypted so other users can't intercept it. For example, JiWire Hotspot Helper is one such VPN; it costs $24.95/year to use, and you can download the appropriate software from www.jiwire.com/hotspot-helper.htm.

Surreptitious Spyware

Another way for a tech-savvy ID thief to pilfer your personal data is to install a Trojan horse-type computer virus or spyware program on your computer—without your knowledge, of course. This type of malicious software sits in the background, monitoring everything your computer does. When it finds something interesting, it goes online and transmits that data to the ID thief over the Internet.

> > > **N O T E**

Learn more about spyware programs in Chapter 19, "Computer Viruses and Spyware: How Big a Problem?"

How does your computer get infected with data-stealing malware? There are a number of ways—you can unwittingly download infected programs from the Internet, click on links to the malware sent to you via email (but labeled as something different, of course), and especially by downloading unknown files from various file sharing sites. You can protect against malicious software by running both anti-virus and anti-spyware programs on your PC, but the effort does require some diligence.

Physical Theft

The old ways are still the best—as far as thieves are concerned, anyway. We're talking about old-fashioned theft, of a person's wallet or purse. And when a thief steals a wallet or purse, he also steals the victim's credit cards, driver's license, and the like. It's much easier than trying to sniff out information online, and the thief gets a bigger haul for his efforts. On the downside (for the thief), when you have your wallet or purse stolen, you immediately know it—and can then put a hold on all the affected accounts.

Observation and Eavesdropping

This is another oldie but goodie—in which the thief simply keeps his eyes and ears open. The thief may overhear you giving your credit card number over your cell phone in a public place, observe the number on your credit card as it lies on the table waiting for the waiter at a nice restaurant, or even copy the credit card numbers from an openly visible receipt in a retail store. Not surprisingly, this method is typically used by store employees to steal credit card numbers from the store's customers.

CAUTION!!!

In addition, you should beware of entering any personal information on your computer or mobile phone while you're out in public. Many thieves like to "shoulder surf"—that is, look over your shoulder as you enter your credit card information, Social Security number, or whatever. (This is also an issue when entering your PIN at a public ATM.)

Inside Information

This approach requires a "plant" inside an office that handles lots of sensitive information. That might be an assistant in a doctor's office, a part-time employee in a hospital, a clerk in an insurance company, or something similar. The insider either takes the job with the intent of stealing all available data or is co-opted at a later date; he typically receives some sort of flat fee for his efforts.

The bad thing about this approach, from the victim's perspective, is that large volumes of data can be stolen over a relatively brief period of time. It's not just one or two people who are affected; it's hundreds or thousands who have their information stolen.

Dumpster Diving

You'd be surprised how common this method really is. As the name implies, the thief (or a lower-level accomplice) rifles through a business' or household's trash, looking for discarded records, receipts, and account statements. As most individuals and many businesses don't shred their paperwork, there is much valuable data here for the taking—as long as the thief doesn't mind getting his hands a little dirty.

Mailbox Theft

This is a less-grimy version of dumpster diving, taking place earlier in the data chain. In this method, the thief steals incoming or outgoing mail from a household or business' public mailbox, including credit card and bank account statements. (The thief can also steal checks that accompany utility payments and such.)

> > > **N O T E**

> According to the United States Postal Service, 2% of identity theft victims report that the theft of their identity was somehow mail-related.

Address Hijacking

This one is almost too easy. With this method, the thief doesn't have to steal anything from you; all he does is fill in a change of address form at your post office. He gives his own address as the new address so that all future credit card invoices and bank statements come to him, not you. He can then purloin your personal info from these invoices and statements, and you never know what's happening—until you realize you haven't received any mail for a few weeks!

Recovering Computer Data

What do you do with an old PC when you're done with it? If you're like most users, you may toss it in the trash, donate to a school or charity, or maybe (if you're environmentally minded) take it to a recycling center for electronics. Doing any of these things, however, puts your old personal data at risk—even if you think you've deleted it.

It doesn't take much imagination to envision ID thieves trying to recover personal data from the hard drives of discarded or recycled computers. Thieves can steal used computers from your trash or from the junkyard, or even from those charities to which you donate. They can then access the computer's hard drive and the data stored on it, even if the computer itself isn't working (by connecting the hard drive to a separate working computer).

And don't think that simply deleting personal files from the hard drive before you toss the computer will do the trick. Your computer's "delete" operation doesn't actually delete the data;

it merely erases the pointer that enables your operating system to find the file. The original data is still there, capable of being accessed via data recovery software. Even if you format your hard drive, the data remains vulnerable to the tech-savvy thief.

So how do you permanently delete sensitive data files from your computer's hard drive? You have to "wipe" the data from the disk using a special data shredding program—which we'll discuss in Chapter 2, "How to Keep Your Personal Information Personal." (Alternately, you can remove the drive from the computer and physically destroy it—with a big hammer!)

Skimming

Skimming is the process of electronically tapping into a business's credit card reader to obtain card numbers. It's a high-tech way to obtain credit card numbers without having to physically steal the credit cards themselves. Like the inside information method, skimming requires the participation of an employee to attach the skimmer device to the credit card terminal or phone line.

This approach gets even higher tech when the dishonest employee uses a special device to remotely read information stored on the RFID chips found in "smart" debit and credit cards. Because RFID chips transmit their data wirelessly, the skimmer doesn't have to attach any wires or devices to intercept the card data.

Scanning

Not all wireless data theft has to be high tech. A lower-tech approach involves using an old fashioned scanner (such as a police scanner) to locate the frequencies used for cordless phone conversations. After he is dialed in, the thief can tap into nearby cordless phone conversations and write down everything he hears—including credit card numbers used to place catalog orders over the phone.

Pretexting

This is another old-fashioned approach—but one that unfortunately works. With pretexting, the thief calls up an unwitting victim on the phone, pretending to be a representative of a trusted business or organization, such as the victim's bank or insurance company or such. The thief smooth-talks his way into the victim's confidence and then asks the victim to provide personal information—for example, to give his Social Security number in the pretext of verify- ing account information. With that information in hand, the ID thief is now set to act.

A talented pretexter can con almost anyone, but this crime happens to be particularly com- mon among elderly victims, who are by nature more trusting of (seeming) authority. After all, if you get a call from someone saying they're from your bank and need you to verify your account number (perhaps because there has been suspicious activity on your account), isn't your first instinct to provide the information as requested? It's a particularly insidious crime.

Data Theft

Our last type of physical ID theft is also the one with the most impact—the large-scale theft of database information from large companies or organizations. It doesn't happen often, but when it does it's a big deal. Imagine your credit card company having a tape or hard drive full of customer data stolen, or a large online retailer having its customer records go missing. Unfortunately, both have happened, leaving tens of thousands (if not millions) of customers vulnerable to misuse of that data.

This type of ID theft is so important that it warrants a complete section in this book. Learn more by reading the chapters in Part II, "Protecting Against Data Theft."

What Happens When Your Identity Is Stolen?

So someone gets hold of your credit card number, Social Security number, bank account number, or other personal information. What happens next—what might the ID thief do with this data?

There's a long list of fraudulent activities an ID thief might engage in, including:

- Withdraw some or all of the funds in your checking account.
- Open a new bank account in your name and then write bad checks against that account.
- Create (and then pass) counterfeit checks, using your name and account number.
- Take out a bank loan in your name, for which you are then responsible for paying.
- Make unauthorized purchases against your credit card.
- Open new credit card accounts in your name—and then make purchases that you're responsible for.
- Change the billing address on your credit card so you don't see the bills they're running up—which means it will take longer for you to notice the stolen card.
- Use your ID to rent an apartment.
- Use your ID to obtain other utility services, such as electricity, gas, or cable television.
- Establish a new telephone or cell phone account in your name—and then rack up large numbers of expensive long-distance calls.
- Get a new driver's license issued in your name but with the thief's picture.
- Use your name and Social Security number to obtain government benefits.
- File a fraudulent tax return, using your information.
- Use your Social Security number to get a job (popular among illegal immigrants).
- Use your ID to obtain medical services.
- Pretend to be you online, to cause mischief on MySpace, Facebook, and other social net-

working sites.

- When captured for criminal activity, give the police your personal information—which puts your name on police records.

Any one of these activities can cost you time, money, and lots of grief. This is why you need to protect yourself against identity theft—which you'll learn to do in Chapter 2, "How to Keep Your Personal Information Personal."

> > > N O T E

Want to learn more about identity theft? Then check out the following resources online: The Identity Theft Resource Center (www.idtheftcenter.org), the FTC's Identity Theft site (www.ftc.gov/idtheft/), and the Privacy Rights Clearinghouse Identity Theft Resources page (www.privacyrights.org/identity.htm). Another good resource is Jim Stickley's book, *The Truth About Identity Theft* (Que, 2008).

Is It Safe?

So with all the hype and hysteria about identity theft, how much should you worry about the problem?

It's important to state right out front that even if the risk is low, identity theft is still a big problem for any who has their identity stolen. This isn't like somebody breaking into your car and stealing your car radio; this type of theft is the gift that keeps on giving. An identity thief might start by charging up your credit card but progress to all sorts of criminal activities, all done in your name. That's major.

That said, the risk *is* low. There is much less full-blown identity theft than the media leads you to believe. It isn't happening to everyone; in fact, it's probably never happened to anyone in your circle of friends and family.

What you're probably more personally familiar with is credit card theft, which while technically a subset of identity theft, is far less damaging. I've had my credit information stolen on a couple of occasions, as have most of my friends and family. It's a relatively common crime, yet also one in which the damage is fairly limited, thanks to precautions practiced by the credit card companies.

So is it safe to expose your personal information online? Based on the potential damages that accrue from full-blown identity theft, the answer is a definite no. Even if the risk is low, the damage is high.

You can reduce your risk, of course, by limiting the amount of personal information you disclose both online and in the physical world. Be very circumspect about what information you give out and to whom; most websites, retailers, and service firms do *not* need your Social Security number and similar private information, for example. Minimize your profile, and you minimize your risk.

How to Keep Your Personal Information Personal

You don't have to be a victim.

When it comes to protecting yourself against identity theft, there's a lot you can do. It all involves making sure that as few people as possible have access to your personal information; the less visible your info, the less likely it is to be appropriated by ID thieves. In addition, you need to be cautious about handing out your personal information, and skeptical about any person or institution who requests this information. It's a matter of keeping your information secure and keeping yourself from being conned.

To that end, this chapter examines the steps you can take to harden your defense against identity thieves—and reduce your chances of becoming a victim of ID theft.

Step One: Be Aware

Your first line of defense is one you're already working on—becoming aware of the problem. When you're aware that ID theft exists and the many ways your information can be appropriated, you're well ahead of your less-informed contemporaries. Knowing what can happen and how makes you more alert—and less likely to fall victim to the most common forms of identity fraud.

If you're not aware of the ID theft problem, you're more likely to be a victim—and not to know it. Not only will you be less cautious about revealing your information, you're also less likely to be aware if your data has been compromised. In other words, you won't even know what to look out for. Better to be a little cautious (without becoming paranoid), which comes from being informed of potential dangers.

Step Two: Keep Your Data Secure

When it comes to protecting yourself against identity theft, deterrence is one of the keys. That means taking steps to safeguard your personal information, both online and in the physical world—because, as you know, identity theft can happen anywhere and at any time.

How do you safeguard your personal information? There are many things that you can do, most of which require a liberal application of common sense. In other words, there's nothing top secret here; most of these are things you should be doing as a matter of course.

Protecting Your Computer Data

Let's start with steps to protect the information stored on your personal computer and information you access online. There are lots of little things you can do to make your data more secure.

Create a Password-Protected User Account

Every user of your computer needs to create his or her password-protected user account. How you accomplish this depends on the operating system you're using, but it's not that hard to do. With your own account created, no one can access your data and programs without logging in with the correct user name and password—which only you should know.

< < < TIP

> To create a new user account in Windows Vista, open the Control Panel, go to the User Accounts and Family Safety section, then click the Add or Remove User Accounts section. You need to assign each new account a password after it's been created.

Without a password-protected account, anyone can log on to your computer and access your files and programs. Not only does that leave your data vulnerable to prying eyes within your household, it also makes it very easy for a thief to access your data if your computer is ever stolen. Using a password-protected user account puts one more layer of protection between your data and potential thieves.

< < < T I P

If you're afraid to create a password because you might forget it and get locked out of your entire computer system, Windows offers a nice safety net in the form of a password reset disk. Create this disk ahead of time; then insert it if you ever forget your password. To create a password reset disk in Windows Vista, open the Control Panel, select User Accounts and Family Safety, select User Accounts, select your user account, and then click the Create a Password Reset Disk link.

Protect Individual Files

Even with a password-protected user account on your computer, you can go one step better and password-protect individual computer files that contain personal information. This ensures that anyone trying to open a given file has to first enter the correct password, a valuable extra layer of protection. Unfortunately, Windows does not have its own universal password protection; you have to rely on the password protection features found in individual software programs (when they exist).

Alternately, if you're using Windows Vista Business, Enterprise, or Ultimate editions (as well as Windows XP Professional), the operating system features an Encrypting File System, which lets you encrypt individual files and folders. After a file or folder has been encrypted, it can be unencrypted only when someone enters a password or uses a special key stored on a smart card.

> > > N O T E

You can also use third-party file encryption utilities to encrypt files and folders on your hard drive. Popular encryption programs include Advanced Encryption Package (www.secureaction.com), File Encryption XP (www.cp-lab.com/filecrypt/), Invisible Secrets (www.invisiblesecrets.com), and PGP (www.pgp.com).

Install Anti-Virus and Anti-Spyware Programs

Because computer-based data theft is often accomplished via Trojan horse computer viruses and spyware, it's a must to protect your system against these malicious software programs. Viruses and spyware aren't the same, however, which means you need to install both anti-virus and anti-spyware programs on your computer. These utilities protect against rogue programs that may access your stored information and send it surreptitiously across the Internet to an ID thief.

> > > N O T E

Learn more about viruses and spyware in Part VI of this book, "Protecting Against Computer Viruses and Spyware."

Practice Safe Computing

You can further protect your computer from spyware and viruses by being smart about what you download and open on your computer. You should never open computer files sent to you unexpectedly or from strangers, via either email or instant messaging. In addition, never click hyperlinks sent to you via email, even if it's from someone you know; some viruses hijack other users' email programs and replicate themselves via bulk email mailings. Further, don't download programs from websites you don't know and trust—and avoid downloading programs and files from file-sharing websites, which are often rife with embedded spyware.

In other words, don't open or download anything unless you're absolutely, positively sure you know where it came from!

Install a Software Firewall

Another way to keep data from being unwittingly pulled from your computer is to block unauthorized incoming and outgoing transmissions with a firewall program. This is a program that sets up a virtual "wall" between your computer and the Internet to keep hackers from accessing your system (and its stored information) without your knowledge or approval.

Windows includes its own built-in firewall, which works okay in most instances. In addition, there are a number of third-party firewall programs that offer enhanced protection; many Internet security suites include their own firewalls, as well.

> > > **NOTE**

Learn more about firewalls in Chapter 23, "Defending Your Personal Computer from Attack."

Browse Securely

It's all too easy to send personal information over the web; if you do so cavalierly, your data could eventually end up in the hands of ID thieves. For this reason, you want to make sure you browse the web with a secure browser, such as Internet Explorer, and keep it up to date with the latest security updates.

Further, you should avoid entering personal information into web forms on sites with which you're not familiar. And, when shopping or providing personal information online, look for the "lock" icon on the browser's status bar; this ensures that information is sent and received in a secure fashion.

Create Secure Passwords

Over time, you'll end up managing a lot of your personal accounts over the web; many websites also request that you register before you can use them. Whenever possible, you should create passwords for all these online accounts. Do not leave any important account not password-protected.

When you're creating a username or password for an online account or website, do not use any common identifiers, such as your birth date or the last four digits of your Social Security number. Create as long a password as you can, using a mix of letters and numbers. Make the password as nonsensical as you can while still being able to remember it; it should not be a simple password to guess.

To make an even stronger password, you need to increase the length of the password. Remember, 8 characters is better than 6—and way better than 4. You should also use a combination of letters, numbers, and special characters (!@#$%). Avoid using real words you might find in a typical dictionary; any standard dictionary cracker can crack that password in less time than it takes you to type. Also, don't use easily guessed words, such as your middle name or your wife's maiden name or the name of your dog or cat. Better to use nonsense words, or random combinations or letters and numbers—anything that isn't found in a dictionary.

One approach to creating a memorable but unguessable password is to think of a passphrase—a complete sentence or string of words that mean something to you. Then use the first letter of each word to create the password, followed by a relevant number. For example, you may think of the passphrase "my dog spot is 3 years old." Take the first letter of each word and you get the password **mdsi3yo**; add Spot's birth year and you get **mdsi3yo2005**. Not very easy to guess, but not impossible to remember, either.

Most important, you should remember that your password should never be shared—with anyone. As blatantly obvious as that sounds, many people feel no compunction about providing others with their passwords, for whatever reason. This is a huge security risk; your password is yours and yours alone, and should never be shared or compromised.

> > > **N O T E**

The practice of gaining access to passwords by gaining the trust of the user is called *social engineering*. This may take the form of a phone call or email from someone purporting to be from your ISP or your company's IT department, asking you to confirm your user ID and password. When you reply, the budding social engineer on the other end of the line now has the information he needs to directly access your computer. For this reason, you should *never* give out your password, no matter how official-sounding the request.

Minimize Your Notebook Risk

One of the most common sources of stolen data is notebook theft; when a thief steals a notebook PC, he also steals all the data stored on the notebook's hard drive. For that reason, if you own a notebook PC, you should store as little personal and financial information as possible on it; delete all files that aren't absolutely necessary to take with you. And don't forget to create a password-protected user account for yourself on the notebook—and, if possible, encrypt the data on the notebook's hard drive.

> > > **N O T E**

Learn more about securing your notebook PC from theft in my companion book, *Your First Notebook PC* (Que, 2007).

Don't Toss It—Shred It

When it's time to dispose of an old computer, don't just toss it into the trash. You want to delete all the personal information stored on the PC's hard disk—and, as you learned in the previous chapter, your data is not completely erased when you think you've deleted it. You see, deleting a file only removes the "pointer" to that file; the bits and bytes of the data file still remain on the hard disk until they are overwritten by a newer file. A tech-savvy thief with a standard-issue data recovery program can easily restore these pointers and retrieve almost any deleted data. Bad for you.

< < < **T I P**

Formatting a disk doesn't actually delete old data, either—so don't think you're safe if you reformat the hard disk before you get rid of your computer.

The key to completely clean old files from a hard disk is to use a secure disk "wipe" utility, which overwrites and shreds the data into an unrecognizable series of 0s and 1s. The best of these data scrambling utilities include Active@ Kill Disk (www.killdisk.com), CBL Data Shredder (www.cbltech.com/data-recovery/software/data-shredder.html), Eraser (www.heidi.ie/eraser/), Master Shredder (www.secureaction.com/master-shredder/), Secure Delete (www.secure-delete.net), and WinShredder (www.anti-software.com).

Protecting Your Physical Data

What about all your personal information that exists in the physical world—receipts, statements, blank checks, even plastic credit cards? Fortunately, there's a lot you can do to protect yourself from physical ID theft. Let's take a look.

Carry Only What You Need

The less valuable information you carry around in public, the less valuable information can be stolen. You should carry in your wallet or purse only those credit and debit cards that you actually use on a regular basis. Carrying fewer cards limits the potential damage if your wallet or purse is stolen. In addition, you should never carry your Social Security card in your wallet or purse; leave it at home in a safe and secure location.

And, just in case your wallet or purse does get stolen, be prepared by keeping a list of the cards you carry in a safe place at home. You want to be able to quickly alert your credit card companies if a theft does take place; scrambling around for old statements and contact numbers only slows your response time.

Don't Give Out Your Social Security Number

Speaking of Social Security numbers, you should give out your SSN as infrequently as possible—even though you'll probably be asked for it a lot. Provide your Social Security number only to those institutions that legitimately need it, such as your employer, bank, and other financial institutions.

In most instances, your Social Security number is used for wage and tax reporting purposes, although some businesses may need it to perform a credit check—especially if you're applying for a loan, renting an apartment, or signing up for utilities. If you're unsure whether your Social Security number is really necessary, ask the firm why they need it, how it will be used, how they protect it from being stolen, and what happens if you don't give it to them.

In addition, you should never write your Social Security number on a check. Retailers and other institutions cannot, by law, require your Social Security number; if a retailer insists, ask to provide another identifier or choose to shop elsewhere.

And here's something else you might not have thought of. Find out whether your health insurance company uses your Social Security number as your policy number. (Many do.) If so, ask to use a different policy number instead.

Shred Your Paperwork—and Your Charge Cards

As repulsive as it might sound, dumpster diving is a productive way for thieves to obtain personal information. You can thwart these efforts by not putting anything valuable in your trash.

Hard to do, you say? What about all those pieces of paperwork that you throw away every single day? Simple: Buy a document shredder and use it to regularly shred all documents and paperwork that contains personal information. This includes credit card statements, purchase receipts, insurance forms, medical records, and the like—as well as all those offers for new credit cards you receive in the mail and any blank credit card checks you receive from your credit card company. If it has personal information on it, shred it.

For that matter, you should also shred or cut up all your old credit cards. Never throw out an intact credit card; when you need to discard an old or expired charge card, cut or shred it into multiple pieces, to keep thieves from reassembling the card and retrieving the card's numbers.

Opt Out of Credit Card Mailings

Think about all those unsolicited credit card offers you receive in the mail—any of which could be used to an ID thief to establish a new credit card in your name. You can thwart would-be ID thieves by opting out of offers of credit via the mail; just call 1-888-5-OPTOUT (1-888-567-8688) or visit www.optoutprescreen.com.

> > > **N O T E**

The opt-out service is operated by the major credit reporting companies.

Keep Your Personal Information Secure

If a burglar breaks into your house, you want to make it as hard as possible to find and steal your valuable documents—including your Social Security card, birth certificate, and the like. The best course of action is to keep all your personal information in a secure place in your home, ideally in a locked drawer, lockbox, or safe. Alternately, you can keep your valuable documents offsite, by renting a safe deposit box at your bank.

Don't Use Your Mailbox

Here's another one that most people don't think of. Your mailbox is accessible to you, to your postman, and to anyone who wanders up to it. Which means, of course, that any stranger can open your mailbox and steal your incoming or outgoing mail.

There's little you can do to protect your incoming mail, short of waiting by the mailbox every day for the postman to arrive. Your outgoing mail, on the other hand, is a different story.

Keep thieves from stealing the account information on all the bills you pay by not using your household mailbox. Instead, place all outgoing mail in the collection box at your local post office, which is secured against just such theft.

Pick Up Your Checks in Person

That said, there are some items you probably don't want sitting around in your mailbox after your mail has been delivered. For example, do you really want a box of blank personal checks just sitting in your mailbox, waiting for a thief to steal them away? It's much better, when you order new personal checks from your bank, to pick them up at the banking office—rather than having them sent to your home.

Hold That Mail

The less mail sitting in your mailbox, the better. For that reason, if you're going to be away from home for an extended period of time, put a hold on your mail delivery. This keeps your mail (which contains your credit card and bank statements, remember) from piling up in your publicly accessible mailbox.

> > > **N O T E**

To put a hold on your mail delivery, call 1-800-275-8777 or go to the Postal Service's website at www.usps.gov.

to call or mail your personal information.

Your response to a mailing like this should be the same as if you were called or emailed for the same information—don't provide it. That is, don't call the number listed within and most certainly do not mail the information to the address provided. Instead, look up the real phone number of the firm in question and call them directly. If it was a legitimate request, they'll be glad to take your info. If the request was a scam, you've just saved yourself a world of trouble.

Step Four: Monitor Your Situation

Finally, you have to stay on top of what's happening. If you're unfortunate enough to become a victim of ID theft, the faster you react to the situation, the less damage you'll incur—and the faster you'll get your accounts back under control.

Check Your Accounts

The worst situation is to be a victim of ID theft and not know about it for weeks or months. The longer the ID thief has to work, the more damage he can do. With time on his side, the scammer can bleed your bank accounts dry, charge your credit cards up to their limits, and use your pilfered ID to establish a completely new identity for himself. Unnoticed, ID theft becomes a larger and more unmanageable problem.

If you nip the theft in the bud, however, you can minimize the potential damage. The sooner you notice the fraudulent activity, the sooner you can shut off access to bank and credit card accounts, essentially shutting off the tap for the fraudster. With all your accounts on alert, the ID thief can't make further use of the stolen data, thus closing the case before extensive damage is done.

The key, then, is to constantly monitor all your financial accounts, as well as other places where your personal information is used. Check your bank and credit card balances online on a weekly if not daily basis, and be alert for any unknown or suspicious activity. Do not wait for your monthly statement to arrive; sign up for online account access so you can keep a constant eye on all your accounts.

Be Aware of Suspicious Activity

You should also be aware of any suspicious activity that may be caused by identity theft. In particular, be alert to the following:

- **Credit card declined**—If a store declines your credit card for an otherwise normal purchase, it's possible that your credit line has been eaten up by fraudulent purchases.

- **Credit denied**—If you sign up for a new credit card or apply for a loan and find that your application is denied, it could be because your credit has been trashed by an ID thief.

- **Unexpected bills**—If you get a bill for something you don't remember purchasing, that's not a good sign. Also suspicious are statements for credit cards you haven't applied for or received—which an ID thief may have opened in your name.

- **Missing bills**—Also bad are bills you expect to receive but don't. If you didn't get it, an ID thief might have stolen it out of your mailbox—and may well be on the way to use that account for his own nefarious purposes.

- **No replacement card**—If your credit card is due to expire and you don't automatically receive a replacement card, it may not be the card company's screwup. Instead, your new card might have been hijacked by an ID thief along the way.

- **Phone calls and letters**—If you ever get a call from a store or financial institution or collection agency about a purchase you didn't make, it's time to take immediate action. Same thing if you get a letter in the mail to the same effect.

Inspect Your Credit Reports

As a longer-term project, you should make a point of requesting and inspecting your credit reports on a regular basis—at least once a year. These reports are generated by the three major credit reporting firms, and list every piece of past and present credit opened in your name, as well as your bill-paying history.

It pays to inspect these reports for accuracy (mistakes are sometimes made) and to be sure that there are no new accounts that you don't know anything about. An unknown account on your credit report could have been opened by an ID thief.

{ P E R S O N A L   E X P E R I E N C E }

The credit reporting companies sometimes make honest mistakes. It's happened to me, due in part to my very common name. On more than one occasion I've found accounts in my credit reports that belong to some other "Michael Miller." In each instance, a quick call or letter to the credit reporting firms cleared up the confusion.

How do you get a copy of your credit reports? It's easy—and it's free. Federal law requires each of the three nationwide credit reporting companies to provide you with one free copy of your report each year, if you request it.

The three companies have created a single service you can use to request all the reports at once. To order a copy of your free reports, you can do the following:

- To order over the Web, go to www.AnnualCreditReport.com.

- To order by phone, call 877-322-8228.

- To order by mail, write Annual Credit Report Request Service, P.O. Box 105281, Atlanta, GA, 30348-5281.

If you prefer, you can also contact each of the three services directly. The companies' contact information is as follows:

- **Equifax**, www.equifax.com, 800-685-1111, P.O. Box 740241, Atlanta, GA, 30374-0241

- **Experian**, www.experian.com, 888-397-3742, P.O. Box 9532, Allen, TX, 75013

- **TransUnion**, www.transunion.com, 800-916-8800, P.O. Box 6790, Fullerton, CA, 92834-6790

> > > **N O T E**

The only way to get free reports is to use the joint Annual Credit Report Request Service. If you contact a company directly, you will have to pay for their credit reporting service.

C A U T I O N ! ! !

Many third-party firms sell access to your credit reports. Often they'll offer one free look but then sign you up for a monthly subscription; if you don't look closely, you'll think you're getting a free report but then find a monthly charge on your credit card bill for their ongoing service. Avoid this problem by not dealing with any "credit reporting" firm other than the Big Three or their Annual Credit Report service.

ID Theft Protection Services—Real or Con?

If you listen at all to talk radio, you've probably heard ads for products like Identity Theft Shield (www.prepaidlegal.com), LifeLock (www.lifelock.com), and TrustedID (www.trustedid.com). These companies offer services that promise to completely protect you from the ravages of identity theft. (For a fee, of course—typically around $10 per month.) Some even guarantee their services—up to $1 million, in the case of LifeLock. Sounds like a good deal, doesn't it? Well, maybe it is—and maybe it's not.

How Do These Services Work?

The reality is, services like LifeLock and TrustedID don't do much of anything you can't do yourself. In essence, each service works by contacting each of the three major credit reporting bureaus and placing a fraud alert on your account. With such an alert placed, credit issuers are obligated to contact you for verification if anyone attempts to open a new credit account in your name. This then alerts you that a thief is trying to use your identity; you tell the credit issuer not to create the new account, and the ID theft is averted.

The thing is, you don't have to pay LifeLock or TrustedID $10 or $12 a month to do this. You can place your own fraud alerts with the three credit reporting services. In fact, you only have to place an alert with a single service; that service then notifies the other two services. Each fraud alert lasts for 90 days, so you just set your schedule to request new alerts every three months.

< < < **T I P**

> To sign up with LifeLock and similar services, you have to provide them with all your personal informa-
> tion—including your Social Security number. They say it's because they need to know whose account
> they're protecting, and that may be valid. But by sending yet another party your personal information, you
> make it that much more likely for it to be stolen. These companies say that they have secure systems, but
> what if the company's database gets compromised? That's not a risk you have to take.

That's if you really want to place a fraud alert on your accounts . By requesting ongoing fraud
alerts, you make it next to impossible for you yourself to establish new credit. If that's not a
problem, okay. Know, however, that red-flagging your account like this bogs down everybody's
systems; in addition, lenders aren't officially required to respond to fraud alerts in this fashion.
For these and other reasons, repeated use of fraud alerts is not a recommended form of ID
theft prevention.

These companies also contact the opt-out list to remove your name from unwanted credit
card solicitations—something else you can do yourself, for free. They also claim to examine
your credit reports once a year (something you should be doing anyway, as discussed previously in this chapter) and say they'll help you contact your credit card companies if your wallet is ever stolen. They don't say they'll actually do it; they just say they'll "help." Oh, boy.

> > > **N O T E**

> Although TrustedID and Identity Theft Shield appear to be reputable services, LifeLock is more suspect.
> LifeLock's founder, Robert J. Maynard, Jr., previously ran a credit repair business that was shut down when
> authorities discovered it was making unauthorized charges to its customers' credit card accounts (itself a
> form of identity theft); that firm eventually went bankrupt. Although Maynard's current firm claims to be
> entirely legal and have no customer complaints, critics are less enthusiastic. And, for what it's worth, the
> Experian credit bureau has filed a Federal lawsuit against LifeLock, charging that the company's "illegal and
> fraudulent activities" (in placing constant credit alerts on customers' accounts) is costing Experian millions
> of dollars a year. You can read more about the exploits of LifeLock's Robert Maynard in a detailed May 2007
> *Phoenix New Times* exposé, located online at www.phoenixnewtimes.com/2007-05-31/news/
> what-happened-in-vegas/.

Should You Sign Up?

So should you pay for the services of an ID theft prevention firm? The reality is that there is no
such thing as complete protection against identity theft. The measures these firms take could
reduce the chances of theft, but aren't nearly as effective as the steps you yourself can take, for
free. And, given the fact that you have to provide these firms with all your personal data, you
may actually be increasing your risk rather than reducing it. I can't recommend them.

What About ID Theft Insurance?

Don't confuse ID theft protection services with ID theft insurance, such as that offered by Nationwide and other traditional insurance companies. ID theft insurance is just what its name says—insurance against identity theft. You pay a monthly premium, just as you do with other types of insurance, and if you're ever a victim of identity theft, the insurance company reimburses you for the theft-related losses. Many firms also offer additional services, such as credit monitoring (you're alerted if new credit is opened in your name) and assistance in calling affected companies and credit bureaus, as well as replacing stolen documents.

Insurance companies that offer this coverage typically let you add it to your homeowner's coverage at a discounted rate, or purchase a standalone policy for a higher rate. As an example, Nationwide's standalone policy costs $99 annually, or just $45 if added to an existing policy. With $25,000 worth of coverage and no deductable, this isn't a bad deal—especially if you're already a customer.

Is It Safe?

Can you keep your personal information personal? Or are you fated to become a victim of identity theft?

To answer the first question first, of course you can keep your personal information personal—to a point. While your local video rental store doesn't need to know your Social Security number, your bank does. And, while you might try to keep your phone company from eliciting a complete credit history when you sign up for new service, resisting too hard might result in you not getting a phone number. In other words, providing some personal data is necessary to keep the wheels turning in the machine.

That said, you can control to a large degree the amount of personal information you make public. And, more important, you can reduce the risk of having that information stolen, by protecting the paperwork and electronic data within your control. I hate to state the obvious, but in this regard a paper shredder is a good investment.

As to that second question, of course you're not destined to be a victim—as long as you employ a modicum of common sense. Act as privately as possible, keep your personal data close to your vest, and stay alert to any misuse of that information, and you'll sleep more soundly at night.

Repairing a Stolen Identity

ven if you take all the steps outlined in Chapter 2, "How to Keep Your Personal Information Personal," you can still be a victim of identity theft; there is no foolproof way to protect against this type of crime. What happens, then, if you are a victim—how do you stop the crime, minimize the damage, and work to repair your identity and credit?

That's what this chapter covers—how to recover from identity theft.

How Do You Know Whether Your Identity Has Been Stolen?

Millions of people each year are victims of identity theft. How do you know if your identity has been stolen?

If you're lucky, you find out quickly—typically via a phone call from your bank or credit card company, inquiring about a suspicious purchase, maxed-out credit line, or overdrawn account. Not that there's anything lucky about having your accounts infiltrated, but rather you're lucky to find out quickly.

If you're unlucky, you don't find out you're a victim until much later in the process. Maybe it's when you get your next month's credit card bill, or when you go to apply for a loan or new credit card, or even months or years later when a collection agency (or even the police!) knock on your door. By this point, a lot of damage could be done.

> > > **N O T E**

It does take some time for information to filter through the system. The FTC reports that it takes 12 months before the average victim of identity theft becomes aware of the problem.

This is why you want to constantly monitor your bank and credit card accounts, as well as regularly check the information on your personal credit reports. (We discussed all this in Chapter 2, if you recall.) The sooner you know something's wrong, the sooner you can start working to stop the crime and undo the damage.

And those are the two steps you must take. First, you have to put a halt to any further fraud resulting from the theft of your personal information. Second, you have to work to minimize the effect of the theft and repair your damaged credit. You have a lot of hard work ahead of you.

Stopping the Fraud

When you become aware that your personal information has been compromised, the very first thing you should do is stop the fraudulent activity. Don't assume that just because you know of a compromised account, the ID thief will quit using it. You must block all access to any account you know is compromised—and *then* work on undoing the damage done.

Closing Compromised Accounts

The fastest way to freeze out an identity thief is to close the account(s) to which he has access. As soon as you suspect that an ID thief is using a particular account, you need to call the institution that issued the account, notify them of the problem, and close the account.

You can contact most credit card companies and financial institutions by phone—which is the fastest way to proceed. There should be a phone number to contact in case of fraud on the back of all your credit cards, and on your credit card and bank statements. You can also find contact information on the companies' websites.

When you call, ask for the security or fraud department. Tell them everything you know, and why you think your account is compromised, and instruct them to close the account immediately. You should then ask to examine a list of recent purchases, and note those that you didn't make yourself; the company should automatically discharge those purchases for which you weren't responsible. If the company has forms that need to be filled out to clear up the situation, ask for them to be sent to you as soon as possible.

{ P E R S O N A L   E X P E R I E N C E }

The times I've had my credit card information stolen, the credit card company worked quickly to identify the suspect charges, close down the existing account, and then open a new account with a different number. It took just a few days to receive the credit cards for my new account.

After you've completed the phone call, you should follow up in writing to the company.

Compose a letter that details what just transpired—the compromised account info, the fraudulent transactions, and the actions taken by the phone representative. Send the letter, along with copies of any supporting documents (such as your account statement with the fraudulent transactions circled), to the security or fraud department of the company via certified mail with return receipt requested; ask for verification that the disputed account has been closed and that the fraudulent transactions have been discharged. And keep a copy for your own records, just in case there's a dispute at a later date.

Repeat this process for all compromised accounts. Naturally, the particulars may be different depending on the type of account (a checking account has slightly different issues than a credit card account), but the procedure should be similar in all cases.

< < < **T I P**

When you open new accounts to replace the closed ones, make sure they have different account numbers and that you use new PINs and passwords. You don't want the ID thief to have easy access to your new accounts by using your old information.

< < < **T I P**

When you replace a compromised credit card with a new one, remember to notify all the companies that had recurring fees automatically charged to the old card. For example, if you have your auto insurance automatically billed to your credit card, you need to have the insurance company change their billing to the new credit card.

Dealing with Your Other Cards and Accounts

One question that ID theft victims often ask concerns their other credit cards and accounts—those not stolen. Should you cancel these cards and accounts also, just to be safe?

The answer is a resounding *no*. If there is no evidence these accounts have been compromised, they should still be active and usable. And you might need them in the future; if the theft of other cards has damaged your credit rating, it may be difficult for you to obtain new credit for some period of time. Best to hold on to your existing cards and accounts—if, indeed, they have not been compromised.

That said, you probably want to change the PINs and passwords associated with these other cards and accounts—especially if you used the same or similar PINs and passwords for the stolen cards. You want to reduce the possibility that the ID thief can access your other accounts with the information obtained from the stolen cards.

You may also want to notify the security departments for your other cards and accounts, and let them know that you had another account that was the victim of ID theft, just so they can be on the lookout for suspicious activity. It's also a good idea to set up a fraud alert with the credit reporting firms—which is discussed next.

Placing a Fraud Alert on Your Credit Reports

One longer-term risk from having a credit card or personal information stolen is that the thief may use that information to open new loans and credit accounts in your name. You can guard against this by placing a fraud alert on all your credit reports. With such an alert in place, any attempt to open a new account is flagged automatically, and you'll be personally contacted for approval. This should effectively block any future attempts on the part of the ID thief to open new accounts in your name.

To place a fraud alert, contact any one of the major credit reporting firms:

- **Equifax**, www.equifax.com, 800-685-1111, P.O. Box 740241, Atlanta, GA, 30374-0241

- **Experian**, www.experian.com, 888-397-3742, P.O. Box 9532, Allen, TX, 75013

- **TransUnion**, www.transunion.com, 800-916-8800, Fraud Victim Assistance Division, P.O. Box 6790, Fullerton, CA, 92834-6790

When you place a fraud alert with one of these firms, they automatically notify the other two companies, who then initiate fraud alerts of their own. A fraud alert stays on your credit report for 90 days; you can call the reporting agency at the end of 90 days to issue another fraud alert, if you like.

> > > **NOTE**

  Placing a fraud alert also entitles you to free copies of your credit reports. You should examine these reports for any open accounts that are not your own, or for other suspicious activity.

Filing a Police Report

If you're the victim of ID theft, you're a crime victim just as if you'd been held up at gunpoint. For that reason, among others, you should always file a report with your local law enforcement officials when you've experienced ID theft.

Having a police report in hand may also help you with creditors who've been affected by the ID theft. To clear you of any fraudulent transactions, they may want proof of the crime—which a police report provides. Make sure you get a copy of the police report to use in this fashion, if asked.

> > > **NOTE**

  A police report of an ID theft crime is technically called an Identity Theft Report. So if a creditor asks you for an Identity Theft Report, this is what they're asking for—a copy of the police report.

Know, however, that not all police departments are eager to take reports of ID theft; some agencies view it as a waste of their time, or think that the report should be filed by the credit card company, not you. If this is the case, you can ask to talk to the head of the department's fraud or white collar crime unit, file a "miscellaneous incidents" report instead, or take your problem to another jurisdiction, such as your county or state police.

{ P E R S O N A L   E X P E R I E N C E }

My acquisitions editor notes that some police departments are terribly slow about providing copies of theft reports—which was a problem for him when he was recently trying to move quickly in a case of credit card fraud. You need to be persistent to get the paperwork you need in a timely fashion.

Filing a Complaint with the FTC

After you've filed a police report about the fraudulent activity, you should also file a report with the Federal Trade Commission (FTC). Although the police report provides local officials with key information regarding the ID theft, the FTC report has wider impact; it's used by law enforcement officials across the country to track down whomever stole your personal information.

You can file an FTC report in any of the following ways:

- Online, at www.ftc.gov/idtheft

- By phone, at 877-ID-THEFT (877-438-4338)

- By mail, addressed to Identity Theft Clearinghouse, Federal Trade Commission, 600 Pennsylvania Avenue NW, Washington, DC, 20580

Repairing the Damage

After you've stopped the current fraudulent activity resulting from ID theft, you need to start the long and involved process of repairing the damage done. That involves reversing fraudulent transactions, replacing stolen credit cards, resetting compromised user names and passwords, and similar activity.

Disputing Unauthorized Transactions

You don't want to pay for any purchases or withdrawals you didn't make. How do you go about removing the fraudulent transactions from your accounts?

Credit Card Theft

Let's start with any purchases that the ID thief made using a stolen credit card. Your first step is to contact the security department of the company that issued the card in question. You should be able, over the phone, to run through a list of recent transactions and identify those that were the responsibility of the ID thief.

After the fraudulent charges are identified, what happens next is up to the card issuer. Most credit card companies simply remove these charges from your account, and you're done with it. But what do you do if the company *doesn't* remove the disputed transactions?

> > > **N O T E**

Who ultimately pays for fraudulent transactions? When the credit card company removes those charges from your personal bill, it charges back the retailer for those purchases. So the ultimate victim of ID theft isn't you, it's the retailers who got scammed—and are left paying for what is essentially "stolen" merchandise.

In the case of credit card fraud, the Fair Credit Billing Act limits your liability for unauthorized charges to just $50 per card. So even if the thief charged $5,000 of merchandise to your stolen card, you only have to pay $50 of that charge. And if you have a personal (not a business) credit card with MasterCard or Visa, you don't even have to pay the $50; both companies have a zero liability policy for their personal credit cards.

If the credit card company doesn't want to work with you in terms of removing the disputed charges from your account, or at least not over the phone, you'll need to argue your case in writing. The Fair Credit Billing Act requires you to write to the charge card company (at their address for "billing inquiries"); include your name, address, account number, and description of the disputed charges, as well as copies of the police report or other documents that support your case. Mail this letter within 60 days of the first bill that includes the disputed charges, and send the letter by certified mail with return receipt requested. The charge card company is required to resolve the dispute within two billing cycles after receiving your letter.

< < < **T I P**

Need help composing this or any other type of letter regarding an identity theft problem? Then check out the letter templates on the Identity Theft Resource Centers website (www.idtheftcenter.org/artman2/publish/v_templates/index.shtml)—they can help you get started.

Unauthorized Electronic Withdrawals

The situation is similar if the fraudster made an unauthorized electronic withdrawal from your bank account, using either a credit or debit card and an ATM. Your first step, of course, is to notify your bank by phone when you first discover the unauthorized withdrawal; and under the Electronic Fund Transfer Act if you do this within two business days of discovery, your loss is limited to $50. If you report the loss after two business days of discovery (but within 60 days), you're liable for the first $500 stolen. If you wait more than 60 days to report the theft, you could be liable for the complete amount stolen.

> Both MasterCard and Visa have voluntarily agreed to limit your liability for unauthorized use of their debit cards to just $50 per card, no matter how much time has elapsed since discovery of the crime.

As with standard credit card theft, you need to notify your banking institution in writing of the fraudulent electronic withdrawals. Send your missive via certified letter, return receipt requested. Your bank then has 10 business days from receipt of your letter to investigate your claims.

Bad Checks

Check fraud is one of the oldest forms of financial ID theft; it's been around long before the advent of the Internet and online banking. This could take the form of stolen checks or counterfeit checks with your account number. In either case, the money comes out of your checking account, without your permission.

If you discover that your checks have been stolen, you can act before the thief has a chance to use the checks. Contact your bank via phone, stop payment on the stolen checks, close your checking account, and ask your bank to notify Chex Systems, the national check verification service, of the theft. Chex Systems then notifies its retailers not to accept the checks in question.

> Chex Systems works kind of like the major credit reporting firms, but with a particular focus on checking accounts. You can contact the company directly via phone at 800-428-9623, on the web at www.chexhelp.com, or via mail at 7805 Hudson Road, Suite 100, Woodbury, MN, 55125.

Unfortunately, there is no federal law to limit your losses from check fraud, as there is with credit card or electronic withdrawal fraud. That said, many states do have such laws in place; you need to check with your local Secretary of State to see how you're protected in your state. (Most states hold the bank responsible for these losses, not you.)

> You may also want to contact directly any merchants who were victims of the check scam, so they know it wasn't you who passed the bad checks.

Closing Fraudulent Bank Accounts

Some of the worst cases of ID theft occur when the thief uses your stolen data to open new banking accounts in your name. If this happens to you, you want those accounts closed post haste. Contact the host institutions directly and plead your case, via phone initially and later via mail to confirm your conversations.

If the banking institution isn't cooperative, you can kick it up a level by taking your case to the appropriate regulatory agency, as shown in Table 3.1.

Table 3.1   Banking Regulatory Agencies

Type of Institution	Agency	Website	Phone	Address
State-chartered banks that are part of the Federal Reserve System	Federal Reserve System (The Fed)	www.federalreserve.gov	202-452-3693	Division of Consumer and Community Affairs, Mail Stop 801, Federal Reserve Board, Washington, DC 20551
State-chartered banks that are not part of the Federal Reserve System	Federal Deposit Insurance Corporation (FDIC)	www.fdic.gov	800-934-3342	Federal Deposit Insurance Corporation, Division of Compliance and Consumer Affairs, 550 17th Street NW, Washington, DC, 20429
National banks (a bank with the word "National" or initials "N.A." in its name)	Office of the Comptroller of the Currency (OCC)	www.occ.treas.gov	800-613-6743	Customer Assistance Group, 1301 McKinney Street, Suite 3710, Houston, TX, 77010
Thrift institutions (including many savings banks and savings and loan institutions)	Office of Thrift Supervision (OTS)	www.ots.treas.gov	202-906-6000	Office of Thrift Supervision, 1700 G. Street NW, Washington, DC, 20552
Credit unions	National Credit Union Administration (NCUA)	www.ncua.gov	703-518-6360	Compliance Officer, National Credit Union Administration, 1775 Duke Street, Alexandria, VA, 22314

> > > **N O T E**

If you're not sure which agency has jurisdiction over your financial institution, call your bank or visit the National Information Center website (www.ffiec.gov/nicpubweb/nicweb/nichome.aspx).

Replacing Compromised Documents

Having your credit card company issue you a new credit card to replace a stolen one is one thing. Dealing with a stolen driver's license or Social Security card is quite another.

Let's start with the case of the stolen driver's license—or any other government-issued identification, for that matter. For a stolen driver's license, start by contacting your state's department or bureau of motor vehicles. Each state has its own procedures (which may or may not be outlined on the department's website); you need to follow those particular procedures to cancel the stolen license and have a replacement issued.

< < < **T I P**

> If your state uses your Social Security number as your driver's license number, ask to substitute a different number on the new license.

Same thing with other government-issued IDs. Contact the issuing agency and find out what you need to do to cancel the stolen one and get a replacement.

If the thief has stolen your passport, you need to contact the U.S. Department of State to report the theft. You can do so online (travel.state.gov/passport/), or at any local USDS field office.

What should you do if your Social Security number has been stolen? One thing *not* to do is try to change your number. Your SSN is attached to many accounts and official documents, including your credit reports, tax filings, and so on—and if you change your SSN, your new number is still attached to all your old reports and accounts, so you really don't gain anything. Besides, there is no bigger hassle than trying to get the Social Security Administration to change your SSN; the net results, which are minimal, are simply not worth the effort.

Recovering from Bankruptcy Fraud

In the event an ID thief has used your stolen information to file for bankruptcy in your name, you need to write to the U.S. Trustee in the region where the bankruptcy was filed. You can find a list of regional offices on the UST website (www.usdoj.gov/ust/). In your letter, describe the situation and provide proof of your identity; the Trustee contacts the appropriate law enforcement authorities, as necessary.

That said, this sort of ID fraud is big and complicated enough that it warrants your retaining an attorney to fight your cause in bankruptcy court. Find a law firm that specializes in this sort of fraud and let them go to work on your behalf.

Recovering from Investment Fraud

If an ID thief has accessed or tampered with your securities investments or brokerage account, you're the victim of investment fraud. After contacting your investment firm or broker about the specific activity, you should then have a word with the U.S. Securities and Exchange Commission (SEC). You can contact the SEC's Complaint Center online (www.sec.gov/complaint.shtml), via phone (202-942-7040), or via mail (450 Fifth Street NW, Washington, DC, 20549-0213).

Recovering from Website Fraud

Here's one we haven't discussed much yet, but could be a major issue. Some ID thieves use stolen identities to register Web domain names and then launch websites that support phishing activities or offer illicit software for sale. Although this type of activity doesn't harm you directly, you don't want to have your name associated with the scam.

If you discover that your name has been used to register a website without your permission, you need to contact Network Solutions (www.networksolutions.com, or via phone at 800-333-7680), the entity that manages all domain registrations. If you can discover where the illicit site is hosted, you can also contact that website host to get the site pulled.

Recovering from Criminal Fraud

If someone who has stolen your identity is arrested, it's your personal information that enters the criminal justice system, even though you're not the criminal. How do you clear your record?

This can be a long and painstaking process, one that might benefit from the hiring of legal counsel. Although procedures vary from state to state, you'll probably want to start by contacting the office of your state's Attorney General to determine any special procedures available to identity theft victims. This gives you a roadmap of what to do next.

In most instances, your next step is to contact the police or sheriff's department that arrested the person falsely using your identity, or the court agency that issued the warrant for the arrest. You'll need to confirm your identity and then file an impersonation report with the department or court agency. That probably means heading down to the police station, having them photograph you and take a full set of fingerprints, and make copies of your driver's license or other photo ID. You'll then need to ask the police to compare your prints and photo with that of the imposter.

> > > **N O T E**

> If the imposter was arrested in a locale distant from where you live, you can ask your local police department to take an impersonation report and send it to the department in the other jurisdiction.

Your identity fully established, the law enforcement agency should then recall any standing warrants and issue a clearance letter or certificate of release; this document clears of you any crimes committed by the imposter. You'll want to keep this document with you at all times, in case you're wrongly arrested in the future.

You should also ask the police to file the record of this follow-up investigation with district attorney's office or court where the crime took place. This results in an amended complaint. However, it's unlikely that your name will be completely removed from the official record; the best you can hope for (and ask for) is for the primary name be changed from your name to the imposter's name, with your name noted as an alias.

> > > **N O T E**

It's also important for you to clear your name in the court records. Again, this is where a lawyer (specifically, a criminal defense attorney) can be of help. The process varies from state to state.

Dealing with Collection Agencies

One of the lingering effects of ID theft is the unpaid debt that the thief rings up in your name. When a retailer sells merchandise to an ID thief and doesn't get paid for it, they hold you responsible for the debt—which means, in time, turning your debt over to a collection agency. And nothing is more annoying that being hounded by debt collectors, either via mail, phone, or even in person.

Fortunately, the Fair Debt Collection Practices Act prohibits debt collectors from unduly hounding consumers—including victims of identity theft. All you need to do is send a letter to the collection agency, telling them you do not owe the money in question because you were a victim of identity theft. You should include copies of any documents that support your position, including a copy of the police report of the crime. Because the collection agency is responsible for proving that you're wrong, this should stop the unwanted calls and letters.

Know, however, that although you can stop a collection agency from contacting you, that doesn't get rid of the debt itself. You still need to contact the company that holds the account in question to dispute the debt. There's nothing stopping a company from sending your debt to another collection agency, which forces you to go through the whole letter-writing process yet again. Better to deal with the debt at the source, via phone calls and letters, as necessary.

Monitoring and Correcting Your Credit Reports

You've been a victim of identity theft. You've discovered the theft, filed a police report, and even contacted the FTC. You've worked with your credit card companies and banking institution to close down the affected accounts, open new ones, and discharge all the debts arising from the stolen data. It was a lot of hard work, but you've finally put the ID theft behind you—right?

Wrong.

Unfortunately, identity theft is often the crime that keeps on giving. You may have corrected all the initial effects of the ID theft, but that doesn't mean that the thief is done with you. Simple credit card theft is often a fleeting thing, but the theft of your more personal information—birth date, address, Social Security number, and the like—provides the thief with material to commit even larger and longer-lasting frauds.

After all, after the fraudster has control of your personal information, why should he stop using it? As you learned in Chapter 1, "Identity Theft: How Big a Problem?," a stolen Social Security number can be used for all sorts of pernicious activities. Just because the low-hanging fruit is no longer available doesn't mean that the ID thief is done using what he has stolen.

For this reason, you need to be constantly vigilant for suspicious activity involving your name, your credit cards, your bank accounts, and such. You also need to be aware of any new financial activity and accounts issued in your name. You want to know right away if the ID thief has something new up his sleeve.

You do this by constantly monitoring your personal credit reports, available from Equifax, Experian, and TransUnion. Look for new accounts that you didn't create, as well as unauthorized activity on your current accounts. Then, if something is amiss, contact the firm where the suspicious behavior occurred, get the necessary details, and work through the obligatory steps to shut down and correct any fraudulent activity.

You also want to remove evidence of this and previous fraudulent activity from your credit report. Under the Fair Credit Reporting Act, both the credit reporting company and the business that gave that information to the reporting company are responsible for correcting any fraudulent information in your report. You need to contact both firms—the credit reporting company and the company that was the victim of the ID fraud—and instruct them to remove the fraudulent information from their records. Obviously, you need to make these requests in writing, and provide whatever evidence you have of the fraud, including copies of the identity theft report. The credit reporting company has four business days to correct the fraudulent information; it's also obligated to inform the victimized firm that it is blocking the distribution of the fraudulent information.

Is It Safe?

The effects of identity theft can be repaired—it just takes a lot of work. But even if you jump through all the correct hoops to repair the damage, the effects of ID theft can last for years to come. How long you have to deal with it depends on the type of theft involved, how aggressive the thief was in using your stolen data, whether the thief sold your information to additional parties, and what firms were victimized by the use of this fraudulent data. The whole thing could be behind you in a month, or you may be dealing with the aftereffects for several years.

Because damage from ID theft lingers, you need to continue monitoring your credit reports for at least three years—five to be safe. I recommend obtaining new copies of each report every three months for the first year after the theft, and then once a year thereafter. You can never be too safe; increased diligence is a necessity, for as long as your stolen data remains valuable to the ID thief.

The good news is, of course, that the incidence of ID theft is gradually decreasing. The bad news, however, is that it's still a significant crime, and one that can cost you both time and money to recover from. So be vigilant and act immediately if you become a victim—and prepared for a long and involved fight to repair your reputation and credit.

Data Theft: How Big a Problem?

ata theft is a defined subset of identity theft—in particular, the large-scale theft of customer records from businesses and other organizations. These stolen records are then used to perpetrate identity fraud upon the unsuspecting customers whose data was stolen.

We touched upon data theft in previous chapters because stolen corporate data contributes to a significant portion of today's identity theft problem. What makes it different from simple identity theft is the magnitude; when a corporate database goes missing, it can affect hundreds of thousands, if not millions, of individuals.

What Is Data Theft?

Data theft is, quite simply, the unauthorized copying or removal of confidential information from a business or other large enterprise. It can take the form of ID-related theft (the theft of customer records) or the theft of a company's proprietary information or intellectual property.

ID Data Theft

ID-related data theft occurs when customer records are stolen or illegally copied. The information stolen typically includes customers' names, addresses, phone numbers, usernames, passwords and PINs, account and credit card numbers, and, in some instances, Social Security numbers. When transmitted or sold to lower-level criminals, this information can be used to commit all manner of identity fraud.

A single data theft can affect large numbers of individual victims. There are many examples to cite.

Let's start across the Atlantic, in England. In January, 2008, two laptop PCs were stolen from Brent's Central Middlesex Hospital. Each laptop contained hundreds of confidential patient records. Not a large theft (389 records in all), but one particularly disconcerting to the patients whose personal data were compromised.

Then there was the case of the Wilkes-Barre driver's license center in Hanover, PA, which was broken into in late November, 2006. In addition to assorted office supplies and materials, the thief got away with a computer containing driver's license information for more than 11,000 citizens.

Not even those companies charged with keeping our data safe are immune from data theft. For example, ChoicePoint, Inc., is a company that collects personal and financial information on millions of computers. In February, 2005, ChoicePoint reported that it had suffered a security breach and inadvertently sold personal information on 145,000 people to a criminal enterprise. Oops!

A much larger theft occurred in October, 2007, when the financial institution GE Money discovered that a computer tape containing information on 650,000 J.C. Penney customers had gone missing. Although not yet officially confirmed as a theft (it was just "missing"), the tape in question included more than 150,000 Social Security numbers.

Retailers store a lot of valuable data about their customers, which makes them a prime target of data thieves. Thus the story of shoe retailer DSW, which in June, 2005, had 1.4 million customer records stolen. Among those customers affected was then-FTC chairwoman Deborah Platt Majoras—a nice little irony for those that care.

Of course, data theft isn't limited to the retail sector. Witness the U.S. Department of Veterans Affairs, which had the home of one of its employees burglarized in May of 2006. Stolen in the burglary was a laptop computer and external disk drive that contained the Social Security numbers of about 26.5 million veterans. That was a big breach—but the story has a happy ending. Thanks to some excellent police work, the hard drive was eventually recovered; it was later determined that the sensitive data had not been accessed.

An even bigger breach was the June, 2005, "security incident" reported by Atlanta-based payment processor CardSystems Solutions. The company handles payments for all the major credit cards, including MasterCard, Visa, American Express, and Discover. Intruders used malicious software code to breach the company's systems, exposing more than 40 million credit card accounts to potential fraud. Fortunately, only about 200,000 of these accounts were found to be actually stolen, but the FBI was still called in to investigate.

But all these incidents pale compared to the largest reported case of data theft on record. In December, 2006, the TJX Companies (parent to T.J. Maxx, Marshalls, and other retailers) reported a massive computer breach on that part of its network that handles credit card, debit card, check, and merchandise transactions. It appears that hackers made off with more than 94 million records from customers in the U.S. and abroad.

Take a look at that last case again. A single data theft compromised the identities of an esti-mated *94 million individuals*. That's just an incredible number—and indicative of the impact of this type of computer crime.

> > > **N O T E**

> For what it's worth, TJX disputes the 94 million number, which comes from a group of banks suing the com-pany over the breach. The company says that *only* 45.7 million records were stolen—which is still a very big deal.

Non-ID Data Theft

Customers' records aren't the only kind of data that can be stolen from a large organization. Companies of all sorts are hosts to various types of confidential information; this information, if accessed by a competitor, could often lead to a diminishment of the company's position in the marketplace.

Non-ID data theft occurs when an employee makes one or more copies of a company's confi-dential information, and then uses that information either for his own personal use or trans-mits that information to a competitor for the competitor's use. However it's done, this is a theft of the business' intellectual property, every bit as harmful as a theft of money or equipment.

What kind of information are we talking about? A company's confidential information includes its employee records, contracts with other firms, financial reports, marketing plans, new product specifications, and so on. Imagine you're a competitor who gets hold of a com-pany's plans for an upcoming product launch; with knowledge beforehand, you can create your own counter-launch to blunt the impact of the other company's new product. A little inside information can be extremely valuable—and damaging for the company from which it was stolen.

> > > **N O T E**

> One notable example of non-ID theft occurred in 2006, when three Coca-Cola employees attempted to steal the secret formula for Coke. They tried to sell the trade secret to rival PepsiCo; unfortunately for them, Pepsi contacted Coca-Cola management, who alerted the FBI. The Feds used this information to conduct a sting operation that landed all three culprits in the big house.

How Do Thieves Steal Corporate Data?

Data theft can be a virtual theft (hacking into a company's systems and transmitting stolen data over the Internet) or, more often, a physical theft (stealing the data tapes or discs). It's typ-ically perpetrated by an insider with easy access to the data; the stolen data is then sold over the Internet to professional identity fraud rings, often located in Russia or eastern European countries, or via special-interest websites (dubbed *underground economy servers*). The original thief profits from the sale of the records, while the fraud ring or ultimate buyers of the data profit from merchandise purchases or other fraudulent activity enabled by the stolen data.

Online Theft

Virtually everything today is connected. Information might reside on a company's internal servers, but those servers are connected to the Internet, and anything connected to the Internet can, if not properly protected, be accessed by other Internet-based computers. Even if a company's database is not directly accessible over the Internet, other computers that connect to the database are Internet-connected. All it takes is a clever hack into one computer in a company, and that compromised computer can be used to ferret out information hidden deep in the bowels of the company's IT infrastructure.

In other words, a dedicated hacker stands a good chance of infiltrating a company's defenses and accessing confidential data. Obviously, there are protections against these types of intrusions, but a poorly designed system (or one with weak security) is at risk of online theft.

> > > **NOTE**

Learn more about protecting a company's servers from outside intrusion in Chapter 24, "Defending Your Company Network from Attack."

Physical Theft

In many ways, it's easier for a thief to physically steal a company's data than it is to hack into the company's network for the same purpose. Most companies give a lot of attention to Internet-based security, but less attention is typically paid to the individuals who have physical access to the same information.

For example, many cases of ID-based data theft involve the physical theft of the storage media used to store a company's customer records. That's right—it's surprisingly easy for someone to walk away with a computer tape or hard drive containing massive amounts of confidential data. It's even easier if that person is an employee with the proper security clearances—which is why most thefts of a certain magnitude are "inside" jobs.

An even bigger problem is the theft of non-ID data by lower-level employees from their own computers or workstations. Ironically, the growing use of portable storage devices, such as USB flash drives, has made this type of data theft much easier to perpetrate. A disgruntled employee can easily copy confidential information from a company's servers to a flash drive or even an iPod or digital camera connected to his own computer, and thus make off with valuable data burning a hole in his pocket.

This was how Jessica Quintana, a low-level worker at the Los Alamos National Laboratory, allegedly obtained highly classified documents about the design of U.S. nuclear weapons that were later found in the living room of her trailer. Quintana copied the files to a USB flash drive at work and then downloaded the files to her home computer; nobody thought to search her purse for something like a USB drive when she left the secure facility. (Fortunately for all concerned, she was only copying the documents to work on at home, so that she wouldn't fall behind in her job. But still….)

> > > **N O T E**

The act of illegally downloading data from a networked computer to a USB flash drive is called *thumbsucking*. The use of an iPod or other portable music player for the same purpose is called *podslurping*. Because of how easy it is to copy data to these types of devices, some companies are now outlawing the use of any personal, portable data storage devices in their offices.

Another contributor to the influx of physical data theft is the proliferation of notebook PCs. Many employees store confidential company data on their notebooks; if and when a notebook is stolen, the thief has access not just to the PC but also to all the data stored on the notebook's hard drive. If you're a disingenuous competitor who wants a peek at a company's inside info, there's no easier method than tracking a valued employee to the local Starbucks, waiting for him to leave his table to get his drink or use the restroom, and then appropriating his momentarily abandoned notebook.

Witness the example of the Boeing Company. In December 2006, Boeing reported the theft of a notebook PC from an employee's car near their offices in Seattle. The laptop contained confidential information (including home addresses and Social Security numbers) for 382,000 current Boeing workers and retirees; the theft put these individuals at risk of ID theft. And this wasn't the first time Boeing had a valuable laptop stolen; six months earlier, a notebook with 3,600 employee records was stolen, and the previous year another notebook holding information on 161,000 employees also went missing. All instances were simple cases of theft, with no hacking or cracking involved.

What Happens to the Stolen Data?

Okay, now you know how large volumes of data are stolen from large organizations. What does the thief do with all these stolen records?

In the case of most ID-related data theft, the thief doesn't do anything with the stolen data. Not himself, anyway. How the thief makes money is by selling the stolen data to other parties, who then use it however they deem fit—typically for purposes of ID fraud.

How does a data thief sell his stolen data? There are a number of different ways. Perhaps the most common is to use an underground economy server—a website devoted to the illicit trading of stolen data, including credit cards, debit cards, user names, passwords and PINs, and even Social Security numbers.

The people who frequent these sites comprise an underground of thieves, fraudsters, and other low-lifes who trade information for money. These sites have a language of their own (and it's typically not the Queen's English), where a "dump" is a credit card number and a "cob" is a brand new credit card account where the billing address can be changed via a pilfered PIN. On most of these sites, a piece of personal information typically goes for between $1 and $20, depending on the quality and quantity of data available.

Most of these black market sites are based in Russia or other countries in the former Soviet Union, which makes them difficult to police. Eastern Europe represents a kind of Wild West of data theft, where anything goes—and everything goes for a price.

That price is not negotiated on the website, however; that would be too easy for authorities to track. Instead, the dealmakers move off the web onto ICQ, the black market's instant messaging program of choice. (That's because of its almost-total anonymity—no registration required.) Payments change hands via an electronic currency such as e-gold or WMZs.

> > > **NOTE**

E-gold is a digital gold currency issued by Gold & Silver Reserve, Inc., supposedly backed by actual gold bars. WMZ is an electronic monetary unit equivalent to the U.S. dollar, issued by the Moscow-based online payment service WebMoney Transfer.

A lower-level ID fraudster can buy a piece of information and with surprising ease make double or triple his investment by using it to make unauthorized purchases on the stolen card. The fraudster first changes the billing address so that the merchandise is delivered to him, not the original cardholder. After it is received, the merchandise is typically fenced on the black market for pennies on the dollar.

> > > **NOTE**

Experienced users of stolen credit card data typically have purchased merchandise delivered to a safe location ("drop"), rather than to their actual physical address.

Alternately, some thieves provide "cash out" services, where a stolen credit or debit card (and pilfered PIN) is used at an ATM to withdraw cash, up to the daily allowable maximum. Daily withdrawals are made until the account is depleted. (Because there's a risk that the person doing the withdrawal could be arrested, these services typically command a premium.)

The sad fact about this sort of black market data trading is that it's a relatively safe crime for the criminals. The perpetrators are hard to track and catch, the crime itself is difficult to prosecute, and there's little if any violence involved in the profession; most of the criminals operate from the safety of their living rooms. According to the FTC, only about 5% of these cybercriminals are ever brought to justice.

How Widespread Is the Data Theft Problem?

Given the appeal of this type of data theft to tech-savvy thieves, one would expect it to be somewhat widespread. And it probably is—if we truly knew all the numbers.

The problem with trying to size the data theft issue is twofold. First, many companies do not report data theft to the police or do not publicize such thefts; they're trying to avoid bad publicity. And even when data theft is reported, the dollar impact of such theft is difficult to ascertain. (Remember, the actual thief benefits only from the sale of the information, not from its eventual use in fraudulent activities.)

That said, some attempts have been made to put this type of crime in perspective. Unfortunately, the numbers aren't quite in sync.

For example, the Identity Theft Resource Center estimates that more than 79 million data records were compromised in the U.S. during 2007. That's an increase of 295% over 2006's 20 million number.

> > > **N O T E**

> The 2006–2007 increase in data theft is due in large part to the multi-million record theft from the TJX Companies—which, by the way, the ITRC estimated at only about half the size as did Attrition.org.

However, a competing organization, Attrition.org, puts the 2007 number at 162 million stolen records worldwide. (That's worldwide versus U.S.–only, so it's not strictly apples to apples.) That's an increase of 230% over Attrition's 49 million estimate for 2006.

Whichever number is correct, that's a lot of stolen data. Add to that the immeasurable cost of intellectual property data theft, and you get a sense of the size of the problem—it's big and it's getting bigger.

Is It Safe?

Data theft is a worrisome problem. Although the number of individual incidents is relatively low, the magnitude of each incident can be disturbingly large. When a single theft can result in millions of compromised individual records, you know you have a real problem on your hands.

Fortunately, even in these large data thefts, only a small number of the compromised accounts end up being victims of identity theft. My guess is that that's because of the huge volume of stolen records; there are just too many records involved in these large thefts for a thief to unload in a short amount of time. Individual records get lost in the volume.

That said, the last thing you want to hear is that your credit card company or retailer of choice just experienced a big data theft, and your account data was among those compromised in the theft. ID theft is ID theft, no matter how it happens.

Unfortunately, there's little you as an individual can do to prevent data theft; the onus is all on the company holding the data. You could, I suppose, reduce your risk by limiting the number of companies with which you do business, but that may not be practical. The best you can do is stay alert to news reports about data thefts regarding the companies you deal with, and then take advantage of the restitution services (free credit checks and so on) that most companies offer in the wake of such thefts. Being alert is your only defense against this type of large-scale theft.

Protecting Corporate Data

A s you learned in the previous chapter, a single security breach at a large company can result in hundreds of thousands if not millions of individual records becoming vulnerable to identity theft. For this reason, it's vitally important for any entity that stores large amounts of consumer data to protect itself from data theft.

Just how can a company best secure this type of sensitive data? There are many steps that can be taken—just as there are several things you can do to protect yourself in case your personal information is ever part of a larger corporate data theft.

Data Loss Prevention—It's Not Optional

Computer security professionals dub the whole area of preventing corporate data theft DLP, or *data loss prevention*. And, depending on the type of data we're talking about, DLP may not be optional. The fact is, many large companies are subject to various governmental or commercial regulations regarding the security of various types of information.

For example, the Health Insurance and Portability and Accountability Act (HIPAA), enacted in 1996, has a set of provisions called Administrative Simplification, or AS. These provisions address the security and privacy of patient health data. Any company in the health care industry must secure its patient data according to these provisions.

In the area of finance, the Gramm-Leach-Bliley Act (GLB), enacted in 1999, dictates how financial institutions must keep customer data secure. The act's Safeguards Rule requires financial institutions to develop a written information security plan that describes how the institution should protect its customers' personal information.

In addition, the Sarbanes-Oxley Act (SOX), enacted in 2002, must be taken into account. Most non-accountants think of Sarbanes-Oxley as a response to the widespread accounting scandals and corporate malfeasance of the late 1990s, but it also impacts data security management. In particular, it regulates organizations' internal control structures in a way that impacts the security of employee and customer data.

Finally, the major credit card companies have their own guidelines for securing customer information. The Payment Card Industry Data Security Standard (PCI DSS) specifies 12 requirements or "control objectives," including installing a firewall, encrypting transmission of cardholder data, restricting physical access to cardholder data, regularly testing security systems and processes, and so on. Providers are periodically audited to ensure PCI DSS compliance.

The point is, the type of data security you enact may be dictated to you by these governmental and industry guidelines. Find out what obligations your firm has before you enact your own data security plan.

Discouraging Copying to Portable Storage Devices

Let's start with the lowest level of corporate data theft—the theft of intellectual property by a company's employees. This most often involves the theft of company secrets and other confidential information, often to the benefit of a company's competitors in the marketplace.

Most crimes of this sort are small scale, typically perpetrated by a single disgruntled worker. The weapon of choice for this type of data theft is most often a portable data storage device, such as a USB flash memory drive or an iPod configured for data storage. These devices plug into a USB port on the worker's computer; confidential information is then copied from the worker's hard disk or the company's network to the portable storage device, in techniques informally known as thumbsucking or podslurping, respectively.

> > > **NOTE**

Let's not forget the old school approach to copying data—using a floppy disk or writable CD. This is why most large corporations purchase computer workstations without these writeable drives.

Banning Portable Devices

One way to guard against this type of low-level data theft is to ban the use of portable storage devices and iPods in the workplace. This type of device ban is honored more in the breach than in the observance, however; it's devilishly difficult to part these little devices from their owners. In fact, short of searching everyone's pockets and briefcases when they enter the building each day, this is one approach that is likely to fail.

<<< TIP

It should be noted that none of these approaches is 100% foolproof. A physical block of a USB port can be removed. BIOS settings and the Windows Registry can be re-edited. An enterprising thief can even go to the extreme of using a PS2-to-USB port converter, or connecting an external drive via the computer's parallel or serial port. Still, in most cases just the attempt of blocking USB access is enough to discourage would-be data thieves; it's certainly worth the effort.

Disabling USB Ports via the Windows Registry

A more effective approach is to disable the USB drives on all the company's computers. This can be done by purchasing computers sans USB drives; disabling existing USB ports via the computers' operating systems (in Windows, typically via a simple Registry hack); or physically blocking the open USB ports, using masking tape or a plastic plate.

For the technically minded, you can disable writing to all USB devices in Windows XP and Vista by using RegEdit to edit the Windows Registry. Navigate to the `HKEY_LOCAL_MACHINE\SYSTEM\CurrentControlSet\Control\StorageDevicePolicies` section, then add the following command:

```
"WriteProtect"=dword:00000001
```

With this hack enabled, any worker trying to write data to a portable USB drive sees the error message shown in Figure 5.1.

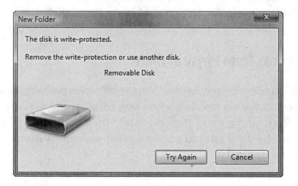

Figure 5.1
What a would-be thief sees after USB drive access has been disabled.

> > > N O T E

You can also disable a computer's USB ports by altering the BIOS settings on the computer—and then locking the BIOS with a password known only to the system administrator.

Software Solutions for Portable Data Theft

You can also disable or restrict access to USB drives via administrative software. These programs let you monitor and control access to removable storage devices via the USB ports of your network's computers.

For example, GFi offers its EndPointSecurity package (www.gfi.com/endpointsecurity/), which controls access to computer ports and external devices on the administrative level. Pricing is on a per-computer basis; for example, the 100-computer package runs $1,800.

A similar program is Reflex Disknet Pro from Check Point Software Technologies, Ltc. This program manages access to all I/O on network computers, including portable storage devices, PDAs, printers, and so forth, via USB, FireWire, Bluetooth, and other technologies. Contact the company at www.checkpoint.com/reflexmagnetics/products/disknetpro/ for more details and pricing information.

Locking Down Corporate Laptops

Another common form of data theft involves the theft of notebook PCs—and the data stored on their hard drives. In today's highly mobile workforce, there's little or no likelihood of outlawing the use of notebook PCs; every employee who travels or works from home needs a laptop. What you can do, however, is minimize the risk of notebook theft.

Protecting Notebooks from Physical Theft

If all employees did was use their notebook PCs in the office, we probably wouldn't have to worry a lot about theft. But when mobile workers take advantage of the portability and use their notebooks on the road, the risk of theft increases. When a notebook PC is publicly visible, it's also publicly vulnerable. How can you protect against someone walking off with a notebook PC when no one's looking?

Anti-Theft Cables

The first thing to do is invest in a physical anti-theft device. The most common such device is a simple locking cable. This cable connects to the Universal Security Slot (USS) located on the side of most notebooks. It then wraps around any secure object or piece of furniture, such as the leg of a table or office desk. If a thief wants to make off with the notebook, he has to carry away the table or desk along with the notebook. You remove the cable by keying in the combination to the cable's lock.

Some of the most popular anti-theft-cables include Kensington's MicroSaver Retractable Notebook Lock (us.kensington.com) and Targus' DEFCON CL Notebook Computer Cable Lock (www.targus.com). Both function similar to bicycle locks; you key in a combination to lock and unlock the cable.

Motion Sensors

Other devices use motion sensing technology to alert the user if the notebook is in any way moved from its current location. For example, Caveo's Anti-Theft PC Card (www.caveo.com) is a motion-sensing device that inserts into your notebooks' PC Card slot; if the notebook is lifted up or carried away, the motion sensor takes notice and sounds the alarm. Better still is the Targus DEFCON 1 Ultra Notebook Computer Security System, which features both an anti-theft cable and a motion sensor; the alarm is sounded if the cable is cut or if the notebook is moved.

Notebook Safes

For those workers who use or transport your notebook in their cars, it's not a good idea to leave the PC sitting on the seat for all to see. Better to lock it up in an in-car safe, away from prying eyes and protected by a secure lock.

One such notebook safe is the Ncase Portable Safe (www.car-safe.com). This case looks like an armored aluminum attaché case. Open it up and it's designed to safely store a notebook PC and other small electronic devices. The contents are secured by a lock and a steel cable that fastens around or to any permanent object.

Notebook Tracking Software

If a notebook PC does get stolen, special software can help you track it down. This software, installed on the notebook, connects to the Internet or dials into a special toll-free number the first time an unauthorized person tries to use the PC; the monitoring center can determine its location by tracking the phone number or Wi-Fi location it connected from. When the company receives a signal from a stolen notebook, it tracks the location of the notebook and works with local law enforcement to recover the machine.

> > > **N O T E**

As an added level of security, most of these programs are designed to survive attempted deletion and hard disk reformatting.

The most popular of these tracking programs include the following:

- Computrace LoJack for Laptops (www.lojackforlaptops.com)

- CyberAngel (www.thecyberangel.com)

- PC PhoneHome (www.pcphonehome.com)

- zTrace Gold (www.ztrace.com)

Expect to pay $30 to $70 per year per PC for the software and accompanying tracing service. Some of these programs also provide data encryption and other functionality.

Protecting Notebooks from Data Theft

What happens if a notebook PC does get stolen—how do you keep your company's valuable data from falling into the wrong hands? There are several steps you can take to defend against this possibility.

BIOS Passwords

One way to foil data thieves is to block access to the computer unless a password is entered. I'm not talking about a Windows password, like we discussed in Chapter 2, "How to Keep Your Personal Information Personal;" I'm talking about stopping the computer from starting up by using a BIOS password. This is a password that is entered when the computer is first booting up. If the correct password isn't entered, the computer doesn't start.

> > > **N O T E**
>
> Not all BIOS versions include a password feature.

What makes a BIOS password so secure is that the only way to defeat it is to physically remove the notebook's CMOS battery to clear the BIOS information. Most thieves, even those who are good at hacking passwords, won't go to this extreme.

To set a BIOS password on a notebook PC, you need to enter the computer's BIOS setup utility. You do this when the computer is first booting up, before Windows launches. You should see a blank screen with a little text on it; the text may tell you how to enter the BIOS or CMOS setup. (You may also need to consult your notebook's instruction manual.) Typically, you enter a particular key or key combination; many computers require you to press the DEL key, although this differs from machine to machine.

When you press the proper key, the boot sequence pauses and the BIOS setup utility appears onscreen. Although different notebooks use different BIOS versions, what you see should look similar to what you see in Figure 5.2. You'll want to enter the advanced or security section of the utility, where you should have the option of entering a password. Do so as instructed, then save your changes and exit the BIOS utility. Your computer now resumes the boot process and starts up normally.

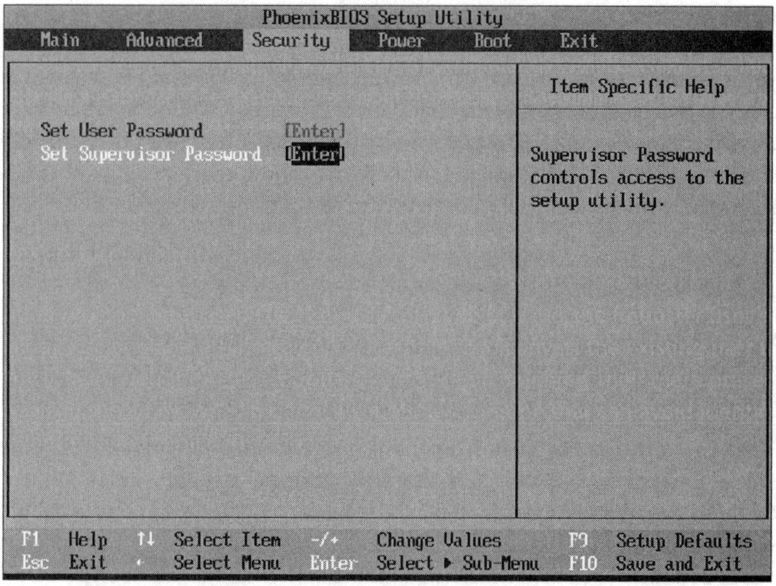

Figure 5.2
Adding a BIOS password to a notebook PC.

Whenever the computer is turned on, the user is now prompted to enter a password at the beginning of the boot process. If the correct password isn't entered (typically within three guesses), the computer doesn't start. That should foil most data thieves.

Fingerprint Readers

Even better than using a password to control access to a notebook PC is biometric security, in the form of fingerprint identification. If a notebook has a built-in fingerprint reader, all you have to do to initiate operation is glide your fingertip over the reader. Your unique fingerprint is entered into the reader's memory; there's no way to duplicate your fingerprint, so no one else can obtain access.

If a notebook doesn't have a built-in fingerprint reader, you can add an external one. For example, UPEK's Eikon USB Fingerprint Reader (www.upek.com) connects to any notebook via USB; the notebook doesn't start unless the fingerprint reader is attached and it's your fingerprint it reads.

File Encryption

Another way to keep unauthorized users from accessing data stored on a notebook PC is to encrypt the notebook's files within Windows. When files are encrypted, no one can open them without first entering the proper password. Without the password, the files are just gibberish.

Microsoft offers what it calls the Encrypting File System (EFS) in the business-oriented editions of Windows Vista—Business, Enterprise, and Ultimate—as well as in Windows XP Professional. In these versions of Windows, you use Windows Explorer to navigate to the file or folder you want to encrypt, then right-click that item and select Properties. When the Properties dialog box appears, select the General Tab and then click Advanced. Check the Encrypt Contents to Secure Data option, then click OK, and the file or folder is now encrypted. The file or folder can only be accessed by the properly logged-on user of the current user account.

C A U T I O N !!!

File encryption does little good if you use an easily cracked password or leave your computer open and running while you're away from your desk. Make sure you lock your computer (from Windows' shut-down screen) if you leave your computer unattended or in a place where it could be compromised or stolen.

Window Vista Enterprise and Ultimate editions also let you encrypt entire drives, using BitLocker Drive Encryption. BitLocker works by encrypting all user and system files on the hard disk, including the swap and hibernation files. No one can decrypt these files without the proper decryption key, which is automatically generated by the BitLocker utility. By default, BitLocker uses 256-bit encryption, which requires a 96-character key to decrypt—long enough to be almost impossible to hack. Access is secured by use of a Trusted Platform Module (TPM) chip in your notebook, in conjunction with a personal identification number or USB device that contains the requested startup key. The encrypted drive can't be accessed without the PIN or startup key.

C A U T I O N !!!

Remember, a thief doesn't have to physically take a PC to steal valuable information; it's all too easy to purloin private information just by looking over the user's shoulder while he's typing. (This is called "shoulder surfing" and is often accomplished by using a cell phone camera to snap a picture of the computer screen.) To keep neighbors from viewing onscreen documents, attach a privacy screen, such as the 3M Notebook Privacy Computer Filter (www.3m.com).

Minimizing Large-Scale Data Theft

The cost of an enterprise-level data breach can run into the millions of dollars. Forester Research calculates that the cost of a data breach runs anywhere from $90 to $305 per record; if a typical data breach involves 10,000 or so records, you can do the math and see why business losses from data theft cost more than $60 billion each year.

Of course, it's not just the money. When a data breach exposes thousands of customers to identity fraud, the company's reputation suffers just as much if not more than its bottom line. Data theft is bad publicity, no matter how you look at it.

With both reputation and money at stake, how do large corporations and organizations protect their data from theft?

What Data Is Vulnerable?

A typical corporation holds many different types of sensitive data, often in different depart-ments and physical locations. It's not just customer data that's at risk; employee records can also be valuable to data thieves.

Here's a quick checklist of the different databases you're likely to find in a typical large organization:

- Customer records database (names and addresses)
- Customer payment database (credit card numbers, and so on)
- Accounting history database
- Human resources employee database
- Employee payroll database
- Employee benefits system database
- Applicant tracking database
- IT department user database (usernames and passwords)
- Facilities system database
- Security system database
- Corporate travel expenses database

And those are just the major systems. It's also likely that individual departments and managers will have more specific databases on their own computes, tracking such things as employee performance, bonuses and commissions, customer contact information, and the like. Add in all the backups and copies of the original files, and you can see the magnitude of the problem.

Bottom line, the typical company has a lot of data and a lot of databases to protect. Let's look at some of the most popular ways to protect this information from theft.

Physical Theft Solutions

Many of the largest data thefts have involved stolen data storage media—hard drives, tapes, and the like. How easy would it be for a would-be thief to sneak into your data storage area, remove a tape or hard drive from the archive, and pop it into his or her briefcase or backpack? If you could imagine yourself pulling this off, then your physical defenses are lacking.

> > > **N O T E**

Computers aren't the only targets of computer data theft. Some network printers include onboard memory that remembers the last documents printed. A thief stealing one of these printers can then print out any confidential documents held in the printer's memory.

The first step in protecting against physical data theft is to consolidate all your digital data into a single area. Don't spread your storage media around the building; centralize the storage of both current and archived media. Putting it all in one place makes it easier to protect.

That done, you want to restrict access to the media storage room. The room should be locked, with access via electronic keycard or keypad access code (or both). Employ stringent physical security; make it as difficult as possible for unauthorized individuals to enter the room and access the sensitive data. (That might mean separate keypad access for storage vaults within the data storage room.)

CAUTION!!!

You should also alert employees to watch for "tailgaters." These are unauthorized people who enter a secured room by following right behind authorized employees, without having to use a keycard or enter an access code.

You also need to restrict the number of individuals who have authorized access to the data storage room. It won't do to employ access cards and keypads and such if you then provide those cards and access numbers to practically everyone in the organization. Pare down the employees who have access to the bare minimum; there must be a real reason for anyone to enter the room and access the data stored within.

The employees who have authorized access to your sensitive data should be worthy of this access. That means conducting background checks to screen out obvious security risks. This might seem like an unnecessary or Big Brother-like step, but it's necessary when you have low-level employees working with the data or technology.

< < < TIP

Remember to change access cards and codes on a regular basis, and to have all ex-employees surrender their cards when they leave the company. In fact, changing cards and codes when any authorized employee leaves may be a good idea.

Finally, your secure data room should be augmented with a monitored alarm system, accompanied by a video surveillance camera. If an unauthorized access occurs—that is, if someone breaks into the room—that access should set off a physical alarm. That alarm should also be monitored by a security company, with the proper response at the ready. Of course, alarming the room means securing not just the main door but also any windows, ventilation ducts, or other means of entrée.

And don't restrict your data theft protection to just digital data. Much sensitive information is still stored physically, typically in manila file folders in somebody's office file cabinet. Regarding these physical records, you need to control who has access to these folders during work hours, who can remove the files from the host office, who can make copies of the files, and who can take files home. It does no good to completely protect your digital data if equally sensitive paperwork can easily be copied by anyone walking down the hall. So put those file cabinets under lock and key, and restrict who has the keys!

> > > **N O T E**

What to do with expired or unnecessary physical records? Don't just put them in the trash—shred them. You should train your employees to routinely shred all sensitive physical data and correspondence, as a matter of course. Larger firms might want to hire a third-party shredding company to shred large amounts of confidential data—typically done on-site, using massive truck-based shredders.

Content Monitoring Solutions

When multiple computers on a company's network have access to sensitive data, it's imperative that that access is monitored, and that inappropriate use of that data is blocked. This is what content monitoring software does—scans network activity to make sure that sensitive data is not compromised.

For example, take the common situation where an employee emails protected documents to his own personal email address, so that he can work on those documents from home. Unfortunately, moving sensitive documents over the Internet to the worker's home computer puts that data at risk. Content monitoring software can detect this activity and block it.

> > > **N O T E**

Remember to include the issues of portable storage devices and laptop theft, discussed previously in this chapter, in your company's data theft prevention plan.

Digital Rights Management Solutions

Digital rights management (DRM) is more popularly known as a technological solution to pirated music, movies, and other digital media. For example, Apple employs DRM on the tunes it offers for sale in its iTunes Store; the DRM software limits how the downloaded music can be used.

What's less known is that companies can also use DRM to protect their sensitive data files from inappropriate use. DRM software lets a company define a file's metadata to control who in the company can access it, for how long, and from which computer(s)—as well as to whom those users can send it and whether or not they can edit, save, or print the file. It's a nifty technological solution to data usage issues.

Encryption Solutions

Hand in hand with DRM solutions are solutions involving data encryption. Although there's no such thing as a perfectly uncrackable encryption, you still need to put up as many barriers as possible to prevent data thieves from being able to access any stolen data—and the most effective solution is a strong encryption scheme.

Put simply, data encryption scrambles the data in question. The data can only be unscrambled after the correct passphrase or passkey is entered. Unless the data thief knows the magic phrase or key, the data remains inaccessible.

Even more important is the dissemination of the de-encryption passwords/passkeys. Encryption is no good if hundreds of people throughout your organization have the keys to unlock the encrypted data. Treat access to de-encryption keys with the same scrutiny as you do access to your data's physical storage area.

Network Intrusion Solutions

Much sensitive data travels over your company's computer network. Anyone with access to the network can intercept these data transmissions—or, even worse, install malicious software to reroute sensitive communications or damage important data.

Your computer network needs to be completely secure from both internal and external intrusion. That means limiting access to authorized users via some sort of password scheme, as well as employing firewalls, anti-virus and anti-spyware protection, and other means to stop malicious attacks and software.

This particular means of protection is so important I devote two sections of the book to the problem. To learn more about defending against malicious software, including Trojan horses, turn to Part VI, "Protecting Against Computer Viruses and Spyware." To learn more about defending against outside attack, turn to Part VII, "Protecting Against Computer Hacks and Attacks."

CAUTION!!!

It should go without saying that any employees leaving the company (even on good terms) need to have their network access revoked immediately. This includes, of course, any means of remote access.

Software Solutions

The data theft problem has inspired a thriving industry to provide enterprise-level solutions. Gartner Research estimated that the data theft prevention industry was worth close to $150 million in 2007, with the most popular programs including content monitoring and digital rights management technologies.

It makes sense to include software solutions as part of your overall data theft protection program. These software programs can help automate some data protection solutions—even if they can't substitute for good old-fashioned diligence and common sense.

Popular data theft protection products include:

- Check Point Media Encryption (www.checkpoint.com)

- McAfee Data Loss Protection (www.mcafee.com)

- Raytheon Oakley Networks SureView (www.oakleynetworks.com)

- Trend Micro LeakProof (www.trendmicro.com)

- Vontu Data Loss Prevention from Symantec (www.symantec.com)

- Websense Data Security Suite (www.websense.com)

Process Solutions

Another way to reduce the risk of data theft is to minimize the risk points. That is, reduce the number of people, processes, and computers that access the data.

To do this, you first have to analyze how data flows in your current processes. Follow the flow of all personal data that comes into your company and see where it goes, who has access to it, and so on. Then work diligently to reduce (a) the amount of data in the system, (b) the number of steps the data follows, (c) and the number of people who have access to that data.

Ask hard questions. Why do you need to collect that particular piece of data? Why does this person or department need access to that data? Why does this data need to be stored after the process is complete? And so on.

For example, do you really need to include an employee's Social Security number as part of a birthday tracking database? Do you need to store a customer's credit card number after a transaction has been completed? Does the shipping department need access to the customer's complete record?

Where you can eliminate data and access, do so. Where the data is absolutely, positively necessary, implement strict access controls and usage restrictions. The only people who should have access to any specific piece of data are those who actually use that data. If access isn't necessary, block it.

< < < **T I P**

> Don't limit your access restrictions to in-house employees. You also need to address remote workers, contractors, business partners, and any third parties that have access to all or part of your in-house databases.

Holistic Solutions

With all these different ways of fighting data theft, which approach should your organization adopt?

The answer, not surprisingly, is probably "all of them." Or at least most of them. You see, there's no one best way to fight data theft; the best protection involves a combination of different defenses.

The key is to integrate all these defenses into a centralized data theft protection program—a permanent initiative responsible to a single manager or corporate executive. The initiative should be treated just like any other corporate initiative, with plans and goals and measurable benchmarks.

What are the goals of a centralized data theft protection program? Your specific goals may vary, but in general you want to address the following:

- Prevent actual data theft (as much as possible)

- Minimize corporate liability for any future data thefts

- Respond effectively to any data theft incidents—minimize damage to employees, customers, and the organization

The data theft protection manager or Chief Security Officer (CSO) should also be in charge of increasing awareness of the problem and training employees on the proper security techniques. Employees must learn that all data, whether from other employees or from your company's customers, is personal, and not to be copied or used anywhere except where absolutely necessary. Personal data must remain secure; if there's no need to store, however temporarily, sensitive data on a worker's personal computer, then that data should not be thus stored. All your company's employees must be trained that there is little or no reason to put most company data at risk. The fewer people who touch the data, the more secure it is.

This training should result not only in a more informed workforce, but also in defined company policies for handling sensitive customer and employee data. It's all part of the whole, and it's the data theft protection manager or CSO who is responsible for constructing and enabling a holistic solution.

Fighting Data Theft on the State and Federal Level

The fight against data theft isn't just a problem in your particular company. Data theft is a problem across multiple industries, and a drain on the entire nation's economy.

This is why various state governments have attempted to address the topic of data theft—in particular, a company's responsibility in reporting and dealing with incidents of data theft. The days of trying to sweep a data breach incident under the rug are long gone; a company cannot ignore its responsibility to its customers and employees in the face of data crime.

The concern is for the violated consumer. Legislators want to protect consumers' rights, to make sure they're contacted in the event their records are compromised, and to minimize their financial risk if stolen records result in identity fraud.

To that end, 38 states now require notification when a security breach presents a risk of identity theft. In these states, a company must inform customers when data is lost or stolen, within a specified period of time. Violations of these laws can bring fines as high as $1 million per occurrence.

In addition, the Federal government is taking the fight against data theft to the thieves themselves. The Justice Department and the Secret Service have worked together in tracking down and arresting known data thieves and users of stolen data inside and outside the United States.

One such investigation, dubbed Operation Firewall, broke up a 4,000-member underground data trading bazaar that had bought and sold nearly 2 million credit card account numbers. This ring had caused more than $4 million in losses to individuals, merchants, and financial institutions.

Still, data crime persists—which is why it behooves the diligent enterprise to go to any lengths possible to protect and secure its sensitive data. Data protection is no longer an option; it's a mandatory part of doing business in today's high-tech environment.

Is It Safe?

If you work in a large organization, can you make your organization's data safe from theft?

Not completely, of course, but you can do a number of things to reduce the risk of theft. Most of these steps require nothing more than a liberal application of common sense and caution—putting sensitive data in secure rooms, tracking all access to said data, restricting the types of data that employees can take with them outside the office, and so forth. As most data thefts are inside jobs, monitoring employee access to sensitive data goes a long way to reducing the risk.

You can then back up these process solutions with the necessary technology-based solutions. That means blocking network access for portable data storage devices, installing data theft protection software, encrypting sensitive data files, and so forth.

Although you can't make your organization 100% safe, you can reduce casual theft by removing the low-hanging fruit and put systems into place to reduce the risk of larger-scale incidents. And, should worse come to worst, you can minimize the impact of any data theft by putting disaster recovery plans in place beforehand—which we discuss in Chapter 6, "Recovering from Data Theft."

Recovering from Data Theft

What should your company do if and when a data breach is discovered? This chapter presents a clear and concise plan of action—whether it's a theft of a hundred employee records from a small company or a theft of a million customer records from a large corporation.

The key, no matter the size of your company or the size of the data theft, is to have a plan in place beforehand so that you can respond rapidly to the situation. The worst responses are the slowest; they leave your customers or employees hanging and in danger of identity fraud, and make your company look disorganized and indecisive. Far better to know how you're going to respond in advance, so that you can then deal with the situation calmly and effectively.

Plan

It is important for any organization that stores large volumes of customer or employee records to plan for the worst—the eventuality of data theft. This planning involves both establishing procedures in advance as well as assigning members of the organization to deal with the situation.

Establish a Rapid Response Team

Before your organization is ever affected by data theft, you need to have a rapid response team in place. This team needs to know ahead of time what steps it will take in response to a data breach, so it can rush that plan into action if and when such a breach occurs.

Without such a rapid response team and plan in place, your company's response to a major data breach is likely to be slow and tentative—which is the exact opposite of what your customers, employees, and the public will demand. You need a fast and sure response, which can only occur if you've planned in advance for such an eventuality.

The task force needs to include members from all affected and relevant departments within your organization. That probably includes human resources, IT, security, risk management, customer relations, public relations, and, of course, senior management. These members need to be defined in advance, and be ready to spring into action when necessary.

Most importantly, the risk management team needs to be empowered to act. The team must be able to do any or all of the following:

- Implement temporary lock-down procedures on the compromised data

- Contact affected customers or employees

- Communicate with the press

- Deal with appropriate law enforcement and government officials

- Work toward recovery of the stolen data

In addition, the team must know which outside resources will be tapped—investigative services, data recovery services, government agencies, and the like. They need to be able to act in an immediate fashion, without having to ask permission before undertaking any of these important activities.

Establishing Procedures in Advance

The rapid response team should also be responsible, in conjunction with your company's CSO or data theft protection manager, for defining all necessary procedures in advance. This may include different procedures for different scenarios—network breach, loss of primary or backup media (tape or disk), loss of physical records, laptop theft, and so forth. Each scenario requires its own specific plan of action; the rapid response team, along with the data theft protection manager, are responsible for thinking through and planning for each eventuality.

As part of these plans, draft communications need to be prepared. You need to know in advance what you will say to your customers, your employees, your partners, and the press/public. You don't want to be composing these important communications in the heat of the moment—or, even worse, risking a company spokesperson to speak to these important constituencies off the cuff.

Your response plan should also detail the chain of command both within the response team as well as regarding how the response team fits into the regular corporate hierarchy. It needs to be clear who is in charge for each task, as well as for the entire operation—and that person needs to be empowered to act.

Respond

If your company is ever the victim of a data breach, the response must be fast and decisive. The longer you wait to respond, the more damage is done—to both the affected parties (in the form of identity fraud) and to your company's reputation. If you wait days or weeks to publicly respond, your company will be perceived as weak, indecisive, and insensitive to customer/employee concerns. You also leave your company open to criticism from customers, others in the industry, the press, and perhaps even the government. (And the last thing you want is undue scrutiny from the government or local law enforcement agencies....)

For this reason, you need to respond as quickly as possible to any data breach—even if your initial response is only partial. Tell your customers/employees/the press what you know, and tell them what you don't know; tell them what you've done, what you're doing, and what you plan to do. And then you have to actually do what you said you'd do. After all, the most important part of your response is to take action, not just to talk about what you're doing.

That said, you don't want to respond with actions or comments that are inappropriate, or with promises that can't be kept. Be honest, be forthcoming, but don't promise or even imply anything that can't be delivered. Don't say "we'll retrieve all the stolen records with no damage" if you really can't do that. (And you probably can't.) Any falsehood you impart, or even management's wishful thinking, could come back to bite you.

Communicate

One of the most important facets of your initial and follow-up response is simple communication. You need to communicate what has happened—what you know and what you don't yet know—to all affected parties:

- Your customers—Those affected by the data breach and those not directly affected (to assuage their fears)

- Your employees—So that they know what's happening and can communicate in line with the rest of the company; or, if their records were stolen, to assuage their fears

- The public (via the press)

- Appropriate government and law enforcement agencies

For the affected customers or employees, your goal is to assuage their fears. They want to know whether they personally are at risk, and how, and what you're doing about it. So tell them—as much as you know, anyway. It's okay to say that X number of customer records were stolen, and it's also okay to say that none of these records have yet been used by the criminals. (If, in fact, that's the case.) Don't minimize the damage, but also don't unduly prolong fear.

For the press, your goal is to minimize the story—and your bad P.R. Get as much information out as soon as possible, and try to make the whole thing a one-day story. The longer it drags on, the more bad press you accrue. Put as good a spin as possible on it (without lying, of course), get all the facts out in the open, and then let the story die of its own accord.

For local law enforcement and state and federal government, your goal is to clearly communicate the facts of the situation. Law enforcement needs to know what happened so they can track down the criminals; the government needs to know the extent of the breach, in accordance with relevant regulations regarding data and identity theft.

Your communications must address the situation directly. You should state what happened, the known extent of the breach, and any not-yet-knowns (how the theft occurred, whether the stolen data has actually been used, that sort of thing).

You also need to reassure all affected parties that your company is on top of the situation. Make it known that an in-depth investigation is underway, that a task force has been empowered to address the situation, and that "lock down" procedures are in place to prevent future occurrences.

Then, as soon as the company has formalized a response, you need to let the press and relevant parties know that all affected customers or employees will be given assistance to (a) protect them from actual identity theft or credit card fraud and (b) reimburse them for any resulting damages or expenses. (This later point should be stated only if, in fact, your company is taking this extra step—which I hope it does.)

> > > **N O T E**

> It should go without saying that you shouldn't make any statements that are speculative or not true, or on which the company has no intentions of following through. To that end, your statements and actions should be approved by all relevant management —and your company's rapid response task force, if it exists.

Contact

A vital component of your communications strategy is contacting those individuals affected by the data breach—those customers or employees whose records were stolen. I'm not talking about a press release stating that 100,000 records were stolen; I'm talking about personal communication with each and every individual who was put in harm's way because of the theft.

Your contact with the affected individuals should be prompt, but doesn't have to (and probably shouldn't) be within the first day or two. That's because this soon in the game you probably won't know enough details to provide a complete response. You may need to wait a few days or weeks in order to communicate fully with the affected individuals.

What do you need to tell the affected individuals? Here's a short list:

- Let them know that their customer records were stolen (or lost or accessed without authorization or whatever the situation is).

- Tell them what information was stolen—name, address, phone number, credit card number, password, Social Security number, or whatever. Be detailed.

- Pass along any information you have as to the progress of the investigation. Tell them whether any stolen records have registered any inappropriate use—or if they haven't been touched (yet). Let them know what you're doing and what law enforcement is doing to track down the thieves and retrieve the stolen data.

- Inform them about any and all assistance or compensation you're offering them. For example, you might arrange with the three credit reporting agencies to offer free credit reports to affected individuals, or you may offer to automatically place fraud alerts on all customer/employee credit accounts.

- If your company has insurance against this type of data theft, and if that insurance includes costs incurred by affected customers/employees, tell them about it. Let them know all sources of assistance and compensation that are available.

- Let them know what they should be doing to look for and protect against any unauthorized use of the stolen data. This could involve checking their credit reports, examining their credit card statements, and the like.

- Inform them of any legal recourse they might have against your company. That's right, give them a little ammunition; they'll find out soon enough on their own, anyway, so you might as well be up-front about it.

This is just the initial contact, of course. You should follow up on this first message with additional communications updating them on the progress of the investigation, as well as any other assistance you're offering. It's important that you constantly keep the affected individuals in the loop; the more you tell them, the less anxious they'll be.

> > > N O T E

You should also contact those customers or employees who were *not* affected by the data breach—and it's okay to do this early in the process. Don't leave your customers/employees hanging; let them know that their records weren't stolen and that they have nothing to worry about. Your customers/employees will thank you for this reassuring contact; it's always nice to receive good news.

Compensate

This is a controversial step. What do you owe those individuals whose records were stolen from your company?

Legally, probably nothing. There have been several instances where individuals affected by a data breach sued the companies where the breach occurred, asking for various damages. Repeatedly, the courts have ruled that the victims were not owed damages by the host company; it was the thieves who did the damage, not the company hosting the records that were stolen.

For example, in August 2007, the 7th U.S. Court of Appeals ruled against victims of a 2005 data breach at Old National Bankcorp. The victims had filed a class action lawsuit against Old National, asking for blanket damages resulting from the data breach. The court ruled that damages were unavailable to victims of data theft if those victims did not suffer economically. That is, blanket restitution was not necessary.

This may or may not be fair to the victims of identity theft, but it appears to be the way things are. That doesn't mean, however, that your company doesn't owe anything to those individuals whose records were compromised.

Some companies try to ward off the eventual lawsuits by offering blanket compensation to victims. For example, TJX responded to their massive 2006 data breach by offering affected individuals a compensation package that included up to three years free credit monitoring, free identity theft insurance, and reimbursement for the cost of having any personal documentation replaced. In addition, customers were offered vouchers if they can prove they shopped at a TJ Maxx or sister store at the times the company's databases were being hacked and incurred losses as a result.

At the very least, you should provide the affected individuals with free credit reports for a year or more. You can arrange this with one or more of the major credit reporting bureaus (Equifax, Experian, and TransUnion).

Should you provide compensation for any individual losses resulting from the stolen data? Certainly not in blanket fashion; just because a record was stolen doesn't mean that it will be used for identity fraud or credit card theft, or that any attempts at fraud will be successful. You can't just say you're giving $1,000 to all individuals whose records were stolen; the likelihood is that only a small percent of stolen records will actually result in financial harm to the affected individual.

That said, what do you do if an individual can prove financial harm resulting from the data breach? Right now, that's an issue between you and your company's lawyers. Some companies do compensate victims for any provable financial losses; some don't. Obtain your own legal advice regarding your company's liability for any personal lawsuits, as well as obligations under applicable state and federal laws.

Recover

Any data breach that involves electronically hacking into your system at least leaves the data intact; the records are more accurately copied than stolen. However, those breaches that involve physical theft—of a tape or hard drive—can actually leave you bereft of important customer or employee information.

In the event of a physical theft, you need to somehow recover the stolen data. With electronic records, this is most easily accomplished by restoring data from a previous backup. If you're diligent about backing up your company's records on a regular basis, at worst you'll be missing a day or two's information.

In the case of stolen paper records, the recovery process may be more difficult. Perhaps copies of the stolen records exist elsewhere in your organization; it's also possible that the physical records were duplicated electronically. If not, reassembling the stolen data may be a long and involved process, accomplished by hand.

In the best of all possible situations, law enforcement agencies may be able to recover the stolen tape, disk, or physical records. This happens more often than you'd think, especially when the data resided on a stolen laptop PC. Recall the stolen Veterans Administration laptop discussed in Chapter 4, "Data Theft: How Big a Problem?" The purloined laptop was eventually recovered by the police, with all data files intact. That's the perfect resolution of a bad situation.

Correct

Finally, you should never let a data breach, no matter how small, go by without reevaluating what factors contributed to the theft. You need to conduct a thorough investigation to learn how the theft occurred, and what could have thwarted the breach.

It's important that you learn from the theft and beef up your security accordingly. If the theft was a physical one, determine where your company's physical security procedures failed. If the theft was electronic, find out how the hacker gained access to your systems. Get to the bottom of how the data breach occurred.

Then, with this new knowledge in hand, you need to change the way you do things. Not only should you plug the hole that allowed this particular data breach, you should examine your entire data security process and bring it up to current standards. Not only do you want to block another similar attempt, you want to guard against the next type of theft. It's unfortunately common to always be fighting the last war (or, in this instance, guarding against the last theft); because thieves seldom attack the same way twice, it's much more important to think ahead and guard against new and innovative ways thieves might attack you in the future.

Bottom line: Your response to a data theft should involve communication, contact, compensation, recovery, and correction—and that correction very well could lead to a complete overhaul of the way your company protects against data theft.

Is It Safe?

If you can't totally protect against data theft (which you can't), you can at least minimize the damage from any incident that occurs. This means taking control of the situation, which is facilitated by the presence of a disaster plan and a named Emergency Response Team. Know in advance how to respond, and you won't be prone to panic and seat-of-the-pants mistakes.

You should also consider investing in data theft or privacy breach insurance—and enough of it to cover the cost of all breach-related expenses (recovery costs, legal costs, PR costs, consumer-reimbursement costs, and so forth). Although this type of insurance can't, by law, cover the cost of regulatory fines penalties, it can save your company from catastrophic financial loss in the event of a TJX-scale data theft.

The key is to know ahead of time how you'll respond to a data theft incident and then minimize the loss and your company's exposure. Although your company may never experience a data loss of that magnitude, you still need to be prepared—just in case.

Online Fraud: How Big a Problem?

on artists prey on the naïve, the ignorant, the gullible, and the greedy. They've plied their trade for untold thousands of years, duping their victims out of their money, their possessions, and even their very identities. Given the profession's durability and adaptability, it's not surprising that today's con artists have embraced the Internet, perpetrating all manner of online fraud.

What types of fraud are we talking about? Most of it is monetary in nature—phony retailers who charge your credit card but never deliver the goods, eBay scammers selling counterfeit merchandise, even buyers who pay with purloined funds.

But here's the thing: Online fraud isn't that much different than the old-fashioned kinds of cons that have occurred forever in the real world. Which means, of course, that online fraud isn't so much about the technology or media used as it is about con artists taking advantage of willing victims.

This chapter addresses the two most common types of online fraud: online shopping fraud and online auction fraud. As you'll see, they all have a lot in common.

Understanding Online Shopping Fraud

The number of consumers shopping online just keeps growing. The U.S. Department of Commerce estimated that total online retail sales in 2007 topped $136 billion, an increase of 19% from the previous year. The Nielsen Online Global Survey found that more than 875 million users worldwide had shopped online, and that half of all Internet users made at least one online purchase in the past month.

Despite this surge in online sales, however, millions of potential consumers shy away from online shopping, afraid of trusting their credit card information to some unknown entity on the other end of the Internet connection. Two out of three U.S. online shoppers say they're concerned about protecting their personal and financial information online, and three quarters say they don't like sending their personal or credit card information over the Internet. Some shoppers say this keeps them from making additional online purchases.

The fear is understandable. Online shopping fraud exists—even if it isn't as widespread as some people seem to think.

The Biggest Risk: Credit Card Fraud

The biggest risk of shopping online is credit card theft. As you learned in Chapter 1, "Identity Theft: How Big a Problem?," theft is always a risk when transmitting your credit card information online, which you do when you're making purchases from an online retailer. It's certainly possible for a tech-savvy thief to intercept the transmission of data packets from the Internet and extract private information from the flow. However, this type of activity is extremely rare, both because it's difficult and because you're just one user out of millions. As you also learned in Chapter 1, it's actually easier and more efficient for a would-be thief to steal credit card numbers by listening in on cordless phone calls via a low-cost scanner, or to go dumpster-diving for discarded receipts behind a local restaurant or retailer. Sniffing and intercepting individual credit card numbers online is a lot of effort for very little return.

A bigger risk comes from large-scale data theft. As you learned in Chapter 4, "Data Theft: How Big a Problem?," your personal and financial records can be compromised when an online retailer or credit processing company has its data stolen. Fortunately, most sites of this type are extremely secure, employing a variety of security measures to keep their customers' information private. But it's also true that this type of data theft does occur—witness the 94 million records stolen from TJX Companies in 2006.

So, yes, it's possible that the credit card information you transmit to complete an online purchase can be stolen, and when stolen used to illegally purchase merchandise using your account and funds. These illegal purchases weigh on the retail community, who shoulder the brunt of the cost of the fraudulent transactions.

From a retailer's perspective, making a sale online or over the phone is a riskier proposition than accepting a physical credit card in person. In fact, the incidence of fraud from online credit card purchases is more than twice as high as the fraud from traditional retail transactions.

A survey by market research firm Celent Communications found that in 2007, the fraud rate for credit card transactions on the Internet was 0.2% percent—that is, two-tenths of one percent of all online credit card transactions were found to be fraudulent. This is a very low number, but not nearly as low as the offline fraud rates of 0.08% for Visa and 0.09% for MasterCard.

For merchants, that means that it's twice as risky to take a credit card sale from an online customer than it is from one in person in a bricks-and-mortar store. This reflects, of course, the fact that it's easier for a credit card thief to use stolen data anonymously online than it is in person.

Not Getting What You Ordered

The Internet Crime Complaint Center (IC3) is a partnership between the FBI, the Bureau of Justice Assistance, and the National White Collar Crime Center; its mission is to receive and refer criminal complaints regarding all manner of cybercrime. Its latest report, covering the year 2005, found that 19% of the complaints registered involved non-delivered merchandise from online retailers.

Now, some complaints about not receiving merchandise translate into not receiving merchandise in a timely fashion. Fortunately, most shipping problems work themselves out in time; when a retailer says the package is in the mail, it usually is—even if delivery is running late.

Sometimes, however, orders don't arrive at all. This can happen even with legitimate retailers, even the best of whom occasionally misplace orders or have systems problems. This is why, if you don't receive your order in a timely fashion, it pays to contact the company's customer service department via either email or phone. Lost orders can be reshipped.

A smaller percentage of non-delivered merchandise comes from placing orders with disreputable merchants, or with con artists posing as online retailers. If a merchant is actually a merchant and refuses to rectify the situation, you have a legitimate complaint—although it might be stretching it to call the situation "fraud." On the other hand, a con artist posing as a legitimate retailer *is* fraud—which is discussed next.

When Is a Merchant Not a Merchant?

A con artist masquerading as an online retailer is a form of phishing fraud. The website in question looks like a legitimate shopping site, but when you place your order and provide your credit card information, you never receive the merchandise you purchased. The site was just a sham, designed to trick you into giving your credit card number—which is then used for unauthorized purchases from another web retailer.

> > > **> N O T E**
>
> Learn more about phishing in Chapter 10, "Email Fraud: How Big a Problem?"

It's difficult to determine phony websites upfront; they often look just like regular retail sites, but looks can be deceiving. It's always wise to look for the secure ordering icon, of course; we discuss this in more detail in Chapter 8, "How to Not Be a Victim of Online Fraud." It's also a good idea to do some research on any website that looks or feels suspicious; if it's a scam, chances are someone else has noticed this and posted about it online. (Google is your best friend in this regard.)

Even better, look for direct contact information on the website—in particular, a real-world address or telephone number. Scammers never display this type of contact info, which you can also use to search for more information about the retailer. If there's no contact info, don't buy there.

Which Merchants Are Riskier?

Although online shopping in general is inherently (but not completely) safe, not all online merchants are equally secure. In general, bigger online retailers are safer than smaller ones. The biggest retailers are every bit as reputable as their big bricks-and-mortar cousins, offering safe payment, fast shipping, and responsive customer service.

Many of the smaller merchants on the web are just as safe as the bigger ones, although they may not have the same level of customer service as the big sites—which may inspire less confidence on the part of wary consumers. Still, if a merchant offers secure shopping and ordering for its credit card transactions, the risk of your data being picked off by a tech-savvy thief is low. (That's not to say that your overall experience with the retailer will be great, however.)

On the other hand, some smaller online retailers are nothing more than garage or basement operations, often not even accepting payments via credit card. When you're dealing with one of these very small retailers, you take your chances. Some of these merchants are as safe and as helpful and as friendly as the store down the street; others are no better than dealing with a stranger at a garage sale.

So although it's difficult to judge the size or stability of any online retailer (any size business can hide behind a fancy web page), chances are if you use a site that is big enough to accept credit card payments (directly, not via PayPal), you're relatively safe.

> > > **N O T E**

> Accepting credit card payments via PayPal or a similar online payment service is not the same as having a merchant credit card account. Any size merchant, or even individuals, can have a PayPal account; only larger merchants qualify for dedicated merchant credit card accounts.

Understanding Online Auction Fraud

If you buy or sell items via online auction on eBay (www.ebay.com), you are at risk for all types of different frauds. Not to be alarmist, but eBay is fertile ground for con artists, simply because the site is so popular; the more users, the more appealing it is to fraudsters.

The Internet Crime Complaint Center reported that online auction fraud accounted for nearly 45% of all complaints it received in 2005. This makes auction fraud far and away the biggest category of online fraud.

This incidence of online auction fraud should be put in perspective, however. eBay claims that the percentage of auctions that end in a confirmed case of fraud account for less than 1/100 of 1 percent of all auctions on the site. That doesn't mean you can't be conned, or that you shouldn't take precautions; it only means that the vast majority of people you deal with in online auctions are honest.

What makes eBay auction fraud problematic is that eBay itself doesn't get involved with individual transactions. The site only *hosts* the auction; it doesn't inject itself into the actual financial transaction between the seller and buyer of a piece of merchandise. Because these are one-on-one transactions between two individuals, it's easy for one individual (typically the seller) to defraud the other.

So, given this structure, what types of auction fraud are you likely to encounter? Let's take a look.

Dealing with Shady Sellers

When you're bidding for and buying items on eBay, you're pretty much in "buyer beware" territory. You agree to buy an item, almost sight unseen, from someone about whom you know practically nothing. You send that person a check or arrange payment via credit card, and then hope and pray that you get something shipped back in return—and that the thing that's shipped is the thing you thought you were buying, in good condition. If you don't like what you got, or if you received nothing at all, the seller has your money—and you've just become a victim of auction fraud.

Not receiving merchandise you've paid for, even on eBay, is a form of theft and should be reported to the proper authorities. If the deadbeat seller can be identified and tracked down, that person can be arrested—and your payment returned, if possible.

> > > **N O T E**

Fortunately, eBay and PayPal have buyer protection plans in place to ward against auction fraud, and refund (most of) your money if you're a victim. Learn more in Chapter 8.

Considering Second Chance Offers

Some unscrupulous sellers like to manipulate eBay's Second Chance Offer feature. This feature lets a seller offer a similar item to nonwinning bidders; that is, if someone else wins but the seller has another unit of the same item, he can sell that item to the second-highest (or third-highest or whatever) bidder.

The problem occurs when a seller offers a quasi-official second chance offer—an offer to purchase a similar item *outside the eBay system*. An official Second Chance Offer takes place within the confines of eBay and offers the buyer all the protection of a standard eBay sale; it also costs the seller the same as a normal sale. Shady sellers game the system by sending you an email making you the offer, rather than the official Second Chance Offer notification. He offers to sell you a similar item for the agreed-upon price but requires direct payment (not via PayPal).

If you bite on this outside-the-system offer, you lose the buyer protection offered by eBay and PayPal. And if you never receive the merchandise (a likely possibility in this scenario), you're up the proverbial creek without a paddle.

Dealing with Counterfeit Merchandise

Another problem facing eBay buyers is the issue of counterfeit merchandise. Perhaps you bid and won what you thought was an expensive Rolex watch, only to find out it was a cheap "Rollexx" knockoff. Or maybe you paid your money for what you thought was an authentic fig-urine or model kit, only to be shipped an inferior recast of the original piece. It happens—more often than you'd think.

eBay vigorously pursues sellers who offer counterfeit merchandise, even when they're clear about what they're selling. The site tries to maintain good relations with name-brand sellers, and doesn't allow knock-offs to be advertised or sold. That said, eBay knows about offending sellers only when someone points them out—which means the onus is on the other members of the eBay community to sniff out and report sellers offering counterfeits. This is done via eBay's Verified Rights Owner (VeRO) program, more details of which can be found at pages.ebay.com/help/tp/vero-rights-owner.html.

If you have been the victim of a seller substituting fake merchandise for the real thing, you've received merchandise that was not as described and have recourse via either the PayPal Buyer Protection program or eBay's Item Not Received or Significantly Not as Described process. We discuss both programs in Chapter 8, so turn there for more details.

Dealing with Deadbeat Bidders

Sellers can also be victims of online auction fraud. Fortunately, this type of fraud is normally less painful.

This type of auction fraud occurs when an individual makes the high bid in an auction, but then doesn't send payment. If you're the seller, your only inconvenience is that you have to relist the item in another auction; you aren't out any money. (That's assuming you haven't shipped the item before receiving payment, which would be a very dumb thing to do.)

The key to protecting yourself as a seller is to hold onto the item until you've received pay-ment, and until that payment has cleared the bank. If you don't get paid, you don't ship—period.

How many buyers end up not paying? eBay isn't saying, but I know from personal experience that it happens—but not often. It's more common to have a buyer complain about what he received after the fact; even eBay users sometimes get buyer's remorse. That said, if you have a winning bidder who doesn't pay, you can recover your eBay fees, relist your item, or even offer the item to the next-highest bidder via eBay's Second Chance Offer program. You're not out anything, financially.

Dealing with Counterfeit Cashier's Checks

Here's another scam affecting eBay sellers. It's relatively rare, but costly when it does occur.

C A U T I O N ! ! !

Counterfeit cashier's check fraud can strike any online seller, not just eBay sellers.

This fraud involves counterfeit cashier's checks, and the buyer is typically located outside the U.S. After winning your auction, the buyer offers to pay via cashier's check, but he only has a check for an amount higher than the item price. He'll send you the larger cashier's check, and you'll send him back the merchandise and the balance between the cashier's check amount and the price of the item. This is typically not a small dollar amount.

In some instances, you see the additional wrinkle that because the buyer is in another country, the cashier's check comes from an associate of his in the U.S. You're then asked to ship the item to the associate, and wire the monetary difference to the buyer in his foreign location.

In any instance, the fraud is that the cashier's check is counterfeit. (Yes, it's possible to counterfeit cashier's checks and money orders; not common, but possible.) Because most banks treat cashier's checks as cash, the funds are immediately added to your account, and you think everything is cool. However, when the cashier's check is later found to be fraudulent, your account is then docked for that amount. You're left with nothing deposited, a hefty fee from the bank for the bad check, and real money sent to the buyer—along with the merchandise he "bought."

Dealing with eBay Identity Theft

In recent years, some eBay users have become victims of an eBay-specific type of identity theft. This takes the form of an unauthorized user hijacking the eBay ID of a legitimate user, and then using that ID to stage fraudulent auctions. The scam artists make a quick buck by taking money from unsuspecting bidders, with the legitimate user (the one whose ID was stolen) left holding the bag.

eBay blames these identify thefts on that form of password crack known as a *dictionary crack*. This happens when a tech-savvy fraudster uses an automated program to take a known user ID and then match it with a list of common passwords and a dictionary of common words. It's a brute force method of guessing a password, but given time, it can work.

This type of identity theft typically involves user accounts that have not been active for some time. The fraudster assumes (correctly, in most cases) that the user of an inactive account is less likely to notice suspicious activity under his name. By the time he notices or gets billed for the fraudulent auctions, the identity thief has moved on to another victim.

As a seller, you want to beware of having your account hijacked in this fashion by identity thieves; that means not falling prey to phishing scams and being constantly vigilant in regard to your account's activity. As a buyer, on the other hand, you want to avoid buying from thieves using hijacked accounts—because you probably won't receive the merchandise you paid for.

You can avoid falling victim to fraudulent auctions from identity thieves by avoiding auctions from sellers who have been inactive for extended periods. For example, if you check out a seller's past auctions and find that his last auction was six months ago, and now all of a sudden he's selling a raft of very high-priced items, it's possible that the seller ID has been hijacked.

Dealing with eBay Phishing Scams

Probably the biggest eBay-related scam today doesn't have to do with buying or selling. Instead, it's the fake email commonly called a *spoof* or *phishing* scheme. This scam comes in the form of an official-looking email message, purportedly from eBay or PayPal, like the one in Figure 7.1. You respond to the email and are greeted with an official-looking eBay logon screen; when you enter your user ID and password, that information is passed on to the identity thief, who uses it to hijack your eBay account for fraudulent purposes.

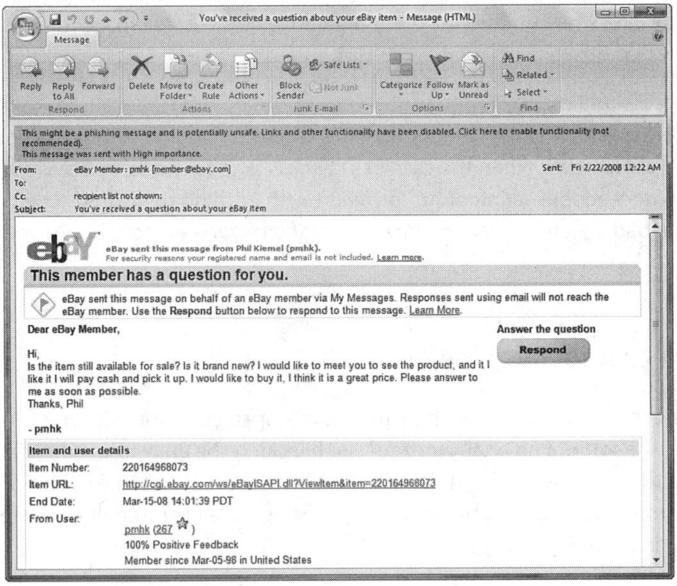

Figure 7.1
A typical phishing email—it's not really from eBay.

How do you tell a fake email from a real one? It should be simple, because eBay never asks for your personal information via email. But when the messages look identical to official eBay messages, and lead you to a real-looking site to enter your ID and password, it's a little trickier.

The best advice is the same as that for any type of phishing email—never enter any information on a page that you get to by clicking a link in an email message. If you need to change your eBay or PayPal information, go directly to the official site; do *not* click to the site from a link in an email message.

We'll talk a lot more about phishing emails in Chapter 10, so I'll hold off further discussion until that time. Know, however, that this is a very visible and consistent problem; some eBay users get one or more phishing emails like this a week. It pays to be vigilant when responding to even official-looking requests from eBay and PayPal.

Is It Safe?

Is it safe to shop online? Is it safe to buy and sell on eBay?

The answer to both questions is a qualified yes.

The incidence of online shopping and auction fraud is much lower than media reports would have you believe. Unfotunately, those rare incidents often get press coverage; dig past the sensationalism, and you find that the numbers don't back up the panic-inducing reporting.

In other words, shopping online and buying and selling on eBay are all relatively safe activities—if you use common sense. I've been an avid online shopper for 15 years and have been participating in eBay auctions for more than 10 years, and I've had nothing but positive experiences. (Save for the occasional deadbeat eBay bidder, of course.) But then, I read the fine print, I compare prices between different websites (and between online and offline retailers), and I don't get suckered into deals that are too good to be true. In other words, I use common sense. I recommend that you do so, too.

How to Not Be a Victim of Online Fraud

Online shopping and auction fraud can be financially damaging to victims. You pay good money and receive either nothing or something unwanted in return. How do you avoid being taken by these online fraudsters?

The keys to protecting yourself against these types of online fraud are homework and diligence. If you do your research before you buy, you'll reduce your risk of falling victim to unscrupulous sellers—on eBay and beyond.

Protecting Yourself from Online Shopping Fraud

Experienced online shoppers know that shopping online is no more dangerous than shopping in the real world. That's not to say that every transaction is 100% safe from fraud or other problems; nothing's that assured. But you shouldn't have any qualms about shopping online or providing your credit card information to pay for a purchase over the web—as long as you take a few common-sense precautions.

Researching Retailers Before You Buy

One of the best protections against online shopping fraud is to research a retailer's reputation before you place your order. Retailers with strong reputations are relatively safe to buy from; retailers with a lot of consumer complaints are more prone to problems and should be avoided.

Where do you research online retailers? On the web, of course. Just as there are sites devoted to customer reviews of specific products, there are also sites devoted to customer reviews of specific retailers.

< < < **TIP**

> You can tell from individual reviews about a retailer just what a specific merchant is good or bad at. You might find one retailer has fast shipping but poor customer service, or another that offers extremely low prices but ships slowly. Learn from your fellow customers' experience!

Some of the most popular sites with reviews of online retailers include the following:

- BizRate (www.bizrate.com), a price-comparison site that also offers one of the largest databases of store reviews on the web. To access BizRate's merchant reviews, click the Store Ratings link; from here you can browse stores by category.

- Complaints.com (www.complaints.com), a site that is all complaints, all the time—the perfect place to find out what kinds of beefs customers have against a particular merchant or with a specific product. To see what complaints are filed against a specific retailer, enter the merchant's name in the search box and then click the Search All Complaints button.

- ePublicEye (www.epubliceye.com), another site that offers customer reviews of online merchants, as well as information about online fraud and scams. The ePublicEye database isn't quite as extensive as that at BizRate, although the information provided for each merchant is more detailed.

- PlanetFeedback (www.planetfeedback.com), which is a bit different from the typical customer review site. With PlanetFeedback, consumers can both leave and read comments about a variety of online and traditional merchants. The letters you write—positive or negative—are posted publicly for all to read, and also forwarded to the retailer in question. It's a valuable service both for letter writers and for users wanting to know more about particular merchants.

- ResellerRatings.com (www.resellerratings.com), which offers merchant reviews from its 120,000 registered members. Merchant reviews are organized by category, or you can search for specific merchants.

> > > **NOTE**

> In addition to the sites listed here, most price comparison sites also offer ratings or customer reviews of the merchants to which they link. Reviews can also be found on Amazon for the third-party merchants in the Amazon Marketplace.

The Right and the Wrong Ways to Pay

How you pay determines the level of risk you assume when buying online. Some methods of payment are simply safer for you than others

What are the safest ways to pay? Here's a quick list that details the safety level of most popular forms of payment, in order of safest to least safe:

- **Credit cards**—Perhaps the safest way to pay is by credit card. When you pay by credit card you can always contact the credit card company and dispute your charges if the item you bought never arrived or was misrepresented. Paying by credit card also provides a very good paper trail, which can come in handy should disputes occur. In addition, credit card companies have a $50 cap on bad transactions ($0 for personal MasterCard and Visa cards), which substantially limits your liability in the event of a fraudulent transaction. (And it doesn't matter whether the retailer accepts credit cards directly or via PayPal; either is equally safe and comes with similar buyer protections.)

- **Personal checks**—Paying by personal check is fairly safe, as you can easily trace whether the check was cashed, when, and by whom. Unfortunately, not all online retailers accept personal checks; in addition, paying by personal check delays the shipment of your item by ten working days or so while the retailer waits for the check to clear.

- **Money orders and cashier's checks**—Believe it or not, cashier's checks and money orders are less safe than personal checks. That's because these forms of payment provide no paper trail to trace if you want to track down the seller. Even though sellers like money orders, you're at the seller's mercy if the payment is in dispute—or if the merchandise never arrives.

- **Cash**—This is the least safe method of payment available today. There's nothing to track, and it's very easy for someone to steal an envelope full of cash. You should avoid paying by cash, if at all possible.

Reporting Fraudulent Business Practices

When you think you're a victim of online fraud, it's time to call in the authorities. If you've had your credit card numbers ripped off, your first call should be to your credit card company. If your card has seen unauthorized use, the credit card company can put a stop to all future purchases and cap your losses, typically at the $50 level.

If you've had a large amount of money ripped off, you should also contact your local police department. In addition, if mail fraud is involved (which it is if any part of the transaction—either payment or shipping—was handled through the mail), you can file a complaint with your local U.S. Post Office or state attorney general's office.

Online, you can register complaints about individual merchants at the National Fraud Information Center (www.fraud.org), which is a project of the National Consumers League. This site transmits the information you provide to the appropriate law enforcement agencies.

Another place to file a complaint is with the Better Business Bureau. The BBB Online Complaint System (complaints.bbb.org) can help facilitate communication between you and the merchant, and possibly get your dispute resolved.

You should also file a complaint about any fraudulent online business transaction with the Federal Trade Commission (FTC). Although the FTC doesn't resolve individual consumer problems, it can and does act if it sees a pattern of possible law violations. You can contact the FTC online (www.ftc.gov/bcp/consumer.shtm) or via phone (202-382-4357 or toll-free at 877-FTC-HELP).

Top Ten Tips for Making Online Shopping Even Safer

Even though the potential for fraud exists, you shouldn't fear online shopping; the incidence of problems of any sort is extremely low. Still, there are several steps you can take to improve the security—and the success—of your online transactions. Read on to discover the Top Ten Tips to make your online shopping as safe as possible.

Tip #1: Trust Your Instincts

Here's the number one rule for shopping online: Trust your instincts. If something smells fishy, avoid it. If you're not comfortable shopping at a specific website, then don't. Determine your own comfortable level of risk for shopping online, and be your best guide.

Tip #2: Shop with Merchants You Know

One of the easiest ways to increase your online safety is to shop only at established and familiar companies. Although it's not a given, it's likely that L.L. Bean's website is more secure than the site for Billy Joe Bob's Online House of Chewing Tobacco. If it's a retailer you've heard of, it's probably legitimate.

Size is also something to look for. The big online-only retailers are just as reputable as big bricks-and-mortar retailers, offering safe payment, fast shipping, and responsive service. Most of the smaller merchants on the web are equally safe, although they might not have the same level of customer service as the big sites. Although it's difficult to judge the size or stability of any online retailer (any size business can hide behind a fancy web page), chances are if you use a site that's big enough to accept credit card payments, you're in safe company.

< < < **TIP**

> If you're hesitant about dealing with a particular online merchant, start by placing a small order. If that goes well, you can consider ordering more merchandise from that retailer.

Tip #3: Check for Complaints

When you're shopping online, it's likely that you'll find some of the lowest prices at merchants you haven't shopped with before. How do you know whether you're dealing with a reputable online retailer—or one that's likely to rip you off?

As you learned earlier in this chapter, one of the better ways to check up on an unfamiliar merchant is to read what others have to say about that retailer. If a retailer has a lot of complaining customers, there's probably a reason for it. Fortunately, you can use the web to check for retailers that have a lot of complaints pending.

You can also check out a retailer's reputation with the Better Business Bureau (search.bbb.org). You can search the BBB database for reliability reports on more than two million different businesses.

Another place to check for complaints against a retailer is with the attorney general's office of the state where the seller is located. View a contact list for the various states' attorneys general at the National Association of Attorneys General (www.naag.org).

Tip #4: Look for the WebAssured Logo

Many quality online retailers subscribe to the WebAssured (www.webassured.com) service. To display the WebAssured logo, shown in Figure 8.1, a merchant has to agree to a high level of conduct encompassing accurate delivery, ethical advertising, full disclosure of product information, fast response to customer complaints, and consumer privacy.

Figure 8.1
WebAssured merchants "deliver what we promise and promise only what we can deliver."

As a consumer, you can use the WebAssured site to search for approved online merchants, request merchant background reports, file complaints about questionable retailers, and engage WebAssured's Automatic Dispute Resolution Service (AdDResS).

Tip #5: Look for a Secure Site

Data sent over the Internet can be picked off by dedicated hackers—unless that data is handled by a secure server. Secure transactions of this sort employ a technology called Secure Sockets Layer (SSL) that encodes information sent over the web, using a form of digital encryption. If both your browser and the website feature SSL security, you know that your transaction has been encrypted and is secure.

Most major shopping sites feature SSL-encrypted ordering and checkout. You'll know you're using a secure site when the little lock icon appears in your web browser. In Internet Explorer 7, the icon is at the far right side of the address bar, as shown in Figure 8.2; in older versions of Internet Explorer, the icon is in the lower part of the browser. If a site's ordering process isn't encrypted, don't shop there.

Amazon.com - Order History: Open and Recently Shipped Orders - Windows Internet Explorer
← → ▾ 🔖 https://www.amazon.com/gp/flex/sign-in/select.html?ie=UTF8&protocol=https   ▾ 🔒 ↔ ✕

Figure 8.2
When this icon appears in Internet Explorer, you're shopping securely.

> > > **N O T E**

> Don't expect to see the secure server icon on regular shopping pages. On most sites, only the checkout
> pages are encrypted in this fashion.

In addition, many secure sites are authenticated by a company called VeriSign (www.verisign.com). If a site displays the VeriSign Secure Site Seal, shown in Figure 8.3, you can be assured that ordering is performed over a secure server.

Figure 8.3
The VeriSign Secure Site seal ensures secure transactions.

Tip #6: Look for Real-World Contact Info

Here's a piece of advice I always follow: Shop at only those sites that have real-world contact information. Let's face it, if something goes wrong with your order, you're going to need to contact somebody. Beware of sites that don't even include an email contact address, and try to target sites that prominently list their phone number (toll-free, ideally), fax number, or street address for post-sale support.

{ P E R S O N A L   E X P E R I E N C E }

> Personally, I won't shop at merchants that don't provide a phone number. There has been the rare occasion
> where something has gone wrong and I need to talk to a real honest-to-goodness human being; as far as
> I'm concerned, no phone number, no order.

Tip #7: Don't Provide Any More Information Than You Have To

One of the risks of shopping online is having your identity stolen during the checkout process. Fortunately, you can limit your exposure to identity theft by providing only information that's absolutely necessary.

When it comes time to place your order at an online shopping site, you're typically presented with a large form with many blanks for you to enter various pieces of personal information. In most cases, fortunately, you don't have to fill out every blank on the form.

Essential fields on the checkout form should be indicated in some fashion, either with shading or an asterisk or something similar; you have to fill out these fields. Other fields are optional and are typically used to collect information that can be sold to marketing companies. (Be especially wary of fields that ask about your hobbies or likelihood to purchase items in the near future.) To keep as much information private as possible, fill in only those blanks that are required by the site.

In particular, you should never provide your Social Security number to an online retailer. (Online banks and brokerages are exceptions to this rule, of course.) There's no reason why an online retailer needs anything more than your name, address, email address, and maybe your phone number to do business with you—along with your credit card number, of course, for payment purposes. *Never* give out your Social Security number needlessly!

Tip #8: Safeguard Your Password

Some online retailers offer rapid checkout to repeating customers, assigning each customer a username (sometimes your email address) and password. Someone who knows your username and password might be able to make purchases from the retailer without providing a credit card number.

Obviously, the weak link in this process is the password. That's not because passwords are inherently not secure, but because most users choose passwords that are too easy to guess. (That's human nature, of course; if a password is hard to guess, it's also hard to remember—and we often compromise security for convenience.)

To create a password that can't easily be guessed, all you need to do is increase the length (eight characters is better than six) and include both letters and numbers—and special characters (!@#$%), if you're allowed. You should also use a combination of uppercase and lowercase letters if the account recognizes both cases. Even better, you should make sure that you don't use the same password on multiple sites; you should also change your passwords on a regular basis.

< < < **T I P**

Want to check the strength of your password? Then use Microsoft's Password Checker, located at www.microsoft.com/protect/yourself/password/checker.mspx.

Tip #9: Pay by Credit Card

It's ironic that some people are afraid of paying via credit card online, when it's the credit card payment that provides the most security for your online transactions. When you pay by credit card, you're protected by the Fair Credit Billing Act, which gives you the right to dispute certain charges and limits your liability for unauthorized transactions to $50. In addition, some card issuers offer a supplemental online shipping guarantee that says you're not responsible for *any* unauthorized charges made online. (Make sure you read your card's statement of terms to determine the company's exact liability policy.)

If you're still uncomfortable sending your credit card information over the Internet, many online retailers let you call in your payment information over the phone. Look for a toll-free number somewhere on the checkout page.

And remember, if you can't get a retailer to refund your money for a bad transaction, you can dispute the charge to your credit card company. Chances are that the credit card company will be able work things out with the retailer, and credit your account for the amount in question.

< < < TIP

If you want your children to shop online and they're too young for their own credit cards, check out Visa Buxx (www.visabuxx.com), a parent-controlled online payment card just for teenagers. You can specify a variety of parental controls, including predetermined spending values and online transaction monitoring. In addition, many online retailers offering services popular with children and teenagers (such as Apple's iTunes Store) allow parents to set a monthly budget for their children so that kids can make purchases up to a set amount with their parent's credit card.

Tip #10: If It Sounds Too Good to Be True—It Probably Is!

Here's one last bit of common-sense advice. You'll find lots of incredible offers on the web, most of which fall under the strict definition of that word—that is, they lack credibility. Do you really think you can get a brand-new notebook PC for less than $200? Or a 40" flat-screen TV for $299? Or a month's supply of Viagra for less than $10? Of course you can't. If the deal appears to good to be true, it probably is. Legitimate retailers present legitimate offers. Don't get burned by dubious offers from shady retailers—let the buyer beware!

> > > NOTE

For more tips on how to shop safely online, visit the Safeshopping.org website (www.safeshopping.org), sponsored by the American Bar Association.

Protecting Yourself from Online Auction Fraud

One of the biggest fears of newbie auction buyers is of getting ripped off in an auction trans-action. Yet, in spite of occasional hysterical news stories to the contrary, eBay is an extremely safe environment. Even though there are bad seeds out there, most people are honest.

Still, because there *are* bad seeds out there, it's possible that you'll run into a shady retailer who never sends you the item you purchased or a buyer who never sends you a check. What can you do to protect yourself against other users who aren't as honest as you are?

Protecting Yourself from Phishing Scams

Let's start with one of the most common online auction scams going today—the so-called "phishing" scam. As already discussed, this type of scam isn't limited to eBay; it happens when an unscrupulous third-party tries to masquerade as a legitimate site, using official-looking email messages, to con you out of information or money.

If you receive this type of email, for either your eBay or PayPal account, you can be sure it's a scam. eBay will never, ever send you emails asking you to update your account and then pro-vide a link in the email for you to click for that purpose. Although eBay does send you emails (and lots of them—either informational or promotional in nature), they don't send out any email that requires a direct response.

It goes without saying that you should never respond to this type of email, no matter how official-looking it appears. If you want to make changes to your eBay or PayPal account, never do so from an email link. Instead, use your web browser to go directly to the official site and make your changes there. No one from eBay or PayPal will ever ask you for this information via email. Be warned!

There are some tell-tale signs of a phishing message, including:

- Many phishing messages just don't look right; they don't use the right logos, or they don't use any logos, or there are obvious misspellings and the like.

- When you hover your cursor over a link and look at the URL, in most instances, it's quite obviously not the right eBay or PayPal domain name.

- If you're using Microsoft Outlook 2007, the program will probably notify you that this is a potential phishing message; it does this when the actual URL doesn't match the visi-ble URL in a message.

- If you install the eBay Toolbar (download for free at pages.ebay.com/ebay_toolbar/), it includes an Account Guard feature that warns you if you go to a potential spoof web-site.

So what should you do if you receive a suspicious email? It's simple—ignore it. Delete the thing from your inbox, and forget about it.

If you want to check for official messages from eBay, you can do so directly from your My eBay page. All you have to do is click the My eBay link at the top of any eBay page and click the My

Messages link. This displays the My Messages page, shown in Figure 8.4, where all your recent messages are listed. These are official communications from eBay and from other eBay users. It's safe to read the messages listed here, because they've been confirmed authentic by eBay. Click any message subject to read the full message—and then ignore any spoof messages that end up in your email inbox!

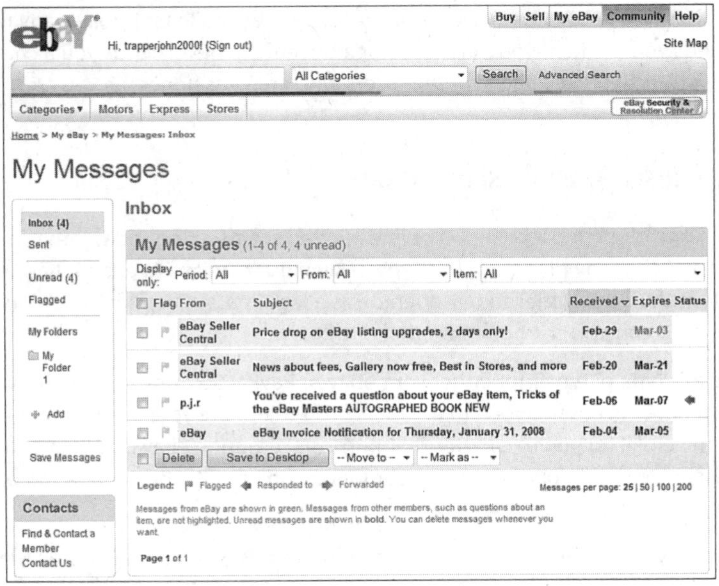

Figure 8.4
My Messages—the safe way to access your eBay messages.

> > > **NOTE**

For more advice on protection against phishing emails, turn to Chapter 11, "Avoiding Email Fraud and Phishing Scams."

Protecting Yourself Against Fraudulent Sellers

Anytime you buy something on eBay, you run the risk of not getting what you paid for. Damaged goods, counterfeit items, used merchandise, products that don't match what was advertised, or goods that were never delivered—these are all issues you can encounter when shopping the eBay site.

As a buyer, you assume more risk than the seller does. You send your money to an individual, and hope that you receive merchandise in return—and that the item is in good condition, as described in the auction listing. Fortunately, there are steps you can take to reduce your risks of being taken advantage of by fraudulent sellers in the eBay marketplace, including the following:

- Always check the seller's feedback rating. And not just the numerical rating—look at the individual comments left by previous buyers. Beware of sellers with a low percentage rating, and with an undue amount of similar negative comments.

- Always pay by credit card. All banks offer strong buyer protection programs; if something goes wrong with the transaction, your credit card company investigates the claim and, more often than not, refunds your money.

- When at all possible, use your credit card to pay via PayPal; the service offers a strong buyer protection plan. In addition, PayPal never transmits your personal financial information to the seller, so that's another level of protection.

- Never pay via cash. Cash is untraceable, which is just asking for trouble. And, besides, reputable sellers never offer cash-only transactions.

> > > **N O T E**

The Internet Fraud Complaint Center notes that of those individuals reporting online auction fraud, 80% used personal checks or money orders to pay for the undelivered merchandise. In other words, the buyers sent the money, and the seller received it and scrammed. Because the payment was in paper form, there was little that could be done to recover the payment after the fact.

- Don't respond directly to second-chance offer emails; scammers often use this approach to try to phish your personal information. Instead, log on to the My Messages in My eBay; if the second-chance offer is there, it's legitimate.

- Be cautious about buying from some foreign countries, especially third-world countries such as Nigeria. These countries are havens for scammers.

And, finally, my best piece of advice is this: Never buy or bid on something that sounds too good to be true. If it sounds like an incredible deal, it probably is—not credible, that is. Trust your nose, and avoid listings that smell funny.

Protecting Yourself from Wire Transfer Scams

Now let's look at a couple of specific eBay scams, starting with the old wire transfer scam.

If you find a seller that demands payment through Western Union or a similar cash wire transfer service (MoneyGram, eGold, and so on), run away as fast as you can. These services are designed to let you send money to family and friends—people you trust. They're *not* to be used to pay for auction items.

> > > **N O T E**

The warning about wire transfers applies to Western Union cash transfers, not to Western Union Auction Payments—previously known as BidPay—which operates much like PayPal and is perfectly legitimate.

Scammers like to receive payment through Western Union and similar cash transfer services, because it's essentially the same as wiring them cash, no questions asked. Cash wire transfers are particularly vulnerable to criminal abuse because they're not traceable, don't offer any verification procedures, and make it difficult to identify the recipient. In other words, these services offer virtually no protection against fraud—which makes them the payment methods of choice for fraudulent sellers, especially those in certain European nations.

Even Western Union warns against abuse of their cash transfer service:

> …we don't recommend that you use a money transfer service to pay for online auction purchases. Money transfer services are fast, easy and convenient ways to send funds to people you know. They are not designed to be a payment vehicle when doing business with a stranger.

And, as if you needed even more disincentive, eBay does not permit wire transfer as an accepted method of payment. If eBay won't let you do it, don't do it!

So if a seller accepts payment only by Western Union money transfer, chances are you're looking at a real honest-to-goodness scam. And if you get taken in this fashion—if you send cash to a stranger who cuts and runs—eBay can't help you much, outside of their normal $200 Buyer Protection Program guarantee.

In short, when you see Western Union cash transfer in the payments accepted section of an auction listing, don't bid—and report the auction to eBay.

Protecting Yourself from Hijacked Accounts

Here's another nasty eBay scam to be aware of—hijacked eBay accounts. This happens when a hacker somehow gains access to a legitimate member's user ID and password, and then takes over that member's identity to launch a series of fraudulent auctions. Everything looks good about the user—because the hijacker is hiding behind the original user's actual feedback—but the auction is a complete sham. When you send away your payment, that's the last you hear of it.

Obviously, eBay does its best to hunt down and close down these fraudulent auctions and hijacked accounts. But how can you identify a fraudulent/hijacked auction before you place a bid?

Here are some telltale signs of a fraudulent auction from a hijacked account:

- The auction is for a very high-priced item, but the starting price or Buy It Now price is considerably below typical retail price.

- Payment doesn't include PayPal or credit cards, instead insisting on money order, cashier's check, or Western Union cash (as discussed previously).

- The seller's feedback is primarily for buying items, not for selling.

- The seller hasn't completed any transactions for several months. (Inactive accounts are more likely to be hijacked.)

- Although the seller's account is listed in the U.S., if you contact the seller you'll find out he's actually in another country. (Eastern Europe is a popular haven for scammers.)

Remember, even if the address and contact info look legit (because they're from the original user), they'll be false. When it comes to sending payment, you'll be instructed to mail it to somewhere else—typically in another country.

To further confuse the issue, many of these scammers send you a follow-up email that claims to be from eBay, vouching for the seller's veracity, or even offering additional insurance to cover the seller's buyers. Because eBay doesn't endorse individual sellers or sell such insurance, you'll know this is a scam.

Bottom line: If you think there's something fishy about a particular auction, don't bid! And if you *know* something is fishy, report it to eBay.

Protecting Yourself with an Escrow Service

There's another payment option you might want to use if you're bidding on a particularly high-priced auction item. An *escrow service* acts as a neutral third party between you and the seller, holding your money until you receive the seller's merchandise. If you don't get the goods (or the goods are unacceptable), you get your money back; the seller gets paid only when you're happy.

When you and the seller agree to use an escrow service, you send your payment (by check, money order, cashier's check, or credit card) to the escrow service, not to the seller. After your payment is approved, the escrow service instructs the seller to ship the item. When you receive the item, you notify the escrow service that you're satisfied with the transaction. At that point, the escrow service releases your funds to the seller.

The cost of using an escrow service is typically paid by the buyer. eBay recommends the use of Escrow.com (www.escrow.com), as there have been some fraud problems with lesser-known escrow sites.

Getting Help if You've Been Victimized by an Unscrupulous Seller

What do you do if you follow all this advice and still end up receiving unacceptable merchandise—or no merchandise at all?

First, know that eBay doesn't accept any responsibility for transactions conducted on its site. It's not the buyer or the seller, only a somewhat disinterested third party.

However, that doesn't mean you shouldn't contact eBay if you're the recipient of a sour deal—you should, and eBay encourages you to do so. At the very least, eBay will start tracking the seller's other activities and perhaps kick the seller off the site if a pattern of fraudulent activity can be shown. Best-case scenario, eBay will actually refund some of the money you've lost.

> > > N O T E

At the very least, you should leave formal negative feedback about any bad sellers you encounter. It's your duty to warn other buyers before they get suckered, too.

eBay used to offer a formal purchase protection program, but that program has been discontinued. Instead, eBay relies on PayPal's Buyer Protection Plan to take care of dissatisfied buyers. This is another very good reason to use PayPal to pay for all your eBay purchases.

Under the Buyer Protection Plan, PayPal reimburses you for up to $2,000 if you don't receive an item you paid for, or if the item is significantly not as described. Note that this $2,000 protection limit is only for items purchased from qualified sellers; for other sellers, PayPal offers a $200 refund limit. To make sure you're buying from a protected seller, look for the PayPal buyer protection message in the Buy Safely portion of an auction listing, as shown in Figure 8.5.

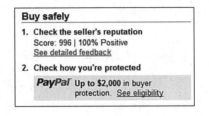

Figure 8.5
This seller is protected via the PayPal Buyer Protection plan.

> > > **N O T E**

> You must file a PayPal claim within 45 days of the date of payment. In addition, you can file only one claim
> per auction listing, and a total of three claims each calendar year.

If you haven't received an item or if the item you received isn't what you think you bought, and if you made your purchase via PayPal, here's how to proceed:

1. **Contact the seller**—If, after a reasonable waiting period, you haven't received an item (or think the seller pulled a "bait and switch" on you), try to work it out with the seller first. Email the seller directly (and politely) and see how he responds.

2. **Open a dispute**—If the seller doesn't respond to your satisfaction, go to the PayPal website (www.paypal.com), select the My Account tab, then click the Resolution Center link. When the Resolution Center page appears, click the Report a Problem link. When the next page appears, select Item Dispute and click the Continue button. You'll now be prompted to supply the ID number for that transaction, as well as provide additional details.

3. **Negotiate with the seller**—PayPal now sends an automated email to the seller, encouraging him to contact you and work out the problem. More often than not, this prompting causes the seller to resolve the issue. If the issue is resolved, the dispute is closed. If not…

4. **Escalate the dispute to a claim**—If you're still not satisfied, you can now escalate the dispute to a formal claim. You must do this within 20 days of first filing the dispute. To file a claim, go to PayPal's Resolution Center and follow the instructions there.

5. **Wait for PayPal to investigate**—PayPal now investigates your claim. If it finds you're right, you get your money refunded, per the fine print of the Buyer Protection Plan. If it finds your claim is unwarranted, it closes the claim in the seller's favor.

If you're left unsatisfied at the close of the PayPal process, you can still contact your credit card company to avail yourself of their buyer protection features. And if you didn't purchase via PayPal or credit card, you can use eBay's Item Not Received or Significantly Not as Described process, although it's rather toothless; it merely sends some automated emails to the seller asking him to acquiesce. To use this process, go to your My eBay page, scroll to the Shortcuts pane, click the Report an Item Not Received link, and follow the instructions from there.

> > > **N O T E**

Be reasonable before you file a dispute. For example, if you paid by personal check, the buyer holds the check for up to two weeks before he ships the item—so you can't expect to receive the item in ten days. Also factor in weekends and holidays before you determine that you're not going to receive an item.

Beyond eBay, you can contact other agencies if you've been disadvantaged in a deal. Follow the same policies as discussed in the "Reporting Fraudulent Business Practices" section, earlier in this chapter, and you'll be well served.

Protecting Yourself Against Fraudulent Buyers

Buyers aren't the only ones at risk in the eBay marketplace. Sellers can also get scammed, from non-paying buyers and from credit card scammers alike.

When selling on eBay, follow these tips to make sure you don't get taken advantage of:

- Never ship your goods until you receive payment. When payment is by personal check, hold the goods for 10 business days to make sure the check clears before you ship.

- Try to funnel payment for as many sales as possible through PayPal. Not only do buyers like PayPal, the service also offers sellers protection against fraudulent and non-paying buyers.

- Be cautious about selling to certain foreign countries, especially third-world countries such as Nigeria. These countries are havens for fraudsters using stolen credit cards; you may think you get paid, but then find a big chargeback on your account when the credit card is reported as stolen.

Savvy sellers also know to avoid some specific eBay scams. For example, consider the situation where you're selling an item, the auction ends, and you get an immediate notice of payment (typically via PayPal) with a request to ship to a different address, as a gift to someone else. Unless you can verify the legitimacy of this request, do *not* ship the item—it's likely that someone has hijacked the buyer's account and is trying to get the item shipped to their own address. (And the payment is likely fraudulent, as well.) If you ship the item to the second address, you are likely to lose both the item and the payment. When in doubt, double-check with PayPal, or hold onto the item long enough for the payment can be verified or cleared.

Another scam revolves around escrow payment. The trick here is that the buyer, after winning the auction, decides he'd rather pay via an escrow service. Now, there are many legitimate escrow services out there, but that's not how this scam works. The buyer recommends a particular escrow site that you've never heard of, and shortly thereafter you receive an email from the site confirming that the buyer has paid and that you should ship the item. The problem, of course, is that the site is fraudulent, the buyer hasn't paid anything, and you've just shipped an item for which you'll never receive payment. To avoid this type of escrow scam, deal only with Escrow.com, eBay's officially authorized escrow service; in addition, you should not respond to any escrow messages sent via email; no legitimate escrow site will send "confirmed to ship" messages via unsecured email. Also check out the discussions on eBay's Escrow & Insurance discussion board; it's a great place to learn about all the latest escrow-related scams!

Is It Safe?

Shopping online can be safe—if you follow the common sense advice imparted in this chapter. Deal only with established merchants, pay only via credit card, and avoid deals that sound too good to be true. That means doing your homework before you buy; check out retailer ratings, compare prices both online and off, and know what's real. Most people who get taken by unscrupulous sellers have only themselves to blame.

The same applies to the eBay marketplace. eBay's feedback system is there to help you avoid scam artists and second-rate sellers; take advantage of it. You should also take advantage of all the buyer protections built into the eBay and PayPal systems. eBay wants your experience to be a good one and goes out of its way to make sure that's the case.

All this said, you can still be taken when shopping online. You can be victimized if you don't read the fine print, if you pay via an unsafe method, if you're greedy enough to be taken by "too good to be true" offers, or if you don't use common sense. In other words, you have to willfully be taken; smart buyers seldom become victims.

Fraud on the Corporate Level: Online Advertising Click Fraud

One more type of Internet-based fraud is worth examining—although this fraud doesn't directly affect the consumer. *Click fraud* affects advertisers, when scammers deliberately inflate the click-through rate on an online advertisement, thus making the ad appear more popular than it really is and causing the advertiser to pay higher rates based on the supposedly higher click-throughs.

Click fraud occurs when individuals or automated software programs repeatedly click the links that appear in web ads. Because there aren't real people viewing a real ad, the activity is fraudulent. And, because advertisers pay for these ads based on number of clicks, they end up paying more without getting the benefit of consumer eyeballs.

Who profits from click fraud? Believe it or not, the online advertising networks, run by Google, Yahoo!, and others, benefit because a fraudulent click is as good as a real one, when it comes to charging the customer. And the scammers benefit, especially if they build "link farms" where they're paid for every link clicked. The victims of click fraud are the companies who pay for the advertising—and their customers, who ultimately have to shoulder the cost of that advertising, in the form of higher product prices.

How Does Pay-Per-Click Advertising Work?

The concept of click fraud is dependent on an advertising model called *pay-per-click*, or PPC. With pay-per-click advertising, an advertiser pays the ad service only when customers click on the link in the ad. If no one clicks, the advertiser doesn't owe anything. The more clicks that are registered, the more the advertiser pays.

> > > **NOTE**

> Pay-per-click advertising is in contrast to traditional cost-per-thousand-impressions (CPM) advertising, where rates are based on the number of potential viewers of the ad—whether they click through or not.

Who Pays Who?

With PPC web advertising, it's not just the ad service that gets paid. Typically, the site where the ad appears gets a cut of the ad revenues paid by the advertiser. So the way it works is thus:

1. An advertiser creates an advertisement and contracts with an online ad network to place that ad on the Internet.

2. The ad network serves the ad in question to a number of affiliate websites.

3. An interested customer sees the ad on a third-party site and clicks the link in the ad to receive more information.

4. The advertiser pays the ad service, based on cost-per-click (CPC) advertising rate.

5. The ad service pays the host site a small percentage of the advertising fee paid.

Advertisers typically purchase search words—that is, they purchase ad space that appears on search results pages and other websites that relate to the keywords in question. So, for example, if you sold printer ink cartridges, you might purchase the words "printer," "ink," and "cartridges." When a consumer searches for any of these keywords or goes directly to a website that features content containing these keywords, your ad appears.

Then, when a customer clicks on your ad, you're charged for that click-through based on the agreed upon cost-per-click rate. If no one clicks your ad, you don't owe the ad network anything.

> > > **NOTE**

> The cost-per-click can be as low as a few pennies or as high as ten or twenty dollars; it's all dependent on the quality of the traffic going to the host site and the competition for that ad space.

Getting to Know the Big Internet Ad Networks

At this point in the process, it's important to know the major ad networks that sell clickable text-based ads on the Internet. Although these companies may be better known for their technology or web services, in reality they make almost all their money from this brokering and placement of Internet-based advertising.

Whenever an advertiser pays Google (for either a click or an impression), the site owner receives a cut of that payment, in the form of a commission. How much of a commission is made depends on how much the advertiser is paying Google for that particular ad. The payment varies by advertiser and by quality of content; competition for the most popular content and keywords causes advertisers to bid up the price accordingly.

The big web-based ad networks are, in order:

- Google AdWords
- Yahoo! Search Marketing
- Microsoft Digital Advertising Solutions

These ad networks essentially serve as ad brokers. They arrange ads from individual advertisers, then place those ads on their own and on third-party websites. Their payment comes from a cut of the PPC revenues.

It's not surprising that the three top online ad networks are run by the three top Internet search engine companies. You see, Google and Yahoo! (and to a lesser extent, Microsoft) do not make money from their search engines. Instead, they make money from the ads they place in their search engines' search results pages—and from other sites in their network across the web. The search engines are merely containers for revenue-generating advertising, much as the articles in traditional magazines and newspapers are just filler between the advertisements that actually pay the rent.

So when we examine who benefits from or is harmed by click fraud, these big three online ad networks obviously float to the top of the list.

What Is Click Fraud?

Click fraud is a deliberate effort to defraud advertisers who pay for their ads by the click. Click fraud occurs when a link within an online ad is clicked for the sole purpose of generating a charge per click, with no actual interest in the ad itself or the site linked to within the ad.

Click fraud can be perpetrated by a person, automated script, or computer program. In fact, there are numerous different varieties of click fraud, using various methods to initiate the fraudulent clicks.

> > > **N O T E**

Not only is click fraud a violation of most ad agencies' participation agreements (you agree not to click on your own ads), it's also a crime. In many jurisdictions, use of a computer to commit this type of Internet fraud is a felony, and law enforcement has been eager and willing to go after alleged perpetrators.

Manual Click Fraud

The simplest form of click fraud comes when an interested individual manually clicks the link in an ad, over and over and over. This typically comes when an individual launches a website, complete with PPC advertising. The individual then clicks the links in the ads on his site, generating revenue for himself. (Remember—the website publisher gets a cut of all PPC advertising.)

> > > **N O T E**

Because the number of clicks and their value is often quite small, this type of manual click fraud often goes undetected.

It's not surprising that manual click fraud is also the least effective method; one can only click so fast so long. For that reason, the instances of manual click fraud today are rare and relatively insignificant, in terms of magnitude.

Script-Based Click Fraud

Manual click fraud is small potatoes. Much larger scale fraud is perpetrated when the fraudulent clicks are automated.

One of the easiest ways to automate click fraud is via the use of computer scripts—bits of programming code that simulate manual clicking on ad links. This is typically accomplished by running the script on one or a few computers owned by the website host and his friends; from these few computers come thousands of fraudulent clicks.

> > > **N O T E**

Automated clicking scripts or programs are called *clickbots*.

The problem with script-based click fraud is that it's relatively easy to catch. An ad network, noticing a suspiciously large number of clicks on an ad, can examine the IP addresses of the computers that generated those clicks. If the clicks are concentrated on one or a few computers in a small geographic area, it's a sure sign of script-based click fraud—and the perpetrator is easily tracked down and brought to justice.

> > > **N O T E**

Script-based click fraud is popular with organized crime, who can install click scripts on computers through-out their widespread organization. Because the computers are dispersed geographically, the fraud is harder to identify.

Traffic-Based Click Fraud

Here's another type of tech-based click fraud. In this type of fraud, the fraudster uses script or programming code and something called 0-size iframes to convert the existing user traffic of his site into clicks. Although the users don't in fact click on anything, their mere presence registers as a click in the ad network. It's a tricky approach, but one that can avoid identification from a concentration of similar IP addresses.

> > > **N O T E**

An iframe is an inline frame on a web page that typically contains another document. With traffic-based click fraud, the iframe contains the code that converts views to clicks.

PTR Click Fraud

An even better situation for a click fraudster is to get someone else to click an ad for you. This is the goal of so-called *paid to read* (PTR) sites, where other individuals are paid to repeatedly click on a given ad on the fraudster's website. By spreading out the clicks among a large number of computers, an ad network can't easily identify fraud patterns by IP address.

The way this fraud works is simple. The website owner joins a click-fraud ring or advertises his site to users willing to participate in the scam. Site visitors are then paid small amounts of money (typically a fraction of a cent) to visit the site and click ad links. The more the visitors click, the more money they earn for themselves—and the more revenue is generated by the ads on the fraudster's site. Obviously, the fraudster pays the clickers a subset of the revenue he earns from the PPC ads; some PTR sites have hundreds and thousands of users merrily clicking away in their free time.

> > > **N O T E**

Some participants in PTR rings (the people who do the clicking) claim to make hundreds of dollars a week for their efforts. This is particularly appealing to low-wage workers in some foreign countries—which explains why click fraud is higher in those parts of the world.

Hijacked PC Click Fraud

Another way to use other computers to commit click fraud is to hijack those computers via a computer virus. As soon as the virus is installed on the PC, it is effectively hijacked; it can now be controlled remotely by a host computer. (A hijacked computer used in this fashion is called a *zombie computer*.)

The remote control operation, of course, is focused on using the computer to commit click fraud. The zombie computer is directed to connect to the website in question and repeatedly click the site's ad links, typically via a clickbot script installed on the machine without the user's knowledge. Thus click fraud is perpetrated without the computers' owners ever knowing about it.

> > > **N O T E**

> Learn more about zombie computers in Chapter 19, "Computer Viruses and Spyware: How Big a Problem?"

Impression Fraud

One more variant of click fraud bears discussion. *Impression fraud* is kind of the mirror image of traditional click fraud; fraudsters scheme to disable competitors' ads by creating an artificially low click-through rate on those ads. This is accomplished by making numerous searches for a keyword but then never clicking on the competitors' ad. The result is a high number of impressions with an artificially low click-through rate; the competitor's ads thus get placed lower in the ad queue, whereas the fraudster's competing ads get a higher ranking.

Who Benefits from Click Fraud?

Who reaps the profit from click fraud? It depends on who's doing the clicking, and why.

Most instances of click fraud directly benefit the entity doing the clicking. Typically the ad that is clicked resides on the individual's own website. Because host websites receive a portion of all PPC revenues, every click on a site's ads results in money flowing into the pockets of the site's owner. By perpetrating click fraud, the site owner artificially inflates the revenues his site earns from the hosted ads.

> > > **N O T E**

> Particularly aggressive fraudsters build websites that are nothing more than links to dozens of other websites—which they also own. These so-called "link farms" are frowned upon by Google and others but annoyingly common on the Internet today. Similar to link farms are "splogs," or spam blogs, that are used solely to promote affiliate websites or link farms.

Other instances of click fraud are designed more to harm the advertiser than to benefit the host website. In these instances, non-contracting parties (not part of any PPC agreement) use click fraud to harm their competitors in the marketplace. For example, a competitor of the advertiser might use click fraud to drain the competitor's advertising budget, which is then spent on the increased payment for irrelevant clicks. Or a competitor to the host website might use click fraud to make it look as if the owner of the website is clicking on his own ads, thus harming the website's relationship with the ad network.

Then there are those instances of click fraud that are out and out malicious. Online vandalism does occur, and unwarranted ad clicking is part of that pattern. An individual might use click fraud to perpetuate a personal vendetta against an advertiser or website, or may target a site just for kicks. It happens, often with no rhyme or reason.

> > > **N O T E**

> One of the most famous instances of click fraud didn't involve any actual clicking. In 2004, programmer Michael Anthony Bradley developed an automated clickbot program that he called Google Clique. He used the program to try to extort Google, asking for $150,000 or he'd distribute the program worldwide—resulting in potential click fraud damages of over $5 million. Bradley was subsequently arrested and charged with extortion, although the charges were later inexplicably dropped.

How Widespread Is Click Fraud?

Click fraud exists; no one denies that, not even Google and Yahoo! That said, the amount of click fraud is in dispute. Quite obviously, the big ad networks say that it's far less a problem than others might think.

Measuring click fraud starts with the PPC fee paid by the advertiser when someone clicks on his ad. An advertiser who pays $10 per click, for example, loses that $10 with each fraudulent click.

Note, however, that Google and Yahoo! don't lose money when a click is fraudulent. In fact, they make the same $10 whether the click is legitimate or fraudulent. To that end, many have commented that Google and Yahoo! actually benefit from click fraud—and may, in fact, generate a significant share of revenues from this fraudulent activity.

Click Fraud Is High...

So what percentage of online advertising clicks are fraudulent? Using data collected from more than 4,000 online advertisers and agencies, Click Forensics (www.clickforensics.com) estimates that 16.6% of all ad clicks in Q4 2007 were fraudulent. That's up from a 14.2% click fraud rate during the same period in 2006.

> > > **NOTE**

Click Forensics says the greatest percentage of click fraud came from countries outside the United States—India (4.3% of the total), Germany (3.9%), and South Korea (3.7%).

If this percentage is accurate, at least $1.5 billion in PPC revenue is wasted due to click fraud. For advertisers, it's a serious matter.

Click Fraud Is Low...

The thing is that the 16.6% number may not be accurate. Google and Yahoo! certainly challenge it.

For example, Google claims that the actual click fraud rate on its own ad network is under 2%. That's because a high percentage of traffic counted by Click Forensics is identified as such by Google beforehand, and filtered out before it reaches the ad network. In essence, Google's advertisers don't get charged for these fraudulent hits.

> > > **NOTE**

Why are Click Forensics' numbers so much higher than Google's? Google claims that the Click Forensics report is an "intentional effort to generate fear and drive interest in its own ad performance tracking services." That's certainly possible, and wouldn't be the first time that a consulting or research firm has manipulated data to sell its reports and services.

How does Google weed out fraudulent clicks? It uses four layers of filtering:

- The first layer is an automatic layer, detecting fraudulent clicks in real time before they show up in a customer's account management console.

- The second layer is an automated flagging system that removes invalid clicks from the AdWords system.

- The third layer is a manual process in which more than two dozen Google employees review and remove suspicious clicks.

- The final layer, as it is, relies on the advertisers to detect click fraud and request investigations by Google.

Yahoo! doesn't release its click fraud numbers, but says that the company actively weeds out fraudulent ad hits and charges its customers only for legitimate traffic.

However large the problem, advertisers are getting antsy. There is a growing effort among some of the web's largest advertisers to force Google and Yahoo! to adjust the ad rates to compensate for fraudulent clicks. Whether that's a 2% or a 16% adjustment, however, is in dispute.

What Can You Do to Combat Click Fraud?

We know that Google, Yahoo!, and their competitors are working to identify and block click fraud inside their ad networks. But what can an individual advertiser do to minimize his losses from fraudulent clicks?

Let's look at a few things you can do.

Monitor Click-Through and Conversion Rates

First, you need to constantly monitor your click-through rates and your conversion rates (measured by information requests, leads, merchandise sales, or whatever). If you see a spike in PPC traffic that is not offset by a corresponding increase in conversion rates, you can suspect click fraud for that traffic increase.

For example, if you see your click-through traffic increase by 50%, you might think your ad program is working quite well. But if, during the same period, your conversion rate increased by only 5%, then your know that most of those new clicks aren't converting to leads or sales—a common sign of fraudulent traffic.

Use a Click Fraud Detection Tool

Second, you should consider using a click fraud detection tool. These software programs monitor your website traffic for irregular patterns, and then flag potentially fraudulent clicks.

Some of the most popular click fraud detection tools include the following:

- AdWatcher (www.adwatcher.com)
- ClickDefense (www.clickdefense.com)
- ClickDetective (www.clickdetective.com)
- ClickLab (www.clicklab.com)
- ClickRisk (www.clickrisk.com)
- ClickTracks (www.clicktracks.com)
- KeyWordMax (www.keywordmax.com)
- WhosClickingWho? (www.whosclickingwho.com)

These tools start at around $30/month and go up from there.

Report Click Fraud to Your Ad Network—and Ask for a Refund

If you identify a case of what you believe to be click fraud, you need to report it to your advertising network and ask for a refund. The ad network's fraud team then attempts to identify the source of the fraud, and (you hope) credits your account for the fraudulent clicks.

How do you report suspected click fraud? Here's what you need to do:

- Document the suspicious activity. Include the keyword that was targeted, IP address of the clicker, date and time of the click, referring page (if known), and any other pertinent information (such as if the click is from a foreign IP). Do this for each suspicious click, perhaps in spreadsheet format.

- Include a summary email message outlining the trends you've spotted. In other words, summarize the data you've detailed in the spreadsheet.

- In the summary message, ask for a refund or credit, based on the number of fraudulent clicks documented.

< < < T I P

The data you need to document your claim can be obtained from most third-party web analytics tools or from your server logs.

Send this information via email to the fraud department of your ad network. You should receive a response within a few days.

The good news is that all the major online ad networks care a lot about click fraud. They have staff dedicated to investigating click fraud complaints and improving the overall quality of traffic. Chances are, if your claim is valid, you'll be made whole. Just remember, the burden of proof is entirely on you.

Is It Safe?

For most Internet advertisers, click fraud is a fact of life. Short of a wholesale industry shift to a different payment method, such as *cost per action* (CPA) or *pay per action* (PPA), advertisers are locked into the CPC method embraced by Google and other online advertising agencies. And, seemingly inherent in the CPC model is the possibility—some would say *probability*—of click fraud.

Fortunately, Google and Yahoo! are aware of these attempts to game their systems and are working to reduce the incidence of click fraud. That doesn't help an individual advertiser who finds himself throwing away a measurable percentage of his online advertising budget, but at least it's a light at the end of the tunnel.

For that individual advertiser, the best defense is awareness. That means monitoring your site traffic and being sensitive to traffic that appears to be related to click fraud schemes. Then you need to get aggressive with your ad network and seek compensation for these phony clicks. You shouldn't have to pay for clicks that didn't come from real customers; click fraud, in effect, inflates the ad rates you pay. Stand up for your rights and fight for rates that recognize the click fraud problem.

Email Fraud: How Big a Problem?

In today's connected world, email is a near-ubiquitous means of communication. It wasn't always so; a mere fifteen years ago, few individuals outside of large corporations had their own email accounts. But things changed—and rapidly.

With the increase in email usage, however, came an increase in email-based fraud and unwanted junk email messages. Email scams and spam continue to be a big problem today—big enough to cause some individuals to stop using email altogether.

Personally I don't think email-related problems are bad enough to throw the baby out with the bath water. Still, email is a common medium for all types of scammers; you need to be aware of the problems that exist in the email world.

Understanding Email Scams

Let's start by examining the many different types of fraud perpetrated via email. In this instance, email is just one more way for con artists to reach and fleece their victims.

For example, let's say you receive a message in your email inbox with the subject line, "Make Money Fast." The message describes a way to get rich without doing any work, which has its appeal. All you have to do is send money (maybe a dollar, maybe five dollars, maybe ten) to a list of people, then pass the email along to ten of your friends or colleagues, who also send money along to the list—to which your name has now been added.

This is email fraud because it's a very obvious pyramid scheme—and, of course, it's blatantly illegal. If you fall for such a scheme and can identify the perpetrator—which is not always easy to do—you can take legal action.

Most instances of email fraud are less obvious than the classic pyramid scheme. They promise bigger payoffs, but require bigger investments on your part. In fact, that's the defining factor of most email scams—you need to send someone either money or your bank account or credit account information. If it's the latter, expect your account to be drained in short order.

What types of email scams are you likely to encounter? We'll take a look at some of the most common.

> > > **NOTE**

> Users of all ages can fall victim to email fraud. According to the Internet Crime Complaint Center, for victims aged 60 and older, the most common types of scams were phishing (21%), lotteries (21%), adult services (20%), and the Nigerian Letter Scam (12%). Among victims under 30, the most common email scams were work-from-home scams (44%) and advance fee loans (35%).

Work-from-Home Scams

If you're young and unemployed (or underemployed), this type of scam can be attractive. The email promises you that you can work from home, be your own boss, and make big money with little or no effort.

Of course, any offer that sounds too good to be true generally is. Starting your own business is hard work and typically requires no small monetary investment; money doesn't start flowing in the first day. So the promises are not to be believed.

The fraud, as usual, comes from the fees you have to pay to learn about this great opportunity. You send a check or give them your credit card number to pay for an information kit, which may or may not arrive. The problem is that the kit, even if it exists, doesn't contain any information that you can't find for free over the Internet. And it certainly doesn't help you one whit in establishing your own business. With this scam, the only person making money from working at home is the person who scammed you out of your money.

Merchandise Resale Scams

Most cons start with a story; the more detailed the story, the easier it is to suck in the victim. The story behind this scam is that a foreign-based company is recruiting U.S. citizens to resell or reship merchandise to destinations inside the United States. The email promises big profits for very little work; in this regard, it's a close cousin to the typical work-from-home scam.

The con is that there is no merchandise to resell. What the con artist wants is your personal information—driver's license, Social Security number, and so on—which he obtains as part of the job application process. You know what happens next.

One variation of this scam involves the new employee actually receiving a paycheck in advance. The check received, however, is significantly larger than the amount actually due; the employee is then instructed to wire the difference back to the company. In time, the paycheck is found to be fraudulent, and the "employee" is out any funds he sent back to his "employer."

This is a scam with lots of tentacles, from check fraud to identity theft. Steer clear.

Reshipping Scams

Similar to the merchandise resale scam is the reshipping scam. In this scam, you're recruited (via email) to receive packages at your residence and then repackage and reship the merchandise, typically abroad.

The con here is that the merchandise is stolen, or obtained fraudulently using stolen credit cards. More often than not, you pay for the shipping yourself and wait to be reimbursed; the reimbursement seldom comes. So not only are you aiding and abetting a criminal enterprise, you yourself are being conned out of your time to do so.

Third-Party Receiver of Funds Scams

This is a long name for a very simple but increasingly common scam. You receive an unsolicited email from someone you don't know, typically someone outside the U.S. The subject says he's running some auctions on eBay or posting items on an online classifieds site, but his location makes it difficult to receive payments from U.S. customers. He's looking for a United States citizen, like you, to act as a third-party receiver of funds; you'll receive the payments from his buyers, then resend the money on to him in his foreign location.

The con is that his buyers are victims of auction fraud themselves. You're just acting as an intermediary—a money launderer, as it were. Worse, you could be on the hook if the other victims stop payment to your PayPal account or try to recover their losses.

Sometimes this scam involves you receiving counterfeit cashier's checks or money orders. You deposit the funds, wire fresh money to the scammer, and then find out the payments you received are worthless. In this instance, you're out any funds you've wired to the con artist.

Multilevel Marketing Scams

Multilevel marketing (MLM) works like a pyramid scheme, but in a business setting. You join up to be a distributor of some product or service, but you really don't sell a thing. What you sell are more franchises or distributorships, and these folks sign up more folks, and so on. Every new member who signs up pays a fee to join; the person who signed him up gets a cut of the fee, with the bulk of the fee going to the parent company. The parent, of course, makes money whether any products are sold or not. Investors like you see no funds from later investors.

There are numerous MLM schemes drifting around the Internet, solicited via email. In fact, they make up a significant portion of spam mailings. They should be avoided.

Investment Scams

Investment scams have been around longer than anyone can remember. They predate the Internet not by years or decades, but by centuries. Today, however, they're propagating via email—which makes them no less dangerous.

Put simply, investment fraud is an offer for a stock, commodity (such as precious metals), or other investment that uses false or fraudulent claims. You've seen these emails; they claim that such and such a stock is set to "explode" and that you should invest now to get in on the ground level. The email may look like a formal solicitation, or may be in the form of a private message from a "friend" (whom you've never heard of). The stock is typically a penny stock, something you can buy cheap. And, in some instances, the stock price actually does move up—for a very short period of time, as other gullible victims who received the same email invest their hard-earned money in the stock. But the gains are short-lived; the stock price quickly returns to where it was before, or even lower. Too bad for all those new investors.

Put simply, you should never make an investment based on the recommendation of a stranger. And you should never reply to blanket investment spam.

Advance Fee Loan Scams

This type of fraud is particularly appealing to younger Internet users. The typical email promises to give you a loan or help you get a loan, even if you have bad credit. The fraud comes from the fact that you have to pay a fee in advance before you get the loan, or to accompany your loan application. Obviously, there is no loan; any funds you send are lost.

You can protect against this type of fraud by never paying upfront for anything, especially loans. In fact, you should never have to pay an upfront fee for a loan; if a loan has a fee, it's paid when it's executed, not in advance. In addition, beware of any promise that you can get a loan regardless of your past credit problems; if you have bad (or no) credit, it doesn't look any better to some unknown firm over the Internet.

Bogus Credit Card Offers

Similar to the advance fee loan fraud are scams involving bogus credit cards. You receive an email promising you a major credit card, even (or especially) if you have bad credit. Of course, you have to pay a fee up front to apply, and there's the fraud.

> > > **NOTE**

> An alternate version of the advance fee loan and credit card scams simply requires you to submit a credit application online. This naturally requires you to submit your Social Security number—which is promptly used for identity theft.

As with the advance fee loan scam, the tipoff here is the fee you have to pay in advance. No legitimate credit card issuer requires you to pay them in advance. In addition, most credit card companies don't offer cards to people with bad credit, so that's another clue.

Credit Card Loss Protection Scams

The email in this scam purports to sell you a loss protection policy for your credit card. Sounds good, certainly—especially in light of all the credit card fraud you've read about so far in this book. The problem is, there's no company behind the email, only a fraudster who wants to get his hands on your credit card number. Naturally, you provide that information when you apply for the protection policy; you have to tell them what card you want protected, after all. As soon as you transmit this data, you become the victim of the very type of credit card fraud you were trying to prevent.

Credit Repair Fraud

If you have bad credit, or have been the victim of identity theft or credit card fraud, your credit record may be tainted. Enter this particular email scam, where the scammer offers a credit repair service. Just pay the fee, and the company will work to clear your good name.

The problem, of course, is that no one but you can repair your credit. A credit repair service, even if legitimate, can't do anything you can't do yourself. That is, if there is incorrect information on your credit report (which you can obtain for free, as you've previously learned), you can contact the credit reporting bureaus to have that incorrect information corrected or removed. You don't need a third party to do this for you.

Even worse are the fraudulent credit repair services, which offer no services at all but exist solely to obtain your credit card numbers. You give them this information, of course, as part of the information-gathering process. After they have your account info, however, they use it to charge up your accounts—which only serves to worsen your credit, not repair it.

Debt Elimination Scams

Here's a similar but more substantive type of fraud. You receive an email from a company offering a legal way to discharge your loans and credit card debts. All you have to do is send them $2,000 or so, along with all your loan and credit card information, then give them power of attorney over your accounts, and you'll soon be debt free.

As you can imagine, just the opposite occurs. Not only are you out the $2,000, the con artist charges up your credit card, empties your bank account, and uses that power of attorney for who knows what nefarious ends. This is one of the most extreme methods of identity theft, and the results can be severe.

Buyer's Club Scams

Here's an attractive offer. You receive an email that invites you to join a buyer's club. With your membership, you get great discounts on all sorts of merchandise. In fact, some of the products may be free; all you have to pay for is shipping.

Some buyer's clubs are legitimate. Some are legitimate but don't really offer great deals; once you join up, you discover the club prices are no better than what you can find elsewhere. The more serious fraud, however, occurs when you're charged for a membership that you never agreed to. You sign up for a free trial, make a purchase or two, then later discover that your credit card is being charged a fat fee every month for the club membership. Even worse, you find that the membership is next to impossible to cancel. That's the fraud.

If you can't get the club itself to stop the unwanted membership, you may have to contact your credit card company and dispute the charges. In any instance, you're probably out any existing charges; the best you can hope for is to stop any future payments.

{ P E R S O N A L   E X P E R I E N C E }

Not all buyer's club scams are perpetrated via email. I found myself the victim of just such a scam after I purchased a kitchen gadget from a late-night television commercial. Two months later, a $19.95 charge appeared on my credit card statement; this was the monthly charge for the buyer's club, for which I was signed up for without my knowledge or approval. I eventually had to call my credit card company to have the charges removed.

Magazine Sale Scams

You might remember this scam from your youth, perpetrated well before the Internet era. The con, of course, is that you sign up and pay for magazines that you never receive. Instead of the pitiable young man standing on your doorstep, however, today's solicitation is via email. The con, however, is the same.

As a matter of course, you should just say "no" when you receive an unsolicited email offering magazine subscriptions at discount. Most such offers are a scam.

Charity Scams

Con artists have always preyed on our better natures. Scams involving fake charities exist in the real world as well as online. It's easy to fall for a plea for help sent in a convincing email message, but if it's a charity you've never heard of before, beware.

You should check out all new charities before you donate. A good source of research is the Better Business Bureau's Wise Giving Alliance; call 703-276-0100 or go to www.give.org to find out more.

C A U T I O N !!!

As with all email solicitations, be wary of directly clicking any links in an email charity solicitation. It may look as if you're being taken to the charity site in question, but in reality you may be the victim of a phishing scheme.

Free Government Grant Scams

Nothing in life is truly free. Such is the case with the offer of "free" government grants that you receive via email. These are simply scams trying to obtain your Social Security number (which you have to provide to obtain the grant) or to con you out of an "application fee."

Here's the deal. The United States government does not send unsolicited emails to citizens offering free grants. Nor, for that matter, does the government require fees to obtain a grant. If you receive such an offer, it's a scam. Resist it.

Scholarship Scams

Prospective college students are especially vulnerable to this scam. The email purports to assist you in finding available scholarships—for a fee, of course. You pay the fee, but receive nothing in return. Or, at best, information which is available publicly, at no charge.

Beware such unsolicited offers. And remember—no company can guarantee that you'll receive scholarship funds. That's always up to the university or institution.

Free Prize Scams

This scam entices you with the offer of a free prize of some sort. Maybe it's a free videogame console, or a DVD player, an iPod, or even a brand new car. What happens next depends on the particular scam.

One variation of this scam sends you to an official looking web page that asks you to fill in your shipping information—name, address, and so forth. Nothing too harmful yet, until you're informed that you have to pay $5 or $10 shipping and handling charges to receive your prize. This seems reasonable, and they let you pay this fee by credit card. And there's the scam— once you input your credit card number, you become a victim of credit card theft.

An earlier version of this scam, back in the days of dial-up Internet access, took victims to a web page that required them to download a software program necessary to claim the prize. What was actually downloaded was a background dialing program that automatically dialed into a pornographic service that secretly charged them $3.99 per minute. Another variation used the download link to install a spyware program that skimmed the user's computer for personal data and surreptitiously uploaded it via the Internet.

Lottery Scams

This particular scam tends to be targeted towards older users, although gullible users of any age are vulnerable. The email is simple and direct: You've been randomly selected as the winner of an international lottery. Your winnings, typically in the form of a very large lump-sum payout, are being held and waiting for you to claim. All you have to do is contact the lottery agency to collect the money.

When you respond to the email, you're asked to pay a "processing fee" of $1,000 or more to initiate the process. Sometimes you're asked to provide your bank account number, so that funds can be electronically transferred. Obviously, any money you send vanishes, and any information you send is used against you. Instead of transferring your lottery "winnings" into your bank account, your existing funds are transferred out of your account. It's not a good situation.

C A U T I O N !!!

Some online scams actually start offline. For example, you might receive a letter via postal mail informing you that you're a lottery winner and that you have to visit the website listed in the letter to claim your prize. After you're online, you're asked to provide all manner of personal information, which then leads to all sorts of fraud. The thing is, you shouldn't consider snail mail safer than email; just because the con artist has your street address doesn't make the offer any more legitimate.

Billing Fraud

This is an email scam directed almost exclusively at businesses. It works, more often than you'd like to think, because office workers often do things by rote, without thinking about them or properly following through. Also at play—the fact that many larger companies are so befuddled with paperwork that it's common for invoices and such to get lost in the shuffle.

The con is simple. The scammer sends an email to the billing or accounting department of a large company, requesting payment for services rendered or supplies shipped. Sometimes the email is a "second notice" for an overdue invoice. In any case, no services were rendered nor supplies shipped; the notice is a bogus one.

Unfortunately, sometimes even bogus invoices get paid. It's easy to imagine an overworked employee seeing the "second notice" and expediting payment (often via credit card, which the scammer conveniently accepts) to placate the distressed "vendor." Of course, if the employee simply checked the invoice against the company's records, she'd find that no such vendor or billing existed; unfortunately, many such invoices get paid without such confirmation.

A canny fraudster can con a company out of large "invoiced" amounts. More aggressive con artists can work a company's system to change their processes for electronic invoicing, re-directing all payments for a legitimate vendor to the scammer, instead. In this latter instance, it's not just the host company that is victimized—it's also the company's vendor that doesn't receive the proper payments.

Fake Tax Refunds

Here's one that the IRS warns about every tax season. You get an email in your inbox purporting to be from the Internet Revenue Service, typically from an address like tax-refunds@irs.gov. The message tells you that you have a tax refund coming and includes a link to an official-looking site that requests personal information, such as your Social Security number and credit card numbers.

As you have no doubt guessed, it's all an elaborate phishing scheme. If you enter the requested information, you'll be helping the con artist steal your financial assets and personal identity.

Here's the thing. The IRS will never ask for personal or financial information via an unsolicited email. And you'll never have to complete a special form to obtain a refund; that happens automatically when you submit your normal tax return. Ignore these bogus emails.

Nigerian Letter Scam

I've saved the best scam till last. One of the oldest and most persistent email scams is the decades-old Nigerian Letter Scam. It started out in the 1980s as a postal mail scam, migrated to fax machines, and now lives on via email. In fact, this single scam accounts for 8% of all Internet Crime Complaint Center complaints.

> > > **NOTE**
>
> Believe it or not, but the Nigerian Letter Scam is supposedly the third-largest industry in Nigeria!

In this scam, you receive an email from an alleged Nigerian civil servant or businessman, containing an "urgent" business proposal. The sender has supposedly been put in charge of the proceeds from some business scheme and needs a foreign partner to help launder the money. Because this person's government prohibits him from opening foreign bank accounts, he asks you to deposit the sum (typically in the millions) into your personal account; for your assistance, you'll receive a certain percent of the total. To complete the transaction, you have to email back your bank's name and address and—of course—your bank account numbers. If you do so, you end up not with a few million bucks from the Nigerian government, but with an empty bank account, thanks to your gullibility.

Here's what a typical Nigerian Letter Scam email looks like:

ATTN:

Dear Sir/M,

I am Mr. David Mark. an Auditor of a BANK OF THE NORTH INTER-NATIONAL, ABUJA (FCT). I have the courage to crave indulgence for this important business believing that you will never let me down either now or in the future.

Some years ago, an American Mining consultant/ contractor with the Nigeria National Petroleum Corporation, made a numbered time (fixed) deposit for twelve calendar months, valued $12M.USD (TWELVE MILLION US DOLLARS) in an account. On maturity, the bank sent a routine notification to his forwarding address but got no reply. After a month, The bank sent another reminder and finally his contract employers, the Nigerian National Petroleum Corporation wrote to inform the bank that he died without MAK-ING A WILL, and all attempts by the American Embassy to trace his next of kin was fruitless. I therefore, made further investiga-tion and discovered that the beneficiary was an immigrant from Jamaica and only recently obtained American citizenship. He did not declare any kin or relations in all his official documents, including his Bank deposit paper work.

This money total amount $12M.USD (TWELVE MILLION US DOL-LARS) is still sitting in my bank as dormant Account. No one will ever come forward to claim it, and according to Nigerian Banking policy, after some years, the money will revert to the ownership of the Nigerian Government if the account owner is certified dead.

This is the situation, and my proposal is that I am looking for a foreigner who will stand in as the next of kin to beneficiary, and OPEN a Bank Account abroad to facilitate the transfer of this money. This is simple, all you have to do is to OPEN an account anywhere in the world and send me its detail for me to arrange the proper money transfer paperwork, and facilitate the transfer. The money will then be paid into this Account for us to share in the ratio of 60% for me, 35% for you and 5% for expenses that might come up during transfer process. There is no risk at all, and all the paper work for this transaction will be done by me using my position and connections in the banks in Nigeria. This business transaction is guaranteed. And the first phase of the transfer will be ($4M.USD) FOUR MILLION DOLLARS as advised by our insider in the bank.

If you are interested, please reply immediately through my personal email sending the following details: (1) Your Full Name/Address (2) Your Private Telephone/fax Number. Please observe the utmost confidentiality, and be rest assured that this transaction would be most profitable for both of us because I shall require your assistance to invest some of my share in your country. I look forward to your earliest reply.

Yours,

Mr. David Mark.

If you respond to this email, you receive a follow-up message that requests you forward to Mr. Mark your bank account number, "to enable us to follow up all pursuance for immediate approvals and transfer." Naturally, the only thing that gets transferred at this point is money out of your bank account.

Some variations of this scam change the name of the business, the name of the bureaucrat or diplomat, the country, the circumstances of the fund, and so on. Common features of all these variations, however, include the following:

- Message is not addressed to a specific name

- Message is often marked "urgent" or "confidential"

- The sender claims to be some sort of senior civil servant (important but not too important) working in one of Nigeria's many ministries; a member of Nigerian royalty; a political insider; a spouse or relative of a deposed leader; a Nigerian businessman, lawyer, or doctor; an auditor with strong ties to Nigerian officials; or a religious figure (deacon, pastor, and so on.)

- Message typically contains spelling mistakes and grammatical errors (designed to give you, the reader, a sense of intellectual superiority)

- Often written in all capital letters

- The amounts involved are very large, in the millions of dollars

- Dollar amounts are written both numerically and spelled out ("four million dollars")

- They play on your vanity by saying you've been singled out for your honesty and business savvy

As to the story driving the scam, variations include the following:

- Transfer of funds from accounts of now-defunct companies or deceased individuals

- Forgotten accounts, wills, and inheritances

- Assistance escaping the country with accumulated wealth

- Attempt to defraud the government by milking forgotten accounts, or accounts from former regimes

- Transfer of funds from over-invoiced or over-estimated contracts

- Conversion of hard currency

- Sale of crude oil or other commodities at below-market prices

- Purchase of real estate

Although the details may differ somewhat, the basic mechanism and intent remain the same—to con naive and greedy people out of large sums of money.

> > > **N O T E**

> To learn more about these and other online scams, go to the National Fraud Information Center (www.fraud.org), Internet ScamBusters (www.scambusters.org), Internet Crime Complaint Center (www.ic3.gov), or the FTC's Dot Cons site (www.ftc.gov/bcp/conline/pubs/online/dotcons.htm).

Understanding the World of Phishing

Phishing is a particular type of email scam that extracts valuable information from the victim, using a series of fake emails and websites. The transmission via email makes phishing a type of email fraud; the extraction of financial data aligns it with credit card fraud; and the pilfering of personal information leads to identity theft.

And here's the thing—phishing is a monumental problem, far greater than any other type of email fraud. It's a big enough problem that we'll look at it separately from other types of email scams.

What Is Phishing?

In essence, a phishing email is one designed to look like an official email. In reality, the email is a clever forgery, down to the use of the original firm's logo. The email is designed to get you to click on an enclosed link that purports to take you to an "official" website. That website, however, is also fake. Any information you provide to that website is then used for various types of fraud, from simple username/password theft to credit card and identity theft.

> > > **N O T E**

The term *phishing* derives from the attempt to "fish" for the victim's information. The spelling is influenced by the word *phreaking*, a slang term for hacking into public telephone networks.

As is probably obvious, phishing is a criminal activity, a form of fraud. And the information garnered from a successful phishing scheme is typically used for additional criminal activities, from credit card fraud to full-blown identity theft.

The History of Phishing

Phishing started in the mid 1990s, on the America Online network. Phishers would pose as AOL staff members and send instant messages to victims, asking them to provide their passwords. The scammers lured their victims by asking them to verify their account information or confirm their billing info. When the victim revealed his password, the attacker could access and use the victim's account for all manner of illicit activities, primarily spamming.

The first use of the term "phishing" occurred in March, 1997, when Tatiana Gau, VP of Integrity Assurance for AOL, made this statement in an article for the *Florida Times Union* newspaper:

The scam is called 'phishing'—as in fishing for your password, but spelled differently.

AOL cracked down on this IM-based phishing, which served to drive phishers to other media—most notably, email. Phishers also realized that bigger profits were possible if they targeted users of financial institutions. To that end, June 2001 saw a phishing email aimed at users of the E-gold online payment service. Although that crude text-based email wasn't successful, it was followed by a "post 9-11 ID check" phishing scheme shortly after the September 11, 2001, terrorist attacks.

These amateurish early phishing attacks were just the beginning. Phishers learned from their mistakes and began to create more sophisticated-looking emails, emulating the look and feel of the targeted institutions. By late 2003, phishers expanded their arsenals, creating a fake pop-up login window that appeared in front of the legitimate website window when victims clicked a link in the phishing email. Users were tricked into entering their usernames and passwords into the fake window, thus providing phishers with access to the user's accounts on the targeted websites.

By mid-2004, this technique had morphed into the creation of completely fake websites. Any user clicking the link in a phishing email was now directed to the counterfeit website and enticed to enter all manner of personal information.

More recent phishing attempts target the customers of banks and online payment services, such as PayPal. Some phishers have even posed as representatives of the Internal Revenue Service, to glean Social Security numbers and other information from gullible taxpayers.

How Does a Phishing Scam Work?

A phishing scam includes both the initial email and an accompanying fake website. We'll look at each separately.

The fake email, like the one in Figure 10.1, purports to be from a legitimate company or organization. A savvy phisher uses logos and other information from the targeted institution's actual emails or website to give the fake email an authentic look. The email typically informs the recipient of some recent event or activity, and asks the individual to confirm an operation or review his information on the firm's website.

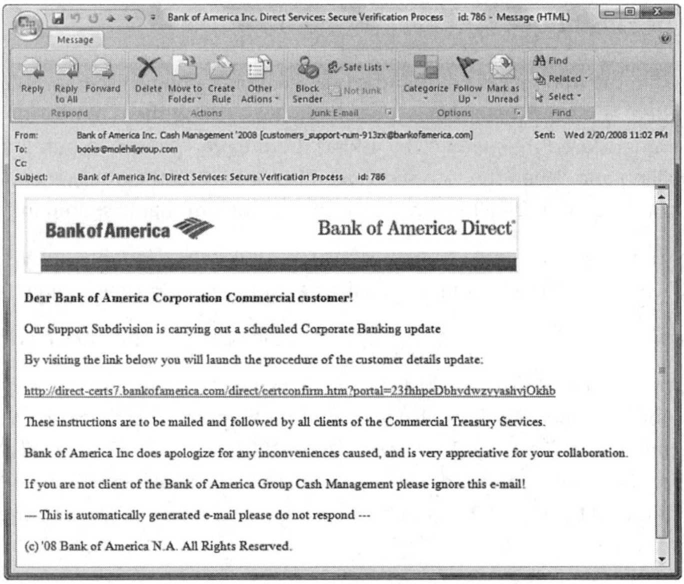

Figure 10.1
A typical phishing email, designed to look like an official communication from Bank of America.

Within the email is a link to that website. At first glance, this appears to be a legitimate link. But if you hover your cursor over the link, you'll see that the actual URL is different from the one visible in the text. In other words, clicking the link doesn't take you to where you think you're going, but to a completely different web page.

> > > **N O T E**

This redirection of a link from one website to another fake one is called *pharming*.

Figure 10.2 shows the actual URL in a phishing email. As you can see, it's a very long and involved address that's actually a bit hard to read. The first part of the address (in this instance, www.commercial.bnc.ca) looks legitimate, but the URL doesn't stop there. If you follow the complete URL, it takes you not to the expected website, but to the phisher's carefully constructed forgery.

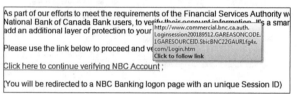

Figure 10.2
Link manipulation in a phishing email—note how the actual URL doesn't match the website in the anchor text.

> > > **N O T E**

The showing of one address in the anchor text while linking to another is known as *link manipulation*.

The counterfeit website is an important part of the phishing scam. Like the official-looking email, the web page on which you land is designed to look as authentic as possible. For example, the site in Figure 10.3 looks like an official eBay login page, but if you look in the address bar at the top of the browser, that is most definitely not eBay's actual URL. This is a spoof web page; if you enter the requested information, that info is transmitted to the con artist behind the phishing scam.

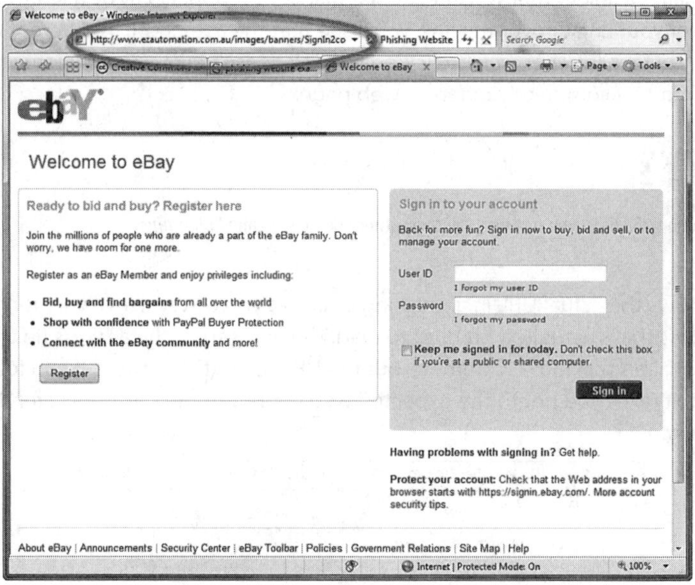

Figure 10.3
A clever forgery—a phishing website designed to look like the official eBay login page.

What institutions are commonly spoofed in phishing emails? The name of just about every major corporation and financial institution has been appropriated to deleterious effect, but some of the more common brands used for phishing purposes include Bank of America, Citibank, eBay, Fifth Third Bank, HSBC Bank, NatWest, PayPal, and Wachovia.

> > > **N O T E**

> Phishing attacks come from all around the world. Although the statistics vary from week to week and attack to attack, the most common originating country is Russia, followed closely by other eastern European countries.

Measuring the Cost of Email and Phishing Scams

The issue of email fraud is difficult to size. This is partly because of the diffused nature of the beast; there are so many different email cons circulating that it's difficult to wrap them all up into a convenient bundle. In addition, there is no central clearinghouse for this type of data; many researchers don't break out fraud by medium (that is, email fraud is lumped in with other types of online fraud); and many types of email fraud go unreported by victims.

Ranking Different Types of Email Fraud

Thanks to the Internet Crime Complaint Center (www.ic3.gov), we know what the most common types of email fraud are. In fact, email fraud constituted half of the top 10 complaints registered with the organization in its last reporting year (2006):

1. Identity theft

2. Shop-at-home/catalog sales

3. **Email: Prizes/sweepstakes/lotteries**

4. Internet services

5. Internet auctions

6. **Email: Foreign money offers**

7. **Email: Advance fee loans/credit protection and repair**

8. **Email: Magazines and buyer's clubs**

9. **Email: Telephone services**

10. Health care

Likewise, the National Consumer League (www.nclnet.org) also says that half of the top 10 Internet scams in 2007 were email-related:

1. Fake check scams

2. General merchandise issues

3. Online auctions

4. **Email: Nigerian money offers**

5. **Email: Lotteries**

6. **Email: Advance fee loans/credit offers**

7. **Email: Prizes/sweepstakes/free gifts**

8. **Email: Phishing/spoofing**

9. Sweetheart swindles

10. Internet access services

> > > **NOTE**

> A sweetheart scam is one where the con artist establishes a personal relationship with the victim in a chat room or on a dating site, and then uses that relationship to swindle the victim out of a large sum of money.

Sizing the Fraud Problem

So how big is the email fraud problem? As I said, this is one type of fraud that's difficult to measure. We do know that the Nigerian Letter Fraud alone is said to generate somewhere between $100 million and $1 billion a year in ill-gotten gains; based on this sole statistic, it's fair to say that email fraud is a multi-billion dollar problem—and getting worse.

On an individual basis, the NCL estimates that the average loss per victim in 2007 for all types of Internet fraud (including but not exclusively email fraud) was $1,507—although this number differs significantly by type of fraud. The more ambitious the fraud, the bigger the cost to victims.

Sizing the Phishing Problem

Of all the different types of email fraud, phishing has become the most dangerous. The statistics are staggering; ICONIX (www.iconix.com) reports that as many as 59 million phishing emails are sent each day. And, believe it or not, recipients actually open 1 in 6 of these messages—10 million fake messages per day.

> > > **NOTE**

Different types of phishing messages have different open rates. For example, fake social-network-related messages have a 24.9% open rate; fake e-cards have a 17.1% open rate; fake financial emails have a 15.5% open rate; and fake dating emails have a 9.5% open rate.

According to an Indiana University survey, 14% of phishing scams are successful in extracting information out of the intended victims. In 2007, according to Gartner Research, this resulted in a staggering $3.2 billion in losses to 3.6 million U.S. adults.

These are impressive and sobering figures. How can you protect yourself against phishing and other email scams? That's what we cover in the next chapter, so read on to get both smarter and safer.

Is It Safe?

With so many email scams hitting inboxes on a regular basis, just how safe is email as a medium? The answer, of course, is as safe as you want it to be.

You see, all email scams, whether we're talking phishing schemes or Nigerian letter fraud, rely on the greed and gullibility of the victim. These aren't tech-based attacks that automatically activate when you open an email message; these cons require the victim to actively participate in the scheme. If you don't play along, you don't get burned.

The key to reducing your risk to email fraud is to never reply to unsolicited emails. It's that simple; just assume that any unsolicited offer you receive is fraudulent. Trust me, you won't be missing out on any legitimate offers.

That said, if you're gullible or greedy or just plain curious and do respond to a fraudulent offer, your risk of being victimized is quite high. That's because few if any legitimate offers will arrive unsolicited in your email inbox; if you opt in to such an unsolicited offer, you risk large financial losses.

To make email safe, simply ignore suspect messages. Trust emails from friends and family, but don't trust much beyond that. If you use common sense, you won't get burned.

Avoiding Email Fraud and Phishing Scams

In the last chapter you learned all about all the many different types of email fraud, including fast-growing phishing scams. With so many scams out there, how do you avoid being a victim?

There is a simple answer to that question: Be smart! Most email fraud is perpetrated on victims that are in some way gullible. Maybe their greed gets the best of them; maybe they're naïve about how the world works; maybe they don't behave in the smartest fashion possible. In any case, most fraud can be avoided just by using common sense.

That said, there are many things you can do to minimize your chances of being taken by email con artists. Read on to learn how to become smarter—and safer—when opening your email.

Minimizing the Risk of Email Fraud

Protecting yourself from the huge number of email scams floating around the Internet is both difficult and simple. The difficulty comes from the sheer number of scams and their amazing variety. The simplicity comes from the fact that the best way to deal with any such scam is to use common sense—and ignore it.

That's right. Most email fraud is easily detectible by the simple fact that it arrives in your inbox out of the blue and seems too good to be true. So if you get an unsolicited offer that promises great riches, you know to hit the Delete key—pronto.

What you can't do, however, is rely on your email program's spam filter to stop scam emails. Spam and scams are two different things, even if they're both unwanted. Although some scam messages are stopped by spam filters, many messages get through the filter and land in your inbox, just as if they were legitimate messages. Which, of course, they aren't.

How to Recognize a Scam Email

Savvy Internet users train themselves to recognize scam emails at a glance. That's because most scam messages have one or more of the following characteristics in common:

- The email does not address you personally by name; your name doesn't appear anywhere in the body of the message.

- You don't know the person who sent you the message; the message was totally unsolicited.

- You are promised large sums of money for little or no effort on your part.

- You are asked to provide money upfront for various fees, or to pay the cost of expediting the process.

- You are asked to provide your bank account number, credit card number, or other personal information.

- The request is labeled "urgent," or the sender says that you must act quickly to take advantage of the offer.

- The message is rife with spelling and grammatical errors. (Scammers frequently operate from foreign countries and do not use English as their first language.)

- The sender requests confidentiality.

- The sender offers to send you "evidence" of legitimacy, often in the form of copies of bank statements, government certificates, or similar documents. (If you actually receive these documents, they'll be fakes.)

If any or all of these attributes apply to a given email message, you can be pretty sure it's a scam—and should be deleted.

How to Avoid Email Fraud

Recognizing a scam email is just one way to reduce your risk of getting conned via email. Here are some more tips you can employ:

- Familiarize yourself with the common email scams discussed in Chapter 10, "Email Fraud: How Big a Problem?" If a message in your inbox resembles any of these common scams, delete it.

- Don't publicize your email address; avoid posting your address in public forums. The less visible your email address, the less likely it is that a con artist will email you scam messages.

- Ignore all unsolicited emails, of any type. No stranger will send you a legitimate offer via email; it just doesn't happen. When you receive an unsolicited offer via email, delete it.

- Don't give in to greed. If an offer sounds too good to be true, it is; there are no true "get rich quick" schemes.

- Research all offers before responding. If, in spite of all the previous advice, you feel you must respond to an email offer, do your homework first. Check the various anti-fraud sites to see whether this message fits a known pattern; query the company's name and reputation on Google. If the offer is a fraud, others will know—and you can learn from their experience.

- Never provide any personal information—including credit card numbers, your Social Security number, and the like—via email. If such information is legitimately needed, you can call the company yourself or visit their official website to provide the information directly.

Finally, it pays to frequent one or more anti-fraud websites, to keep up-to-date on the latest trends in email fraud. The best of these sites include Hoax-Slayer (www.hoax-slayer.com), ScamBusters (www.scambusters.org), Scamdex (www.scamdex.com), and the FBI's Investigative Programs Cyber Investigations (www.fbi.gov/cyberinvest/escams.htm). These sites will keep you on your toes!

> > > **N O T E**

The FBI Cyber Investigations site lets you sign up to receive emails warning of the latest email scams.

What to Do if You've Been Conned

What should you do if you think you've been the victim of an email fraud? The steps are similar to that of dealing with identity fraud:

- If the fraud involved transmittal of your credit card information, contact your credit card company to put a halt to all unauthorized payments—and to limit your liability to the first $50.

- If you think your bank accounts have been compromised, contact your bank to put a freeze on your checking and savings accounts—and to open new accounts, if necessary.

- Contact one of the three major credit reporting bureaus to see whether stolen personal information has been used to open new credit accounts—or max out your existing accounts.

- Contact your local law enforcement authorities—fraud *is* illegal, and it should be reported as a crime.

- Report the fraud to your state attorney general's office.

- File a complaint with the Federal Trade Commission (FTC) by contacting the FTC Consumer Response Center via phone (202-382-4357) or on the Internet (www.ftc.gov/ftc/complaint.htm).

- Contact any or all of the following consumer-oriented Web sites: Better Business Bureau (www.bbb.org), Fraud Bureau (www.fraudbureau.com), Internet Crime Complaint Center (www.ic3.gov), National Consumers League (www.natlconsumersleague.org), and National Fraud Information Center (www.fraud.org).

Above all, don't provide any additional information or money to the scammers. As soon as you suspect you've been had, halt all contact and cut off all access to your bank and credit card accounts. Sometimes the best you can hope for is to minimize your losses.

Guarding Against Phishing Scams

Phishing scams, by their very nature, are harder to guard against. We're used to getting official communications via email from all manner of companies and institutions; email is how corporate America communicates to its customers.

But as phishers continue to impersonate all manner of organizations, our trust in email as a communications medium diminishes. How do we know what emails to trust and which to trash?

Be Aware—and Be Cautious

The first defense against phishing emails is one of awareness. You need to learn what phishing emails look like and what institutions are likely to be targets of phishing scams.

To the first point, phishing emails look like regular emails—to a point. Every phishing email I've ever seen includes a request for you to go to a related website to verify some piece of information. That web link is a dead giveaway, as most legitimate organizations never include a link in their email communications requesting personal information. Even if you think the message is legitimate, you shouldn't click the link to go to the website. Instead, enter the entity's actual web address into your web browser, and go to that site directly—not via the link. If something there needs to be verified, you can do it manually.

Of course, the tell-tale sign of a phishing email is link manipulation, where the printed link in the message doesn't match the actual URL it points to. I always hover my cursor over the link to view the actual URL; if it looks suspicious (overly long, no direct relation to the institution in question), I know I'm dealing with a phishing email.

To emphasize: Never click a link in an unsolicited email message—even if the message *looks* official!

To the second point, phishers tend to target a select group of companies—primarily financial institutions, online payment services (such as PayPal), and online auction sites. So any unsolicited email you receive from a bank, PayPal, or eBay should automatically be suspect.

These emails should be further suspect if your actual name doesn't appear anywhere in the message, or if your real email address isn't visible in the To: field. Most phishing emails are sent to large lists of anonymous recipients, much like spam messages, so if the message isn't personalized, it's probably fake.

Use Anti-Phishing Technology

Until recently, the only guard against phishing scams was common sense. This all changed with the release of the Windows Vista operating system, which includes a new feature called the Microsoft Phishing Filter. This filter works within both Windows Mail and Internet Explorer 7 and compares all the links in your Windows Mail email messages to an online list of known phishing websites. If the link matches a fraudulent site, Windows Mail displays a warning message at the top of the message, as shown in Figure 11.1.

> > > **N O T E**

This same Phishing Filter is also included in Microsoft Outlook 2007.

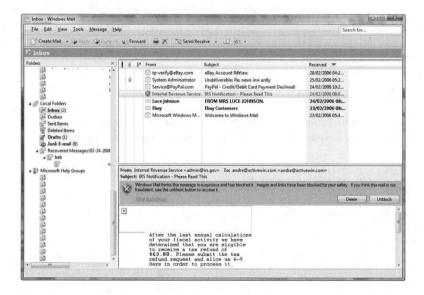

Figure 11.1

Microsoft's Phishing Filter at work in Windows Mail.

If you attempt to click a link to a known phishing site, the Phishing Filter in Internet Explorer blocks access to the site, changes the Address Bar to red, navigates to a neutral page, and displays a warning message, as shown in Figure 11.2. If you attempt to click a link to a site that is not on the list of known fraudulent sites but behaves similarly to such sites, the Microsoft Phishing Filter changes the Address Bar to yellow and cautions you about potentially suspicious content.

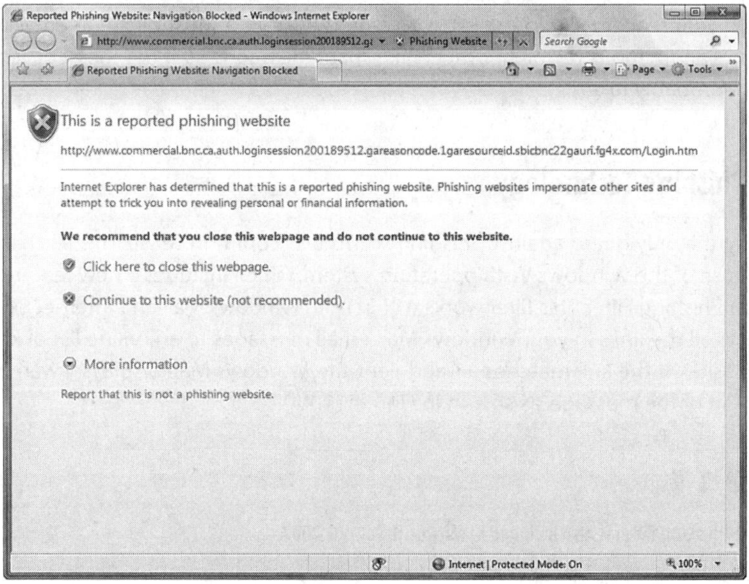

Figure 11.2
What you see if you try to go to a known phishing website with Internet Explorer 7.

< < < T I P

Similar anti-phishing technology exists in recent versions of the Mozilla Firefox and Opera web browsers. In addition, many third-party vendors offer antiphishing technology in their Internet security programs.

Take Advantage of Augmented Password Logins

Some companies are trying to reduce the risk of phishing from their ends, typically by augmenting their login processes with more than just a username and password.

For example, when you first sign up for Bank of America's online banking service, you're asked to select a personal image. Every subsequent time you log in to their website, you're asked to verify this image—in addition to providing your user name and password, of course. If you don't see this image when you log in, you know you're not visiting the official Bank of America site.

Other institutions employ other forms of login augmentation. This may include answering one or more security questions, the use of a graphic captcha (to block attempted automated log in), and the like. The key is to make it more difficult for unauthorized users to log into others' accounts—and to distinguish the real site from phishing sites.

What to Do if You've Been Phished

Cautious as you may be, slip-ups do occur. What do you do if you discover you've entered information into a phishing website?

It all depends on what information you've entered. For example, if you've entered your user-name and password, the first thing to do is change your password. This will keep phishers from accessing your account in the future. If you change your password fast enough, the phisher won't have time to access your account. But if enough time goes by, the phisher can use the purloined information to access your account and do whatever damage is possible. Monitor this account to make sure no unauthorized access has occurred.

If the phisher has accessed your account, your recourse is the same with any type of financial fraud or identity theft. Notify the site/company in question, file a report with local authorities, and notify the appropriate monitoring agencies—as detailed in the "What to Do if You've Been Conned" section, earlier in this chapter.

It's also a good idea to report any phishing emails you receive to the Anti Phishing Work Group, at reportphishing@antiphishing.org. Additional information on how to avoid phishing scams can be found at this group's website (www.antiphishing.org).

{ PERSONAL EXPERIENCE }

I'm probably more cautious than the average person, but even I have been conned by a phishing message. The email in question purported to be a question from an eBay member about an item I supposedly had for auction. I had several items listed at the time, but none that corresponded to that mentioned in the mes-sage, which looked as if it came from eBay's official message system. I clicked the button in the message, saw the expected eBay login page, and dutifully entered my user ID and password—only to discover that it wasn't an eBay page at all. I immediately used my web browser to manually log onto eBay and changed my password. Fortunately, my prompt action kept the phisher from accessing my account—but I could have had my eBay account hijacked. It can happen to anyone!

Is It Safe?

Email can be safe—if you take the proper precautions. Simply not responding to unsolicited emails reduces your risk tremendously. Add to that the use of appropriate anti-phishing technology (in Windows Vista and otherwise) and you should be able to tell the legitimate emails from the phony ones.

That said, it's possible for even the most cautious user to let his guard down on occasion. If this happens to you and you become a victim of email or phishing fraud, follow the steps in this chapter to minimize the damage and start repairing your credit and identity.

Email fraud and phishing don't have to be big problems—unless you act foolishly. Keep your wits about you and you won't fall victim.

Reducing Email Spam

On any given day, I can open my email inbox and find at least one email scam or phishing message similar to those presented in the previous chapters. But that single scam message is insignificant compared to the number of *spam* messages in my inbox; like most Internet users, I receive dozens (if not hundreds) of unwanted spam emails every day.

If you use your email account at all, you know what spam is. Spam—otherwise known as *unsolicited commercial email* or *junk email*—describes any unrequested marketing message sent via email. Spam is typically sent in bulk, so that the one message you see in your inbox has hundreds of thousands of cousins cluttering other inboxes across the Internet.

Understanding Email Spam

Spam messages are sent en masse and indiscriminately, hawking adult websites, male enhancement pills, mortgage refinancing, penny stocks, and other schlocky products and services. It's just like the junk mail you receive in your postal mailbox, except in greater volume and often less tasteful. (And, in some instances, capable of carrying viruses and spyware that can infect your computer.)

The only good thing about spam is that it's easy enough to get rid of—just hit the Delete key in your email program. That is, unless your inbox is so clogged with spam that it interferes with your regular mail, which can happen.

> > > **NOTE**

Spam is said to get its name from the famous Monty Python sketch, with hordes of Vikings singing "Spam, Spam, Spam, Spam" in honor of the Hormel processed meat product.

The History of Spam

Believe it or not, the first email spam hit way back in 1978, when what was to become the Internet was then known as ARPANET. The spam was sent by DEC, one of that era's largest computer companies, to announce the release of a new computer, called the DEC-20. DEC sent email to all ARPANET addresses on the west coast, which broke with existing protocol *not* to use the Net for such commercial announcements. It was small scale in terms of what we see today, but it was unsolicited commercial email, nonetheless.

Over the next decade ARPANET morphed into the Internet. It was on an early version of the Internet that the next recorded instance of spam occurred. On May 24, 1988, a college student named Rob Noha posted individual messages on a large number of Usenet newsgroups. His messages—with the subject "HELP ME!"—pleaded with other users to send money for his college fund, as he was running out of cash. There's no indication whether his pleas were heeded.

> > > **NOTE**

In the early days of the Internet, Usenet newsgroups were one of the primary forums for communicating with other users. Usenet still exists today, but is much less widely used, replaced by various web-based message forums.

Now we fast forward to 1991, when spam was first used to perpetuate that ages-old concept of the chain letter. In this instance, the chain letter took the form of a series of email messages, forwarded from one user to another, about a sick boy named Craig Shergold who wanted to amass enough business cards to set a world record. The chain mailing was almost immediately identified as a hoax, but a lot of business cards got sent to a small hospital in England—and the chain letter, incredibly, still circulates to this day.

The first large commercial spam came on April 12, 1994. That was when Laurence Canter and Martha Siegel, two tech-savvy immigration lawyers from Scottsdale, Arizona, flooded all 6,000 Usenet newsgroups with a spam known as the "Green Card Lottery." This spam message advertised the services of their law firm for obtaining green cards for immigrants; Canter and Siegel purportedly generated close to $200,000 from the mailing, even if they generated the ire of tens of thousands of offended users.

By 1995, spam had pretty much migrated from Usenet to the realm of email. Spammers started sending out millions of emails at a time, thanks to newly developed spam software and the availability of millions of email addresses on CD-ROM. The number of spam messages began to increase faster than the number of new Internet users, with the rate of increase speeding up over time. Today, spam is a fact of everyday Internet life, the bane of every user with an email inbox.

< < < TIP

> Don't confuse unsolicited spam with email advertising practiced by many Internet retailers. This sort of permission-based marketing requires you to opt into future mailings, typically via a check box at the bottom of a shopping cart or order form. After you give your permission, they're free to send you all sorts of ads via email. Because you agreed to receive these messages, they're not spam—even if you don't particularly enjoy receiving them.

How Spam Works

Spam works like any other email message, except in bulk. The spammer creates his message, gathers a list of email addresses, and then bulk emails his message to all the names on his list. The spam message then travels across the Internet to your ISP's email server, and eventually to your email inbox.

The thing is, most ISPs try to block the sending of spam, by monitoring or filtering large numbers of outgoing messages. (Try it yourself; most ISPs return email messages with more than a dozen or two recipients, thinking that it might be a spam message.) To that end, the spammer has to perform some high-tech tricks to get around these outbound message limits.

One such trick is to route the bulk mailing through an unsuspected open mail relay (OMR). This is a separate server (*not* the email server of the spammer's ISP) that forwards—without restriction—email aimed at third parties. Spammers bounce their email off OMRs to mask the true origin of the spam; when you receive a bounced message, it looks like it came from the OMR server, not from the spammer.

> > > NOTE

> The use of OMR servers has decreased in recent years, as many ISPs use DNS-based blocking lists to block mail from identified OMRs. And, thanks to 2003's CAN-SPAM Act, it is now illegal to send spam in the U.S. through an open relay.

A more typical approach today is to use hundreds or thousands of hijacked computers to send the spam. The spammer infects these computers with a virus that opens a backdoor to control the computer via remote control. Then he instructs the email program on each zombie computer to send his spam message to a designated list of addresses; to the recipients, it looks as if the spam came from the hijacked computer—which it did.

Finding Names to Spam

Why is spam such a big problem? It's simple—spam is a low-cost, low-risk way to generate substantial profit. For a budding direct marketer, there is no lower cost medium than email. Unlike postal mail, where you have to put a stamp on every envelope or catalog, email messages are essentially sent for free—assuming, that is, that you have the email addresses to target.

Most spammers don't pay for the email addresses they send to. That's in stark contrast to traditional direct mail, where direct marketers pay several cents for each name and address they use. With junk email, the names are acquired—or created—at little or no cost.

There are several ways a spammer can generate a list of names for his emailings. These include the following:

- **Spam lists**—Spammers can purchase lists of tens of millions of email addresses for just a few hundred dollars over the web, then use these names for their mailings.

- **Email harvesting**—More sophisticated spammers use automated software—called *spambots*—to scour the Internet for publicly available email addresses. These email addresses can come from a variety of sources—public web pages, blog postings, message forums, public directories, and so forth. Aggressive spammers can even scour Google, Yahoo!, and other search engines for publicly posted email addresses; if your email address is on a web page that is listed at the search site, it's visible to a spambot via a quick query of the search engine.

- **Phishing and social engineering**—Some spammers work by tricking you into providing your email address. For example, some spammers send out "blind" spams to all the possible addresses in a given domain, asking you to reply to the message; when you reply, the spammer scrapes your address off the reply email and adds it to their database of valid addresses. Phishing is also popular; when you're lured to a phony website from a phishing message, the email address you enter is used for future spam mailings. (And sold to other spammers, of course.)

- **Automatic name generation**—Perhaps the most common means of generating email addresses today is via *dictionary spam*. This type of spam occurs when the spammer uses special software to guess every possible name in a given domain. For example, the spammer might start sending email to aaa@thisdomain.com, and end with a message to zzz@thisdomian.com. More sophisticated dictionary spammers make sure to include all known given names (and possible first- and last-name combinations) so if you have a common name at a major ISP—mike@hotmail.com or jimbrown@yahoo.com—you're likely to get hit with an inordinate amount of spam.

{ P E R S O N A L   E X P E R I E N C E }

Personally, I receive several hundred spam messages a day—most to multiple email addresses. That's because I use a different email address for each book I write; this way I know which book readers are writing about when they email me. So I'll receive a single spam message sent to each of these dozens of addresses; the spammer is either harvesting addresses from multiple sources or using dictionary techniques to generate all possible names for my single email domain.

Spoofing Email Addresses

Have you ever looked closely at a spam message and discovered that it appears to come from a friend's email account—or even from your own address? Spammers use these fake addresses to trick you—or your spam filter—into not deleting them. This technique is called *email spoofing*.

> One typical trick is for the spammer to spoof the address of a trusted institution, such as Microsoft or eBay. When you see an email in your inbox from one of these companies, you're apt to at least look at it—and thus read the spammer's message.

How does a spammer spoof a specific email address? It's all in the software. There are spoofing programs available today that make it relatively easy to insert any email address into the spam message's header. Some software even works interactively, inserting the recipient's address (that's you) into the sender's address field, so it looks as if the email you receive is actually coming from you.

The problems posed by these types of header spoofs are obvious. Because it spoofs a trusted address or domain, a spam message is less likely to be filtered by spam-blocking software and services. In addition, you're more likely to open a message if it looks as if it's coming from some person or organization you know.

Sizing the Spam Problem

Some organizations spend a lot of time counting spam messages. Even without their efforts, however, we know that spam comprises a significant amount of email traffic today; all you have to do is look at the spam messages in your own personal inbox to realize the magnitude of the problem.

So how big is the spam problem? Well, the Measuring Anti-Abuse Working Group (www.maawg.org) estimates that approximately 82% of all emails delivered are spam; Postini (www.postini.com) says it's more like 90%. Whatever the exact percentage, we're talking more than 12 billion spam messages a year—a humongous amount of junk email.

Fortunately, you don't see most of this spam in your inbox. That's because the offending messages are stopped along the way by one or more spam filters. Chances are your ISP has a spam filter on its incoming email server, and that you have a spam filter in your email program. So your inbox probably isn't filled 82% (or 90%) with junk messages. Still, the problem is significant.

The monetary costs of spam are also significant. All those spam messages, delivered or not, take up bandwidth on the Internet and storage space on your ISP's servers, and both bandwidth and storage cost money. In addition, there is a cost due to lost productivity when you and I have to deal with all those spam messages. How big is this expense? Nucleus Research estimates that the lost productivity alone costs a company $712 per year per employee. Add that to the bandwidth and storage costs, as well as potential damage from virus-infested spam messages, and you're looking at total costs in the neighborhood of $100 billion a year.

> > > **N O T E**

Where does spam come from? SophosLabs (www.sophos.com) found that in 2007, the United States was the top spam-generating country, accounting for 28.4% of all spam messages on the Internet. The other top ten spam generating countries included South Korea (5.2%), China/Hong Kong (4.9%), Russia (4.4%), Brazil (3.7%), France (3.6%), Germany (3.4%), Turkey (3.0%), Poland (2.7%), and Great Britain (2.4%).

Of course, to you as an individual, the cost of spam can't be measured in dollars and cents. Instead, it's measured in minutes and hours, the time you spend dealing with all the junk email in your inbox. It's an inconvenience, and one that also threatens the viability of email as a communications medium. When the majority of the email you receive is spam, how eager are you to check your inbox? How many legitimate messages do you block or delete in your quest to eliminate spam from your inbox? And when do you decide that the signal-to-noise ratio is too low, and cease using email at all?

Good questions all—and questions that beg answers.

How to Reduce Email Spam

Want to decrease the amount of spam in your inbox? Let's look at some of the things you can do to keep off spam lists and reduce the number of spam messages you receive.

Keep Your Email Address Private

The first step to cutting down on spam is to make sure as few people as possible know your email address. If the spammers don't know where you are, they can't bother you much.

What you want is the online equivalent of an unlisted phone number. Although it might be impossible to have a totally anonymous email address, there are ways to minimize your exposure to spammers, and thus decrease the amount of spam that you receive.

Here are some tips for minimizing the public exposure of your email address:

- **Don't give out your email address**—It's simple advice; the best way to hide your email address from spammers is to not give it out. What does this mean, in practice? Well, you shouldn't do any of the following: fill out web-based registration forms, fill out online surveys, include your email address when you post on public message boards or blogs, or add your name and address to any user directory. In addition, you should definitely not put your email address on your website or blog; that's just inviting spammers who skim the web for email addresses. Of course, this approach becomes problematic, especially when a website requires an email address for registration—which might make alternative approaches more viable.

- **Create a less-common email address**—Dictionary spam adds common names to popular Internet domains to "guess" at valid email addresses. For this reason, the address bob@myisp.com will receive more spam that b2qb475@myisp.com. So learn from the dictionary spammers and create an email address that looks as random as possible; it will be harder to guess, and you'll get less spam.

- **Use a spamblock**—If you need to publicize your email address, you can do so in a way that foils automated spambots. The best method is to use a *spamblock*, an email address that has been altered by the insertion of supplementary characters. For example, if your email address is johnjones@myisp.com, you might change the address to read johnSPAMBLOCKjones@myisp.com. Other users will know to remove the SPAMBLOCK from the address before emailing you, but the spambots will be foiled.

- **Use two addresses**—This is kind of a workaround, but it's effective. Use a free web-based email service, such as Gmail or Hotmail, to create a second email address, then use that address for all public correspondence and such. Keep your other, ISP-based email address private, known only to selected friends and family. All the spam will go to the more-public address, which you can easily ignore. Your main address will remain relatively spam-free.

- **Use a disposable email address**—Another alternative is to generate what is called a disposable email address. This provides a working email address to any site that requires it, without divulging your real email address. You can obtain disposable email addresses from Spam Gourmet (www.spamgourmet.com), Spamex (www.spamex.com), ZoEmail (www.zoemail.com), and similar sites.

- **Don't reply to spammers**—Remember, many spammers get your address when you give it to them. For that reason, you don't want to reply to any spam messages—period. It's when you reply that they harvest your email address; don't reply, and they're left empty handed.

C A U T I O N ! ! !

Along the same lines, don't click the "unsubscribe" link found in many spam messages. This link seldom leads to a legitimate unsubscribe function, and more often just adds your email address to the spammer's email database—unlike the functioning unsubscribe link found in legitimate email marketing messages.

Use Your ISP's Spam-Blocking Features

Many Internet service providers provide their own spam blocking services. Some ISPs activate their spam blocking automatically, in the background; others provide a set of tools you can choose to use on the email you personally receive. To cut down on the spam you receive, you should avail yourself of your ISP's spam blocking.

Most ISPs have such spam-blocking features, although they're not often well publicized. If in doubt, check with your ISP's technical support department to find out what spam-blocking services they offer.

Use Your Email Program's Spam Filter

Most email programs include some sort of spam filtering. As you might suspect, newer programs have more robust spam filters than do older ones.

For example, the older Outlook Express program doesn't even have a spam filter built in. Instead, the program lets you manually block messages from known spammers by using the Blocked Senders List feature. When you receive a spam message in your inbox, select the message and then select Message, Block Sender. In the future, all messages from this sender are deleted automatically.

< < < T I P

Outlook Express doesn't actually block any email messages; the messages are still received by your computer, but sent immediately to the Delete folder—where they can still be viewed until you delete the contents of the folder. In fact, it's a good idea to browse through the Delete folder, just in case a "good" message has accidentally been tagged as spam, which sometimes happens.

For more robust spam fighting, you can upgrade to Microsoft Outlook. Outlook 2003 includes four levels of spam filtering, which you can access by selecting Actions, Junk E-Mail, Junk E-Mail Options. The four levels are Low (blocks the obvious spam messages), High (blocks most spam messages, but might also block some nonspam email), Safe Lists Only (blocks all email except from people on your Safe Senders List), and No Automatic Filtering (turns off the spam filter).

Outlook 2007 features the same four levels of protection, as shown in Figure 12.1, but with an even more advanced junk email filter. (The same improved filter is present in Windows Mail, the email program included with Windows Vista.) As with the previous version of Outlook, you can create lists of both safe and blocked senders to further decrease the unwanted messages in your inbox.

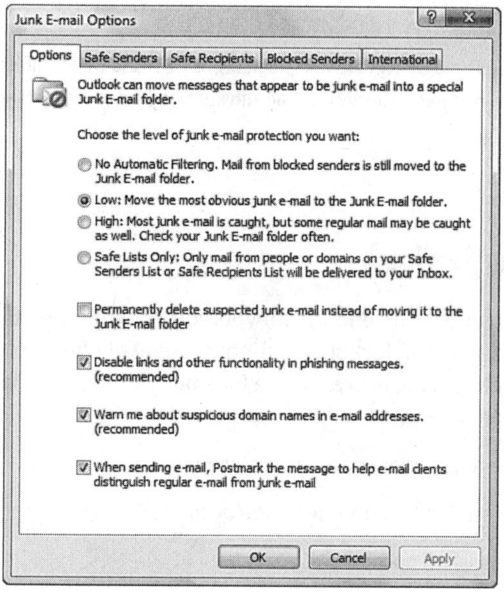

Figure 12.1

Configuring spam protection levels in Outlook 2007.

Bottom line: The newer the email program, the better its spam-fighting capabilities. This may be reason enough to upgrade from Outlook Express in Windows XP to Windows Mail in Windows Vista, or from Outlook 2003 to Outlook 2007.

Use Anti-Spam Software

If the amount of spam in your inbox becomes overwhelming, you might want to consider using an anti-spam software program. Most anti-spam software uses some combination of spam blocking or content filtering to keep spam messages from ever reaching your inbox; their effectiveness varies, but they do decrease the amount of spam you receive to some degree.

The most popular anti-spam software offerings include the following:

- ANT 4 Mail Checking (www.ant4.com)
- MailWasher (www.mailwasher.net)
- RoadBlock (www.roadblock.net)
- SonicWALL Anti-Spam and Email Security (www.sonicwall.com)
- SpamCatcher (my.smithmicro.com)
- Vanquish vqME (www.vanquish.com)

> > > **N O T E**

In addition, many anti-virus and content filtering programs, as well as so-called "Internet security suites," include anti-spam modules. If you're already using an antivirus program or security suite, check whether it offers spam email filtering.

Use a Spam Filtering Service

If anti-spam software isn't powerful enough for you, you can subscribe to one of the several online services that interactively block spam, using a variety of filtering and blocking techniques. Many of these services are also available for small business and large corporate networks; most are priced on a per-month subscription basis.

Here are some of the more popular spam filtering services:

- Brightmail AntiSpam (www.symantec.com/business/)
- Mailshell (www.mailshell.com)
- OnlyMyEmail (www.onlymyemail.com)
- SpamCop (www.spamcop.net)
- SpamMotel (www.spammotel.com)

Report the Spam

If you're feeling particularly vigilante-like, you can go to the extreme of reporting the spam you receive. It's not an approach I particularly endorse, because the sheer volume of spam messages makes it fairly impractical, but some users like to feel as if they're doing *something* about the problem.

You can report spam emails to the FTC by forwarding a copy of the message to spam@uce.gov. You can also send a copy of the spam to your ISP's abuse department—and to the abuse department of the sender's ISP.

Dealing with Blacklists

One feature of most of anti-spam services is that they use *blacklists* to filter out potential spam content. A blacklist is simply a list of known or suspected spammers, either by unique IP address or general domain.

Filtering by blacklist is somewhat effective, as spammers tend to use unprotected computers or domains to do their dirty deeds. If a computer or domain is known to be frequently used by spammers, it makes sense to block traffic from that computer or domain.

The problem with a blacklist is that it blocks *all* traffic from that computer or domain, not just spam traffic. It's inevitable that some messages from legitimate users will get blocked along with the spam messages. That isn't a good thing for either the intended recipients of those legitimate messages or the senders, who can't get their messages out to companies employing those blacklist filters.

{ P E R S O N A L   E X P E R I E N C E }

My personal website, www.molehillgroup.com, is hosted by a web hosting firm that has inadvertently provided services to spammers. I know this because my email has been blacklisted on occasion—along with all the other users of that web hosting service. I found there was nothing I could do about this, short of using an alternate email address until the blacklist expired. It was extremely frustrating—and explains why I'm not a big fan of blacklists.

The issue, then, is how can a legitimate sender get removed from a blacklist? Unfortunately, there's no easy solution.

If you find yourself the victim of an unintended blacklist, your first step is to contact the owner of that blacklist and plead your case. In most instances, that means finding out which anti-spam service a recipient uses, and then contacting that company. Some companies are easier to deal with than others; the bad news is, some companies don't honor any requests for blacklist removal as long as you're using an offending server.

> > > **N O T E**

Fortunately for those individuals or companies that have been inadvertently blacklisted, most blacklists exist for a matter of hours, not days. For example, SpamCop blacklists an offending domain for a maximum of 24 hours after a complaint has been received; if no further complaints are received, the domain is automatically removed from the blacklist.

If you can't get your address removed from the blacklist, your only recourse is to use a different email address for the duration of blacklist. That or, as some companies I know have done, change ISPs or web hosts to one that isn't frequently blacklisted.

Is It Safe?

Spam itself isn't dangerous, but it can be debilitating. When the number of spam messages exceeds the number of legitimate messages in your inbox, email might become more trouble than it's worth.

To that end, you need to use all the methods at your disposal to reduce the number of spam messages that you actually see. Use your ISP's spam filter, turn on the junk email features in your email program, and even purchase a separate anti-spam program if that makes sense. If you can redirect most of the spam to a separate spam folder, you won't have to deal with it—which should make dealing with your normal email messages that much easier.

Online Surveillance: How Big a Problem?

You might think that the Internet is a good place to hide. You can browse most websites without entering a single name or password; no one knows that it was you who visited those sites. Even better, you can create any number of fake names and online personas, and pretend to be anyone you want. It's easy to hide in plain sight.

Except that really isn't the case. Because of the technology behind the Internet, it's possible to track virtually everything you do while you're online. That's right: Every email you send, every message you create, every website you visit can be tracked. And, with all the personal information you leave behind in your wake, it's becoming increasingly difficult to keep your private life private when you're online.

The upshot is that if people want to monitor your online behavior, they can. But who would want to do this—and how big a problem is this online surveillance?

Welcome to the Surveillance Society

In spite of the apparent anonymity of web surfing, the reality is that you leave traces behind every time you do virtually anything on the Internet, thanks to technological tidbits such as cookies, IP addresses, and such. Even worse, it's likely that your name, email address, street address, and phone number are all on the web, somewhere. It's hard to keep private in such a public environment.

You see, the world of the Internet is no different from the physical world. In the physical world, when you buy something from a direct mailer or catalog merchant, your name and contact information enters their database. And most direct merchants generate subsidiary income from selling the names in their database to other companies; make one purchase, and everybody knows who you are.

The same thing happens online. When you buy something online, enter your name and address to register for a specific website, or even reply to a blog posting, your contact information goes into that specific database. The company behind the website can sell your personal information, just as direct mail merchants do; even if the website keeps your information private, much of what you entered is out there on the web, available to anybody doing a rudimentary Google search.

So privacy is an issue online, just as it is in the real world. But the issue of online surveillance goes beyond simple privacy; it's about tracking *all* your movements online, no matter how inconsequential.

C A U T I O N

You might not realize it, but every public posting you make—in blogs, online message boards, Usenet newsgroups, and Internet chat rooms—remains visible to future users of the Internet. Old postings are commonly archived; old web pages are cached by Google and other search engines. So if you made a derogatory comment on a blog three years ago about a co-worker, that comment can still be read three years from now when that co-worker rises to become your boss. The moral here is that you should never post anything in a blog, newsgroup, message group, or chat room that you wouldn't want your future boss—or spouse—to read. After it's out there, it stays out there.

Every website you visit knows a lot about you. Traffic monitoring software can tell which site you came from, which site you go to next, and what pages you visit (and for how long) on the current site. This software also captures your computer's unique IP address, which makes it relatively easy to find out who you are—or at least where you are, and who your ISP is. Cookies saved to your computer's hard disk make it easy to track everything you do on the current site, and retain that information for your next visit, and the visit after that, and the visit after that.

Of course, all this information is also present on your own computer—the sites you visit, the messages you read, and so on. Someone need only steal your computer (or subpoena it in a legal action) to find out more about your online habits than you probably can remember. Think about what the lawyer of an angry spouse in a divorce case might discover!

And what about your work computer? It might come as a surprise to discover that more companies than not these days track everything their employees do online. Not only do companies monitor their employees' web surfing and email communications, they also selectively block which sites you can visit during the workday. One false move and you're apt to get a visit from your company's HR department.

But the worst potential offender of your online civil rights is not your spouse or employer, but your government. The United States government, like many other governments around the world, is increasingly likely to monitor your online activities. It's in the guise of stopping terrorism, of course, but the net is cast so wide as to catch millions of law-abiding citizens. Do you really want the government to know which websites you visit in your leisure time? Is your business *their* business?

The reality is, it may be too late to keep your private online life private. Monitoring of online activities affects millions of users every day. You may be the victim of online surveillance—and not even know it!

Surveillance by Websites

Let's start by examining how any website, no matter how small, can track your online activity. With readily-available technology, a website can follow you as you surf from site to site, logging all the pages you visit and what you do while you're there. It's the online equivalent of someone following you through a shopping mall, snapping pictures of you as you go.

This sort of tracking is facilitated by small text files called *cookies*, which are automatically installed on your computer's hard disk when you visit particular websites. You visit a site, and it downloads a small cookie file to your computer—all in the background, without you knowing it.

And here's the thing: The use of cookies is near-ubiquitous. Most sites, especially the larger commercial ones, use cookies as a matter of course for all their site visitors. So there are a lot more companies tracking you than you might think.

> > > **N O T E**

Learn more about dealing with cookies in Chapter 16, "Covering Your Tracks Online."

The privacy dangers, of course, depend on what someone does with all this potential information. Fortunately, most websites either don't use the available information or use it for relatively benign purposes—typically for marketing.

For example, a site can use cookies to track which website you visited immediately prior to visiting their site. With this knowledge, the current site can serve up advertising based on the nature of the previous site visited. Or a site can analyze your IP address to display local information—time, temperature, local advertising—based on your calculated physical location. As I said, relatively benign.

But the use of cookies and other user-profiling technologies doesn't have to remain benign. Imagine a company using the information contained in your posts to a certain blog, or uttered in an online chat room, and cross-referencing this information with the data stored on a separate website. Even worse, imagine government authorities tracking your online behavior and assembling a profile that indicates you're a risk for terrorist activities, or for child pornography. It might sound Orwellian, but it's technically possible—and, unfortunately, increasingly probable.

Surveillance by Your Employer

Here's an even more common scenario. You're sitting at work, it's a slow day, and you decide to use your work computer to check your stock portfolio or place an order from Amazon.com. Later that day you get an email or a visit from your company's IT or HR department, warning you about unauthorized use of the company's computers for personal activities. How did they know what you were doing?

It's simple: Most large companies today use available technology to monitor their employees' technology usage. This monitoring includes everything from reading all incoming and outgoing emails to tracking website URLs to recording and reviewing telephone messages to physically tracking employees via GPS technology. This is a scary situation.

Here are the statistics, thanks to the American Management Association's 2007 *Electronic Monitoring & Surveillance Survey*:

- 66% of companies monitor their employees' Internet connections

- 65% of companies block connections to what they deem inappropriate websites

- 45% of companies monitor employees' computer keystrokes and the time they spend at the keyboard

- 43% of companies store and review employees' computer files

- 43% also monitor their employees' email messages

- 12% monitor the blogosphere (and 10% monitor social networking sites) to see what their employees are saying about the company outside of business hours

> > > **N O T E**

What is an inappropriate website? Fully 96% of employers are concerned about adult, pornographic, or even romantic sites; 61% block access to game sites; 50% block social networking sites, such as MySpace and Facebook; 40% block entertainment sites; 27% block shopping/auction sites; 21% block sites that offer sports news and scores; and 18% block access to blogs.

And here are the more frightening statistics: 28% of employers have fired workers for misusing email, while 30% have fired workers for misusing the Internet, and 2% have fired employees for inappropriate blog postings. Email abuse includes any violation of a company policy (64%), inappropriate or offensive language (62%), excessive personal use (26%), and breach of confidentiality rules (22%); Internet misuse includes viewing or downloading inappropriate or offensive content (84%), violation of a company policy (48%), and excessive personal use (34%).

Surprised by all this activity? Think your company isn't looking over your shoulder? Then think again. With two-thirds of all employers doing some sort of monitoring, chances are your company is part of the pack. And they don't have to tell you that they're watching; only two states, Connecticut and Delaware, require employers to notify their employees of surveillance activity. (That said, 84% of companies say they inform workers that they're monitoring computer activity, and 71% alert workers to email monitoring.)

> > > **N O T E**

Computers aren't the only technology monitored by employers. Almost half (45%) of all employers monitor their workers' time on the phone and numbers dialed, 9% review all voicemail messages, 8% use GPS technology to track company vehicles, and 7% use video cameras to monitor on-the-job performance.

It's enough to make one paranoid—if, in fact, you weren't actually being watched.

Surveillance by Your Loved Ones

Okay, so know you now that your boss is probably watching you whenever you're at your computer. But it's possible that you're being watched when you're at home, too—by your spouse.

That's right, suspicious husbands and wives who think their spouses might be cheating are increasingly turning to Internet-monitoring software and services rather than to the traditional private eye. It's a simple matter of using technology to fight technology-enabled activities.

In the old days, illicit lovers met in darkened bars and cheap hotels, exchanging furtive phone messages and written notes. Adultery is much more high-tech today. Lovers are likely to meet on web-based chat rooms or adult dating sites, then arrange trysts and send love notes via email and instant messaging. But, as you already know, everything one does online leaves an electronic trail. A high-tech private eye (or equivalent tracking program) can pick up these electronic breadcrumbs and assemble damning evidence against a cheating spouse.

< < < **T I P**

Think a spouse might be cheating on you? Then check out ChatCheaters.com (www.chatcheaters.com) and Infidelity Check (www.infidelitycheck.org), two sites devoted to helping the victims of online infidelity.

Understandably, hard statistics regarding online infidelity are difficult to come by. Michael Fortino, in his 2001 book *e-mergency*, stated that one-third of divorce litigation is caused by online affairs. This may be a specious number, however; there appear to be no surveys or research that confirm this allegation. Still, it's not hard to imagine that the Internet is playing an increasing role in infidelity, thus leading to an increase of online surveillance by suspicious spouses.

> > > **NOTE**

Michal Fortino himself fell foul to the dangers of Internet abuse. In October, 2007 he was convicted and sentenced to 20 years in prison for possessing child pornography on his laptop PC. His crime was discovered when he took his computer to a Best Buy store in Fayetteville, Arkansas, for repairs; employees there discovered the illegal files on his hard drive and alerted authorities.

And here's the thing about tracking unfaithful spouses online—the evidence is damning. Instead of overheard phone conversations or blurry photographs taken with a telephoto lens, Internet surveillance results in very hard evidence about what the spouse was doing and when. IP tracking doesn't lie, and archived emails can be easily retrieved.

Which, of course, should serve as a warning for any spouse with thoughts of straying. Remember, everything you do online is ultimately available to anyone who wants to find it. So don't do anything you want your spouse to find out about—even if it's what you think is a harmless online flirtation.

Surveillance by Your Enemies

If your friends and family can trace your online activities, what's to stop your enemies from doing so, too?

Again, hard statistics are almost impossible to come by. But someone with an axe to grind can certainly find you online and use any unseemly activities to your detriment.

What You've Done in the Past Doesn't Stay in the Past

Imagine a business competitor looking for some sort of advantage in the market place. Now imagine a posting you made to some obscure blog a year or so ago, commenting on your interests and future plans. That seemingly innocuous blog post could contain information valuable to your competitor. And, as with all things online, after it's posted you can't withdraw it.

Worse still, imagine you're a candidate running for political office. Your opponent's campaign is sure to have at least one person running opposition research, and today that research includes scouring the web for each and every word you've ever posted. That expletive-ridden diatribe against big business you made back when you were an angry college student will come back to haunt you in your next campaign.

It's even worse if you've used your computer (personal, work, or public) to visit websites that some might find inappropriate. Imagine the politician found to have visited a steamy porn site, or even a site expounding an opposing political philosophy!

< < < TIP

What can you do to eliminate posts you've made in the past? Unfortunately, not much. If it's your own blog or website, you can delete older posts and comments, but cached versions of your site will still exist at various websites—including Google's search results and the fascinating WayBackMachine at the Internet Archive website (www.archive.org). And if the offending post is on another site, your ability to remove it is directly related to your ability to plead your case to the blog owner or site administrator. Plus, you still have the WayBackMachine to contend with. So it's better not to post in the first place than to try to remove it after the fact.

Online Stalkers and Predators

Of course, the worst kind of enemy surveillance comes when you're being personally stalked online. This could be in the form of a minor being solicited for sex by a older predator, a single woman singled out for unwanted attention in a chat room or online dating site, or just a school bully posting mean messages on your social networking page. Online predators do exist, and sometimes their seemingly harmless online behavior spills out into the real word—with frightening results.

Cyberstalking is the online equivalent of real-world stalking, where one person pays unwanted attention to another, obsessively so. The magnitude of the problem is hard to discern, however, if only because the definition of the crime is somewhat fuzzy. That said, several major organizations—chief among them CyberAngels (www.cyberangels.org) and Working to Halt Online Abuse (www.haltabuse.org)—track cases of cyberstalking reported to their sites; aggregating the cases they report leads to a number somewhere in the 100,000 per year range; other (unsubstantiated) reports say there are closer to 200,000 cyberstalking incidents each year. In any case, it's a significant number, if somewhat lower than sensational news reports might imply.

The number of cyberstalking incidents that turn into sex crimes also appears to be lower than the media might have you believe. In a 2008 article in *American Psychologist*, researchers from the University of New Hampshire's Crimes Against Children Research Center (www.unh.edu/ccrc/) discovered that sex attacks on teenagers actually decreased during the rise of the Internet. From 1993 to 2005, the same years that the Internet came to prominence, teenaged sex assaults decreased 52%. If, in fact, the Internet was such a boon to sexual predators, one would have expected the number of sex assaults to increase with the rise of the Internet, not decrease—which implies that sex predators aren't finding the Internet a fertile hunting ground.

Equally important, this research debunks the myth of the older sexual predator preying on unsuspecting youth. The UNH research indicates that, contrary to common opinion, most online predators don't pose as younger users, but in fact present themselves in chat rooms as the older people they actually are. Their victims are typically older teenagers, not impressionable prepubescents, and are seldom tricked into having sex. Instead, these teenagers willingly agree to meet with their known older correspondents. That doesn't make the crime any less reprehensible, but it does put more of the onus on the younger partners than was previously thought.

So the threats of cyberstalking and online sexual predators both appear to be somewhat overstated. Still, the issues exist, and it's essential to protect both yourself and your children against these types of activities.

> > > **N O T E**

> Learn more about protecting against cyberstalkers in Chapter 17, "Protecting Yourself—and Your Children—from Online Predators."

Surveillance by Your Government

The news isn't surprising. The Chinese government, in the build-up to the 2008 Beijing Olympic Games, is reported to perform constant surveillance on what sites are visited by that country's 80-some million Internet users. It's exactly what you'd expect from a regime with little tolerance for individual liberties.

What might surprise you, however, is that the United States government performs similar monitoring of its citizens, at least on an occasional basis. Some of this surveillance is perfectly legal, some of it not so much. But, like it or not, this high-tech surveillance is a fact of life in the post-9/11 world. Your government *is* spying on you.

To be honest, the U.S. government has always spied on its citizenry, to some degree. In the past, this took the form of opening postal letters and performing the occasional telephone wiretap. But things changed on September 11, 2001; the state of fear evident after the terrorist attacks caused the government to become more aggressive in its surveillance activities—and the public to become more acquiescent to the resultant attack on civil liberties.

Today, the government has many high-tech ways to spy on suspected terrorists and criminals. Letter opening and telephone wiretaps still exist, of course, but now the government can also read your email messages, monitor the websites you visit, and even read along as you instant message friends and family. It's all in the guise of stopping terrorism, but the net is broad enough to catch up lots of non-terrorists as well.

Just how widespread is the government's high-tech surveillance? It's impossible to tell, because the government keeps that information a secret. (We don't want the terrorists to know what we're doing, of course.) The government does admit, however, that it is performing some surveillance—and that some of what it does exceeds its legal authority.

For example, a 2001 survey of travel and transportation companies (including major airlines) found that 64% had provided customer data to the government, often in violation of their own stated privacy policies. And a class action lawsuit filed in 2006 against AT&T charges that the telecommunications giant unlawfully monitored telephone and Internet communications routed over its network—from both its customers and third parties, comprising a large segment of the population, literally millions of individuals and businesses.

> > > **NOTE**

AT&T's actions are related to the National Security Agency's wireless surveillance program, which monitors emails, Internet activity, text messaging, and phone calls from any party believed to be outside the United States—without first obtaining the necessary warrants.

In addition, the FBI acknowledged that during the twelve months of 2006 (the last year reported), it improperly accessed Americans' telephone records, credit reports, and Internet traffic. It also admitted that this was the fourth straight year it had committed such privacy abuses, all allegedly resulting from investigations aimed at tracking terrorists and spies.

Many of these abuses of civil liberties occurred because private businesses—telecommunication companies, banks, airlines, and the like—were willing to give the FBI any and all information it asked for, and then some. That's right, your telephone company (and likely Internet service provider) eagerly offered up more information about its customers than the government even wanted to know.

Even worse, the government is rapidly increasing its ability to monitor average Americans (as well as terrorists, presumably) by tapping into the growing amount of consumer data collected by the private sector. The more information about you is stored online, the more likely it is that some governmental agency will access it. And, as time goes by, that data collection becomes more and more automated. It's easy enough to design a software program to scour the reams of available information; this data mining only increases the odds of your being tracked by the Feds, even if your online activities are purely innocent.

Here's the reality, neatly stated by the American Civil Liberties Union:

"The threat posed by government collection of third-party information is far greater today than it would have been in the 1950s, or even the early 1990s."

That's because the government, for better or worse, now has the Internet and related technology in its collection of surveillance tools. And if that doesn't scare you, it should.

> > > **NOTE**

Learn more about the government's online surveillance in Chapter 15, "Big Brother Is Watching You."

Is It Safe?

Is it safe to take your private life online—or will your private life become public?

The answer, unfortunately, is that the Internet makes most private things public. Anything you post online, no matter how innocuous, remains online and visible for anyone with even rudimentary search skills. Not only are your posts public, they stay visible forever; there is no expiration date on the Internet.

This means that you need to take caution in what you post online. That means taking care with your blog posts and comments, chat room conversations, social network content, instant messages, even emails. If it's on the Internet, it's public; you don't want one ill-thought-out comment coming back to haunt you years later.

You also need to limit the information you post online to avoid attracting online predators. Although the risk of cyberstalking is much lower than the media would have you think, it's still an issue. There's no need to worry unduly about it, however, if you use common sense and take rudimentary precautions.

What you do have to worry about, however, is surveillance by the government. United States governmental agencies are increasing the amount of legal and illegal surveillance of average citizens, and there's little you and I can do about this—save for lobbying our elected officials to protect our civil liberties. It's a simple fact; at some point in time, it's likely that someone in the government will be looking over your virtual shoulder on the Internet. So be careful what you say and do; it very well might be used against you.

Dealing with Surveillance at Work

When you're at work, you're at the mercy of your employer—in a number of different ways, not all of them related to the security of your paycheck. Increasingly, employees find that they're victims of electronic surveillance by their employers; workers' online activities are monitored, recorded, and evaluated, with or without their knowledge. One wrong move online, in many cases, can result in a harsh warning or even termination.

If a company wants to, it can monitor virtually everything their employees do while seated at their computers. Keystroke logger software can track which keys you tap on your keyboard; email sniffers can examine the contents of your incoming and outgoing email; website sniffers can tell the company which sites you visit—and what you do while you're there.

Surveys show that two-thirds of all U.S. companies use some form of online surveillance to spy on their employees. Employers are looking for workers that abuse their Internet and email privileges, who perform personal tasks on company time, and who visit inappropriate websites and send out inappropriate messages. And, in most cases, such surveillance is perfectly legal; workers have few rights in this area.

Why Do Companies Spy on Their Employees?

It isn't mere curiosity or control that drives most companies to spy on their employees. In most instances, there are some very solid legal and security reasons to monitor their workers' Internet usage.

Legal Issues

For example, one of the big no-nos at most workplaces is viewing pornographic material on company computers. This isn't a moral issue; it's a legal one. An employee viewing adult images on his computer creates a hostile work environment for other employees. One employee visiting the wrong website can cost the company big bucks, in the form of a sexual harassment lawsuit.

The attempt to maintain a non-hostile workplace also extends to the issue of email monitoring. What might seem like a funny email joke to you could be construed as sexual harassment by a less open-minded co-worker. Better, then, for the company to monitor email traffic to filter out any possible inappropriate behavior.

For these and similar reasons, legal issues—in particular, the fear of lawsuits—is the number-one reason companies spy on their employees.

Productivity Issues

Of course, much online surveillance is a simple attempt to keep worker productivity at acceptable levels. Every manager fears that his employees are wasting precious work hours playing computer games and surfing ESPN.com. These fears inspire companies to monitor their employees' website use and to block access to certain sites.

For example, one large company I know blocks their workers from accessing online shopping sites (including eBay and Amazon.com), social networking sites (including Facebook and MySpace), online game sites (including Second Life and other virtual worlds), and online sports sites (including the aforementioned ESPN.com). That's in addition to the expected blocks of known pornographic sites, of course.

The goal here is to keep employees working instead of playing, thus boosting productivity. What's not known, however, is whether time spent online is taken away from regular work time or from time previously spent wasted at other non-work activities. In other words, the web may just be the latest way for employees to waste time at work.

Security Issues

Another good reason to monitor employees' web surfing concerns computer security. Visit the wrong site, and you can inadvertently download a computer virus or spyware that could bring down the entire company's computer network. Better, then, for the company to restrict access to those sites rather than risk compromising all the firm's PCs.

Then there's the issue of keeping confidential information confidential. Companies don't want their employees treating company secrets cavalierly; maintaining tabs on email messages helps to keep valuable information out of competitors' hands.

Image Issues

A final issue concerns maintaining the company's image. The wrong internal email leaked to the press or to a hostile organization can result in irreparable damage to a company's reputation. This is why many organizations either monitor or restrict their employees' posts to blogs, web forums, and the like—at least from company computers, but increasingly those made on the employee's own time. This type of surveillance is a little more censorious, and open to more ethical and legal debate. But it's becoming increasingly more common—even if it's more about control than about workplace productivity.

How Do Companies Spy on Their Employees?

Companies employ a number of different technologies to monitor and control their employees' online activities. Let's look at what you can expect to find in a typical large organization.

Web Filters

Probably the most-used type of monitoring software today is the *web filter*, which blocks employee access to specified websites. A company can create a list of specific sites to block, or use the software's filters to describe the kinds of sites to block.

> > > **NOTE**
>
> Web filtering isn't always accomplished by software alone. Some companies also offer web filter appliances (hardware) and web-based filtering services.

In any instance, all web page requests from employees' PCs are routed through the web filter. If the request matches a site or type of site on the block list, the request is turned down and the employee shown a page saying that access to the site was denied. With most software, IT staff can allow specific sites through the filter for specific employees; in practice, most such requests for exceptions must be approved by the employee's manager.

Some of the most popular corporate web filters include

- Barracuda Web Filter (www.barracudanetworks.com)

- iPrism (www.stbernard.com)

- ISSOrangeWebFilter (www.kerio.com)

- MIMEsweeper (www.clearswift.com)

Packet Sniffers

Rather than blocking access to websites, some companies prefer just to monitor which sites are visited. One way to do this is via *packet sniffer* software that monitors, or "sniffs," all traffic flowing over the company's network. The sniffer can be configured in one of two ways. An *unfiltered* configuration captures all the data packets coming over the network; a *filtered* configuration captures only those packets containing specified content.

> > > N O T E

Packet sniffers are also known as *network analyzers* or *protocol analyzers*.

Most employers are likely to use a filtered configuration, and set the sniffer to look for specific types of information. For example, a sniffer might be configured to look at data arriving from websites on a "do not visit" list, or to look for data containing particular words or phrases. Data packets meeting the specified criteria are then stored on a hard disk, for future examination.

Packet sniffers are used not just for monitoring website use, but also incoming and outgoing emails and instant messages. Naturally, some human being, either in the HR or IT departments, must manually read through all the information recorded by the packet sniffer. That's right— your email will be read.

Popular packet sniffers include the following:

- EtherDetect Packet Sniffer (www.etherdetect.com)
- Ethereal (www.ethereal.com)
- Network Probe (www.objectplanet.com/probe/)
- Wireshark (www.wireshark.org)

Log Files

Another way of tracking your online activities is to capture and read the log files created by various software programs. For example, the History list in your web browser is a crude kind of log file; there are also specific utilities that can create log files of user activity over a network.

Any log file that resides on your work PC is the property of your employer. Your company can examine your PC and read the contents of any file on your hard drive—including all log files. For example, your company could confiscate your computer, open your Internet Explorer History list, and look at every website you've visited in the past several weeks.

Desktop Monitoring

There are other ways that your employer can monitor your computer usage. The most common is to use a desktop monitoring program, which routes the contents of one computer screen to a different computer. (The programs typically split the signal going to the original PC's video card, sending a clone of the signal to the monitoring computer.) This way the person doing the monitoring can see everything that the person being monitored is doing on his or her PC.

This type of surveillance is people-intensive, and ultimately quite disturbing. Few employees would feel comfortable about their employer standing over their shoulders and watching everything they do at their computer. This is, however, an effective way to monitor computer usage in real time.

Some of the most popular of these computer surveillance programs include

- SpyAgent (www.spytech-web.com)
- SpyBuddy (www.exploreanywhere.com)
- WinSpy (www.win-spy.com)

Keystroke Loggers

Keystroke loggers do just what the name implies—they log every keystroke typed at an employee's computer. These programs intercept the electronic signals between a worker's keyboard and his operating system, and copy every keystroke into a log file. An employer can then access the log file and see everything entered from the keyboard.

Some of the more popular keystroke logging programs include

- Actual Spy (www.actualspy.com)
- Invisible KeyLogger Stealth (www.amecisco.com)
- KGB Keylogger (www.refog.com)
- Spector Pro (www.spectorsoft.com) .

A company (or individual) can also log keystroke activity by using keystroke logger *hardware*. For example, KeyGhost (www.keyghost.com) is a virtually unnoticeable device, about the size of your thumb, that installs between a keyboard and PC. This device captures keyboard keystrokes and stores them in its own internal memory. The device can then be removed and connected to another computer and the keystrokes retrieved and analyzed.

Email Monitoring

One last way your privacy can be compromised at work is via email. It has been legally established that any correspondence you undertake on your work PC is your employer's property, not yours. That means that your employer has the right to monitor all incoming and outgoing email messages, and to take appropriate action based on the content of these messages.

Even more important, in the eyes of many corporations, is that an organization is legally liable for all communications originating from its computer network. This puts the company at risk for lawsuits if employees engage in harassing, discriminatory, or illegal communications. Hence the need, in some companies' eyes, to monitor all employee emails.

Most email monitoring software scans incoming and outgoing email messages for keywords and phrases that signal inappropriate or illegal use. There are a number of email monitoring programs, including

- EmailObserver (www.softsecurity.com)

- IamBigBrother (www.iambigbrother.com)

- MailMarshal SMTP (www.marshal.com)

- MIMEsweeper (www.mimesweeper.com)

- WebWatcher (www.awarenesstech.com)

In addition, many of the desktop monitoring programs mentioned earlier in this section also have email monitoring features.

Monitoring Employees' Outside Activities

The courts have generally held that companies have a right to monitor and control their employees' online activities—when they're at work and using company-supplied computers. But more and more companies are increasing their surveillance to include online activities undertaken outside of the workplace, on their workers' personal time.

These monitoring activities are typically undertaken under the guise of protecting the company's image—public relations, in other words. Companies don't want their workers revealing company secrets or bad-mouthing the company, even if said bad-mouthing occurs outside of work. It's just not good business, in the eyes of the corporation.

Although a company can control its own PR activities, it's questionable whether they can control the public activities undertaken privately by their employees. Companies hold that any communications that mention their trademarked brands are the possession of the corporation—even if said communications were made by their employees as private citizens. It's not so much controlling their employees, the line goes, as controlling the brand image.

Individual employees, however, often think otherwise. Many people who participate in social networks or write blogs believe that a company cannot control what they post in their personal life. But that belief becomes strained when your employer calls you on the carpet for an unfavorable blog post or out and out fires you for derogatory comments made on your Facebook page.

CAUTION!!!

The comments you make on a blog or social network don't have to be derogatory about your employer to land you in hot water. Racist, sexist, or threatening comments can also be grounds for discipline or dismissal.

The bottom line here is that you need to know what is and is not acceptable to your employer. Some companies let their employees post freely; others are highly sensitive as to what employees post, feeling that any such comments reflect back on the company itself. So ask your HR department before you start blabbing on your blog—or it might come back to haunt you.

Balancing Employer and Employee Rights

This last issue about employer control dovetails into the larger issue of employer and employee rights. Put more succinctly, does an employer have the legal right to monitor or control its employees' online activities?

The answer, disconcerting to some, is an unqualified yes; an employer has every legal right to monitor its employees' activities during work hours, and while they're on company property. This might not give the employer the moral or ethical right to snoop, but ethics are decidedly situational.

Here is the reality. In the United States, at least, there are few legal restrictions on how employers can monitor or control their employees while they're on the job. It's a matter of who owns the computer equipment and network over which these activities take place; because all these are owned by the company, the employees have to walk the company line when using computers, networks, and Internet connections.

> > > NOTE

The Electronic Communications Privacy Act (ECPA) of 1986 explicitly allows organizations with an acceptable business reason to intercept and review email messages transmitted over the firm's network.

That said, it's best if a company has a defined policy in place beforehand, and notifies its employees of that policy. An employee unknowingly breaking an unstated policy has more legal standing than one well-informed before the fact.

This is why it's recommended that a company put its employee monitoring policy in writing and communicate that policy to all employees. At the minimum, this policy should do the following:

- Set out the business purposes for monitoring specific employee activities
- State that the company owns and is responsible for company computers, files, email messages, and networks
- Define the acceptable use of company networks and email
- Set clear boundaries for the personal use of company computers and networks
- Outline which forms of communication are considered inappropriate and banned
- Outline which websites or types of websites are considered inappropriate and banned
- Inform employees of the specific types of monitoring activities that will be employed
- Detail the consequences for any violations of these policies

In addition, it's probably good internal PR to explain how these monitoring activities benefit both the company and its employees.

That doesn't mean, however, that all companies should automatically employ monitoring software and track everything their employees do online. Even though the majority of large companies currently perform such surveillance, the practice is far from universal. For some companies, it's a matter of trust; they trust their employees to do the right thing, and don't want to come across as a monolithic and controlling Big Brother. Employees who feel trusted, these companies feel, will be more loyal and more productive. That's worth a few hours per week lost to personal use of the company's computers, network, and Internet connection.

Is It Safe?

If you're an employee of a company that employs technology monitoring, you should expect that all your online activities will be watched. Expect the company to track which websites you visit; expect your email to be read; expect your instant messages to be monitored. That's a simple fact in Corporate America today.

You also need to know that if a surveillance-related dispute arises, the courts will probably side with your employer. This means that you should use caution when conducting any personal business on your work PC—and be especially careful what you put in your email and instant messages.

And if you do a lot of personal blogging or social networking, be especially careful about what you say about your company in public. You comments might be well intentioned but still offensive to your employer. (This is especially so when you're talking about financial results and other confidential subjects.) When in doubt, just don't say anything.

As an employer, you're probably safe in instituting any type of monitoring activity you like—as long as you inform your employees about it. Your goal is not to trap them in illicit activity, but rather to discourage such activity in the first place. It's not about discovering miscreants; it's about encouraging proper and productive workplace behavior.

In any case, both employees and employers need to know that little of what happens both in the workplace and outside the workplace is private. The Internet makes most things public—whether the company or its workers like it or not.

Big Brother Is Watching You

georg Orwell had it right in *1984*, even if he was off by a few years. Big Brother exists; your government *is* spying on you.

This is not a paranoid delusion. In fact, the United States government readily admits to much of its surveillance activity. Various government agencies are running programs that spy on United States citizens, and it's all legal and aboveboard—well, most of it is, anyway. In addition to the legal spying that goes on, more programs no doubt exist outside the public eye, and who knows how deep they reach?

Of all the threats, real and imagined, that are discussed in this book, this particular threat scares me the most—and it should scare you, too. After all, the risk of having your identity stolen or being attacked by an online predator is relatively low; unfortunately, the likelihood of having your personal information monitored by a governmental agency is relatively high.

Read on to learn more about our Orwellian world.

A Short History of Government Surveillance

You might like to think that governmental spying on its citizens is something that happened in Cold War Communist regimes—and, of course, it did. It's not something one imagines happening in a free democracy like the United States; we're supposed to be guaranteed a certain level of privacy and civil liberty.

But civil liberty is not absolute, and our right to privacy is constantly in battle with our need for security. These battle lines are always in flux, but no more so than after the 9/11 terrorist attacks. In the wake of those attacks, public paranoia fed a government hungry for information and control—and the result is an increase in surveillance unprecedented in our nation's history.

That's not to say, however, that this is the first time that the United States government has spied on its citizens. Far from it; the current threat to civil liberties is not a new one.

Monitoring Minorities

The populace and the government have always been fearful of those unlike themselves. In the early days of the republic, this led to surveillance of "outsider" classes, such as freed slaves and Chinese immigrants. Case in point: The Chinese Exclusion Act of 1882, which not only restricted Chinese immigration to the United States, but forced all Chinese laborers to register with the government so that their activities could be more closely monitored.

This monitoring of minorities continued throughout the 20th century, peaking during the Civil Rights movement of the 1950s and 1960s. Key movement figures, including the Reverend Martin Luther King, were under constant surveillance by the FBI; King and his contemporaries were viewed as "subversives," and subject to many illegal investigations designed to minimize their influence.

Today, minority profiling is more frequently aimed at Muslims and persons of Arabic descent. For example, immediately after the 9/11 attacks, the government rounded up and detained more than 1,200 Muslim and Arab immigrants; these detainees, most of them legal U.S. citizens, were held for extended periods of time without legal representation or having formal charges filed. And, in the eyes of many in the Muslim community, such profiling continues to this day, in the form of additional airport security checks and the like.

> > > **N O T E**

> Christian Parenti, in his book *The Soft Cage: Surveillance in America from Slavery to the War on Terror* (Basic Books, 2003), notes that society's weakest, most disenfranchised, and most alienated are those groups first subjected to surveillance. The surveillance then spreads from these groups into the mainstream.

Watching the Subversives

In addition to monitoring minority groups, the government has always been suspicious of alleged subversives. In some instances, this fear was warranted; however, the government frequently overstepped its bounds in monitoring those thought to be a danger to the system and to the public.

For example, following a series of worker strikes and riots, Congress in 1917 enacted laws allowing the deportation of suspected anarchists and revolutionaries. In reality, these laws were designed to silence the rising voice of the immigrant working class, which threatened the big industrialists of the day.

In the 1920s, this type of surveillance was directed at political radicals, especially workers trying to organize union activity. During the WWII years, surveillance turned to Nazi sympathizers and citizens of German and Japanese descent. Then, during the 1950s, the surveillance spotlight focused on suspected Communists, culminating in the famous McCarthy hearings and various blacklists of supposed fellow travelers.

Widespread, indiscriminate surveillance of U.S. citizens began in earnest during the Cold War years. One well-known example was Operation Shamrock, in which the major U.S. telegraph companies were ordered to secretly turn over to the National Security Agency (NSA) copies of all messages sent to or from the United States. This program began in 1945, and the presidents of all the telegraph companies willingly agreed to participate, playing to their sense of patriotism against the Red Menace. Operation Shamrock continued into the 1960s, when new computer technology enabled keyword searches through each day's traffic.

Between 1956 and 1971, the FBI embarked on a series of operations under the umbrella name of COINTELPRO (COunter INTELligence PROgram). This operation ran a series of covert and mostly illegal projects aimed at investigating and disrupting homegrown dissident political organizations. The motivation behind this program was "protecting national security, preventing violence, and maintaining the existing social and political order." Targets included suspected communist and socialist organizations, black militant groups (such as the Black Panther Party), leaders of the Civil Rights movement and the NAACP, white hate groups (including the Ku Klux Klan), various leftist and anti-war groups (including the notorious Weathermen), and even celebrity activists (including Beatle John Lennon). Agents working in COINTELPRO were instructed by FBI Director J. Edgar Hoover to "expose, disrupt, misdirect, discredit, or otherwise neutralize" targeted groups and their leaders.

> > > **N O T E**

The excesses of COINTELPRO came to light in 1975, thanks to the efforts of the so-called Church Committee, a Congressional committee chaired by Senator Frank Church. The committee investigated all manner of illegal intelligence gathering by both the FBI and the CIA.

Reacting to Crisis

The current call for increased surveillance in time of crisis is nothing new. The government's spymasters have never found a crisis they didn't like—and couldn't exploit.

It's a fact: During national emergencies, the government tends to react overzealously—often with the explicit approval of a frightened populace. That the populace is often manipulated into such fear is part and parcel of the crisis mentality; propaganda feeds paranoia.

This sort of fear mongering dates back to the earliest days of the republic. In 1798, in response to criticism of a looming war with France, president John Adams signed the Alien and Sedition Acts. These were four laws that, among other actions, restricted speech critical of the government and authorized the government to imprison or deport aliens considered "dangerous to the peace and safety of the United States."

Civil liberties have traditionally taken a hit during wartime; this was the case even under Abraham Lincoln, a president known for his support of civil liberties otherwise. Most people today are unaware that during the Civil War, Lincoln declared martial law and authorized military tribunals, not the court system, to try suspected terrorists. While this dismissal of due process was temporary, it reflects how a threatened government reacts defensively.

Government Surveillance Programs Today

Be afraid—be very afraid!

This was the mantra of the Bush administration following the 9/11 attacks, used to drum up support for a series of initiatives that both reinforced executive power and inspired an enhanced level of government surveillance. With terrorists said to be lurking in every darkened corner, a fearful citizenry had little choice but to support these programs—and, in the process, have their hard-won civil liberties slowly but surely chipped away.

Surely, though, these surveillance programs are targeted at would-be terrorists, right? The government would never deem to spy on innocent citizens, would it?

Unfortunately, the government's surveillance programs aren't limited to tracking down a small number of terrorists. These programs, small and large, extend their surveillance to the general public. People, like you and me, who have done nothing wrong, are increasingly being swept up in the government's surveillance net.

Don't believe it? Let's look at just a few of the many examples.

Spying on College Students

The government has always had a thing about college students. Back in the 1960s and 1970s, when college campuses were thought to be hotbeds of leftist radicalism, the FBI kept running tabs on all manner of campus organizations. This surveillance verged on the indiscriminate, with surveillance of anti-war groups, environmental groups, anti-poverty groups, and even the American Friends Service Committee, a Quaker group dedicated to non-violence.

After some letup during the 1980s, the government is at it again, culling personal data from colleges across the nation and putting agents, both visible and covert, on most major campuses. And, to make matters worse, college officials appear to be cooperating; a 2001 ACLU survey found that 195 colleges and universities had turned over private information on students to the FBI, in apparent violation of privacy laws and often without a subpoena.

Spying on Scuba Divers

You might not think that scuba divers as a whole would constitute a serious terrorist threat, but apparently the FBI knows something we don't know. In 2002, the Professional Association of Diving Instructors voluntarily provided the FBI with the names, addresses, and other personal information of close to 2 million people—nearly every U.S. citizen who had learned to scuba dive in the previous three years. Feel safer, now?

Spying on Gamblers

Based on an unspecified terrorist threat against one or more area casinos, the FBI in 2003 obtained the names and personal information of all customers staying in Las Vegas hotels between December 22 and New Year's Day of that year. The FBI also asked for and received information on anyone who flew into the city, rented a vehicle, or used a storage facility. This indiscriminate surveillance ended up scrutinizing the activities of more than 270,000 law-abiding Americans—without their knowledge.

Spying on Travelers

As you might suspect, given the nature of the 9/11 attacks, the government is particularly paranoid about travel arrangements of would-be terrorists. To that end, various government agencies have requested—and ultimately been provided with—information about literally millions of travelers.

We'll start with one of the smaller operators. At the request of the Department of Homeland Security (DHS), JetBlue Airways in 2002 provided the Pentagon with more than 5 million passenger records. These names, augmented with Social Security numbers and other private information, were purportedly to be used by a subcontractor to develop a prototype passenger profiling system.

JetBlue's cooperation with government agencies isn't unique. Also in 2002, Northwest Airlines gave "millions" of passenger records to NASA, which was conducting research on passenger screening systems. When funding for NASA's research dried up, it offered to provide copies of these passenger records to the same contractor working on the DHS' passenger profiling system.

> > > **NOTE**

> Why the National Aeronautics and Space Administration (NASA) was researching civilian air travel systems is a bit of a mystery.

Not to be left out, American Airlines also shared 1.2 million passenger records with the Transportation Security Administration (TSA) in 2002. Like the data from the other airlines, American's records included names, addresses, and credit card numbers—and were assumedly matched with corresponding government records, including Social Security numbers and law enforcement records.

> > > **NOTE**

> In an unrelated security breach, American Airlines, Northwest Airlines, United Airlines, and other major carriers willingly turned over to the FBI millions of passenger records immediately following the 9/11 terrorist attacks —without the passengers' knowledge or consent.

High-Tech Surveillance

Surveillance in the late 20th century has become much more efficient and effective because of computer technology. Computers allow huge databases of information to be stored, collated, and rapidly searched; now surveillance can be undertaken on many more individuals and groups than was previously possible.

In addition, other modern technologies have enabled more precise and constant tracking. For example, the government can now monitor electronic correspondence via email and instant messaging, track which websites a suspect visits, evaluate spending habits via credit card records, and even physically track suspects using GPS technology.

ECHELON and the IAO

This high-tech surveillance began back in 1947, with a project named ECHELON. Run jointly by the governments of Australia, Canada, New Zealand, the United Kingdom, and the United States, ECHELON intercepted and inspected telephone calls, fax communications, email messages, and other data traffic around the globe. The technology used by ECHELON changed over the years, naturally, but included the tapping of publicly switched telephone networks, satellite transmissions, microwave links, and the Internet backbone.

From 2002 to 2003, the U.S. Department of Defense's DARPA unit ran something called the Information Awareness Office (IAO) and the corresponding Total Information Awareness (TIA) program. The IAO brought together several DARPA projects that focused on applying information technology to counter national security threats; if left unchecked, it may have led to the creation of a high-tech mass surveillance system. Fortunately, fears of just such a system led to the IAO being defunded by Congress in 2003—although certain TIA projects have continued, under different funding.

Combining Resources

It appears, however, that the fears of just such a mass surveillance system weren't unfounded. In subsequent years, details have begun to leak about a massive intelligent network built around a collection of governmental agencies and organizations, from the FBI and CIA, to the Pentagon and the Department of Homeland Security, to both big-city and small-town police departments. This system seeks to combine the information gathering and data analysis capabilities of various domestic law enforcement operations, all in the service of spying on suspected terrorists—and on average Americans, as well. It's been reported that this new organization has been given the authority to mine vast amounts of data on both organizations and individuals, including those not suspected of any crime.

The NSA's Warrantless Wiretapping

News of this new surveillance system comes on the heels of a continuing controversy regarding warrantless surveillance of U.S. citizens by the NSA. Under what the Bush administration has dubbed the "terrorist surveillance program," the NSA is authorized by executive order to monitor, without legal warrants, emails, text messages, Internet activity, and other communications involving at least one party believed to be outside the United States. Because monitoring of such communications inside the United States is prohibited without a warrant, the legality of this NSA surveillance is in question—or, at least, it was, before Congress passed the Protect America Act of 2007, which legalized this type of warrantless surveillance.

Related to the NSA controversy was revelation that, beginning in 2003, several large telecommunications companies willingly provided the government with records of millions of individual conversations that took place over their networks. In fact, AT&T was reported to have built secret rooms deep in the bowels of many of its facilities, designed to house computer gear for tapping into Internet communications. The telecom companies' legal liability in this situation was in question, in that they turned over the data without first being provided with a warrant; to absolve the companies from legal action, President Bush asked Congress to provide retroactive legal immunity for the companies involved. As of March, 2008, Congress had not yet acted on this legislation.

Ongoing NSA Operations

Despite the controversy, the NSA continues to monitor huge numbers of electronic transactions. According to a March, 2008, article in the *Wall Street Journal*, quoting current and former intelligence officials, the NSA is actively monitoring so-called "transaction" data from other governmental agencies and private companies (such as an unnamed wireless phone carrier), including domestic emails, Internet searches, bank transfers, credit-card transactions, travel records, and telephone records. The NSA then uses sophisticated software programs to analyze this raw data for suspicious patterns, spitting out leads to be explored by various counterterrorism operations scattered across the government.

While NSA officials say that these investigations remain focused solely on foreign threats, a number of the agency's employees have expressed concerns that the agency is overstepping its authority by performing domestic surveillance. In addition, there is the constitutional question of whether the government can examine such a wide array of data without violating an individual's right to privacy—in spite of the NSA's blanket statement that they strictly follow the "laws and regulations designed to preserve every American's privacy rights under the Fourth Amendment to the U.S. Constitution."

Is It Legal?

All these incidents and operations beg the question: Is it legal for the United States government to spy on its citizens? The answer, in many cases, is yes.

The thing is, the government could always spy on individuals and organizations—with the proper permission. That permission comes in the form of a warrant, issued by a judge. The government presents its case to the judge, and if the judge agrees that there is sufficient prior evidence to indicate a crime may be taking place, he issues a warrant authorizing the surveillance.

In the case of national security, the government can even spy first and ask permission later. The Foreign Intelligence Surveillance Act (FISA) of 1978 (amended by the USA Patriot Act of 2001 to include specific terrorist activities) establishes a special court to hear retroactive requests for surveillance. If the government thinks there is imminent danger, it can immediately put the wiretap or other surveillance in place; it then has 72 hours to obtain approval from a secret FISA court.

The FISA court has a history of approving pretty much everything the government asks for; in the period from 1979 to 2006, it approved 22,985 out of 22,990 requests, or 99.9% of all requests.

Apparently, however, 99.9% wasn't good enough, or maybe the government just thought it was too much trouble to ask permission at all, because in 2005 the Bush administration began circumventing the FISA procedures with its NSA warrantless wiretapping program. For whatever reason, the Bush administration believes that the executive branch has the power to do just about anything it likes without requiring approval from any other branch of government. Hence the blatant disregard for prior law and due process in general.

Of course, defenders of civil liberties take issue with this ask-no-questions approach to surveillance. In their view, the Bush administration's activities are undoing the safeguards placed on law enforcement in the 1970s, after the excesses of the FBI and CIA during the previous decade had been revealed. More important, these activities are rolling back the civil liberties and freedoms that are inherent in the United States Constitution and Bill of Rights. Under the Bush administration, critics claim, the Fourth Amendment is in danger of extinction.

Then there is the issue of "data sweeping," where the government scoops up huge volumes of so-called transactional data—records of phone calls made, subject lines from email messages, and the like, but not the full content of each conversation or email. According to a 1979 Supreme Court ruling, transactional records of telephone calls—but not actual conversations—can be collected without a judge issuing a warrant. However, multiple laws require a court order for transactional records of electronic communications, such as email. Further confusing the matter, the 2001 USA Patriot Act lowered the standard for such a court order in some cases, and in others made such records accessible if a "national security letter" (a form of FBI administrative subpoena) is submitted.

> > > **N O T E**

> The yearly budget for the NSA's data sweeping effort is classified, but one official estimated that it surpasses $1 billion.

The debate is whether there are or should be privacy protections when a large volume of transactional data is brought together—enough data to essentially paint a profile of an individual's behavior. In this instance, the transactional data is informative enough that the government doesn't have to read or listen to the content of individual messages or conversations. How private is such a transaction profile? As I said, the experts are still debating this one.

So are the government's growing surveillance activities legal? It depends: Yes, if a warrant has been obtained in advance. Yes, if the data collected is purely transactional. Maybe, if a warrant is obtained after the fact but you're engaged in suspicious activity. Who knows, if the trends continue—and the Bush administration has its way.

Is It Right?

Legal or not, the recent assault on individual privacy appears to fly in the face of all that America stands for. Life, liberty and the pursuit of happiness are being exchanged for security, surveillance, and the pursuit of evildoers.

And, at least in times of crisis, the majority of Americans appear to support these surveillance activities. In late 2001, in the immediate wake of the 9/11 terrorist attacks, Zogby International polled a cross-section of the citizenry on their views about surveillance and civil liberties. The results were shocking to civil libertarians.

Zogby's poll indicated that 54% of Americans favored allowing telephone conversations to be monitored, 67% approved of roadblock searches of vehicles, another 67% favored having their mail monitored, and a whopping 80% approved of video surveillance of public places. No doubt, this widespread acceptance of government surveillance could be attributed to the fear of further terrorist attacks; as pollster John Zogby noted, "We are in a moment where fear trumps other considerations."

On this issue, however, civil libertarians side with Benjamin Franklin, who in 1759 wrote:

> Those who would give up essential liberty to purchase a little temporary safety, deserve neither liberty nor safety.

Those words were written in response to colonists hesitant to confront the British in the lead-up to the Revolutionary War—Tories who preferred to play it safe rather than fight for their rights and liberties. But the sentiment holds today, when far too many citizens would sacrifice their civil liberties for a short-term and ultimately illusory security from terrorist attacks. Those attacks may never come, but the liberties may be forever forsaken.

Is It Safe?

Some reading this chapter might think it alarmist. So be it. The fact is, the government is increasingly spying on ordinary citizens, most often for no good reason.

What are the odds that the government is spying on *you*? Depending on what activities you engage in, the odds could be very high.

Taking into account the activities that have been revealed to date, it's a good bet that the government has scooped up your personal data if you do any of the following:

- Exchange email or text messages with people outside the United States
- Engage in telephone communications with people outside the United States
- Travel by airplane—either inside or outside the United States
- Belong to any remotely suspicious public or private organization
- Check out suspicious materials from your public library
- Visit websites or chat rooms suspected to be home to terrorist groups

> **> > N O T E**

In this list of suspicious activities, the term "suspicious" is conveniently undefined. When it comes to government surveillance, suspicious behavior is in the eye of the beholder.

Let's put it another way. If the government wants to, it can spy on you. It can read your emails and instant messages, it can track the websites you visit, it can listen in on your phone calls. There is little to stop this from happening, even if you are the most law-abiding citizen in the country.

So, to the overriding question: Is it safe? The answer, in this instance, is no—not unless you and your fellow citizens begin to stand up for your individual rights. Left unchecked, government surveillance can and will become oppressive, even for average citizens; the distance from a security-obsessed state to a police state is a short one.

It is the duty of an informed citizenry to defend its civil liberties; you must defend your liberties by voting into office like-minded representatives. If you feel your rights are being infringed, then vote out those who would take your rights away.

This is, perhaps, the most pressing issue of our time. You can't ignore it—because the government won't ignore you.

> **> > N O T E**

One of the best ways to defend your civil liberties is to support the efforts of the American Civil Liberties Union (ACLU). Learn more at www.aclu.org.

Covering Your Tracks Online

With the government sweeping up all sorts of personal data and individual websites tracking your every move, how can you get a little privacy online?

It doesn't matter who you are or what you do online, sometimes you want to keep your identity secret. Maybe you're browsing websites that your company or family might not approve of. Maybe you're leaking confidential information to a competitor, or to the press. Maybe you have a fear of government surveillance. Maybe you just want to lurk online, without fear of anyone discovering who you really are.

Whatever the case, hiding your identity online is sometimes desirous. Fortunately, there are ways to beat the system—and cover your tracks when you're online. Read on to learn more.

Hiding Your Tracks by Managing Your Cookies

As you learned in Chapter 13, "Online Surveillance: How Big a Problem?," Web browsing is far less anonymous than most people think. Not only do you have to register at numerous sites, most sites track your site visits via hidden cookie files that are automatically stored on your computer's hard disk. The result is a permanent and easily accessible record of all your web browsing activities.

Of course, you can always choose not to visit sites that require you to register. And, not surprisingly, there are ways to beat the other user-tracking technologies—including cookies.

How Cookies Work

On your computer, a cookie isn't a doughy delight; it's a small text file. Websites create and store cookie files on your computer's hard disk; these files contain information about you and your web activities. For example, a cookie file for a particular site might contain your username, password, credit card information, and the most recent pages you visited on that site. The cookie file created by a site is accessed by that site each time you visit in the future, and the information used appropriately.

How might a website use cookies? There are many purposes for cookie files, most of which involve tracking your behavior and tailoring the site's features to match. For example, a site can use cookies to determine whether you've previously visited the site, to store passwords and user IDs, to store any personal information obtained from user registration forms, to track what site you just came from, to display the last product or page you looked at, and so on. While this is great for when you want a site to remember you each time you visit, it's also scary when you think about how much of this type of information can be stored without your explicit knowledge.

What does a cookie file look like? The file itself is a simple text file with the .txt extension. Typically, the name of the file reflects your username on your computer, followed by an @ sign and the name of the website that created the cookie. For example, if your username is "bob" and the cookie was created by the CNN website, the cookie file might be named bob@cnn.txt. (This naming convention isn't universal, however.)

The content of a cookie file consists of a short text string that stores information specific to a given website. A cookie can contain any of six parameters:

- Name
- Value
- Expiration date
- Path (for which the cookie is valid)
- Domain
- Secure (denotes that a secure connection is necessary to use the cookie)

A two-stage process is necessary to use a cookie. First, the website's server creates the cookie file and stores it on your computer, without your knowledge or consent. Second, when you next visit the website, the cookie file is uploaded to the site's web server, where the information is read and used accordingly.

And that's the rub: All this cookie-related activity happens automatically, in the background. You're typically not asked to approve any cookies, nor are you even aware that any of this is taking place. Although this type of behind-the-scenes operation ranks high on the convenience meter, it has serious privacy implications.

Managing Cookies in Your Web Browser

Fortunately, an individual cookie can only viewed by the site that placed it on your hard disk; one site can't read another's cookies. You also have significant control over how cookies are stored on your computer, if you so wish.

Cookie management is a feature of most Web browsers. For example, Internet Explorer 7 lets you adjust the browser's privacy level to determine which types of cookies are automatically accepted—or rejected. You do this by clicking the Tools and selecting Internet Options; when the Internet Options dialog box appears, select the Privacy tab (shown in Figure 16.1). Adjust the slider to the privacy level you want, then click OK.

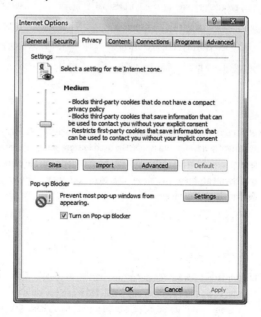

Figure 16.1
Configuring cookie and privacy options in Internet Explorer.

Internet Explorer 7 has six levels of cookie management, ranging from accepting all cookies to declining all cookies, as detailed in Table 16.1:

Table 16.1   Internet Explorer Privacy Levels

Level	First-Party Cookies	Third-Party Cookies
Accept All Cookies	Accepts all	Accepts all
Low	Accepts all	Blocks cookies from sites that don't have privacy policies; automatically deletes (when IE is closed) cookies from sites that use personal information without your implicit consent
Medium	Automatically deletes (when IE is closed) cookies from sites that use personal information without your implicit consent	Blocks cookies from sites that don't have privacy policies, or from sites that use personal information without your implicit consent
Medium High	Blocks cookies from sites that use personal information without your implicit consent	Blocks cookies from sites that don't have privacy policies, or from sites that use personal information without your *explicit* consent
High	Blocks cookies from sites that don't have privacy policies, or from sites that use personal information without your *explicit* consent	Blocks cookies from sites that don't have privacy policies, or from sites that use personal information without your *explicit* consent
Block All Cookies	Blocks all new cookies; existing cookies can't be read (even by the sites that created them)	Blocks all new cookies; existing cookies can't be read (even by the sites that created them)

> > > **NOTE**

Internet Explorer differentiates between first-party and third-party cookies. A first-party cookie originates from the website you are currently viewing, and is typically used to store your preferences regarding that site. A third-party cookie originates from a website different from the one you are currently viewing, and is typically used to feed advertisements from separate ad sites to the current website. In general, third-party cookies are less desirable than first-party cookies.

> > > **NOTE**

Internet Explorer also differentiates between temporary and persistent cookies. A temporary cookie is stored only temporarily in your computer's memory and is deleted when you close your web browser. A persistent or permanent cookie is one that is stored as a file to your computer's hard disk—and are the ones that most concern us.

The default setting is Medium, which pretty much blocks all advertising-related cookies and deletes any cookies that contain personal information when you close Internet Explorer. If you'd rather that no website store any personal information you haven't explicitly approved, choose the High setting.

Internet Explorer also lets you adjust the privacy level on a site-by-site basis. From the Privacy tab in the Internet Options dialog box, click the Sites button. This opens the Per Site Privacy Actions dialog box, as shown in Figure 16.2. From here, enter the address of a specific website then click either Block (to block all cookies from this site, regardless of your general privacy settings) or Allow (to allow all cookies from this site, regardless). Click OK when done.

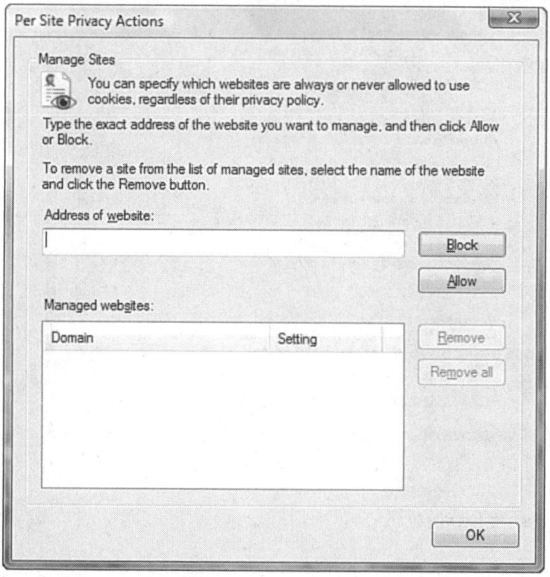

Figure 16.2
Managing cookies on a per-site basis in Internet Explorer.

{PERSONAL EXPERIENCE}

You might think that turning off all cookies would be the way to go, at least in terms of improving your browsing privacy. The problem is, many cookies are actually useful. For example, I recently turned off cookies on my main PC, and then found that none of my favorite websites remembered me! That's right, membership-only sites rely on cookies to store username and password information; with no cookies stored, I had to manually log onto the sites every time I visited. The same thing with using Amazon.com; with cookies deactivated, I was no longer a customer the site remembered. So, in many instances, deactivating cookies actually makes the web harder to use—which means you have to balance convenience with privacy.

Automatically Deleting Cookie Files

Internet Explorer 7 also lets you automatically delete all the cookie files stored on your computer. This is useful if you want to erase all tracks of the websites you've visited; with no cookie files, your employer or spouse won't know your browsing history.

To delete all cookie files in Internet Explorer 7, click the Tools button and select Delete Browsing History. When the Delete Browsing History dialog box appears, as shown in Figure 16.3, click the Delete Cookies button.

Figure 16.3
Deleting cookies in Internet Explorer 7.

> > > **N O T E**

> You can also use the Delete Browsing History dialog box to delete your temporary Internet files (cache), browsing history, form data, and any website passwords you've entered.

Manually Deleting Cookie Files

If you have a PC running Microsoft's Windows operating system, you can also manually delete cookie files from your computer's hard disk. All you need to know is where—in which folder—the cookie files are stored. This location differs, depending on which version of Windows you're using. Table 16.2 details the cookie location for most recent operating systems.

Table 16.2   Cookie Locations

Operating System	Cookie Folder (main)	Cookie Folder (alternate)
Windows Vista	C:\Users*username*\AppData\Roaming \Microsoft\Windows\Cookies\	C:\Users*username*\AppData\Roaming\ Microsoft\Windows\Cookies\Low\
Windows XP	C:\Documents and Settings*username*\Cookies\	C:\Documents and Settings\Administrator\Cookies\
Windows Me	C:\Windows\Cookies\	C:\Windows\Profiles*username*\Cookies\
Windows 98	C:\Windows\Cookies\	C:\Windows\Profiles*username*\Cookies\
Windows 95	C:\Windows\Cookies\	C:\Windows\Profiles*username*\Cookies\
Windows 2000	C:\Documents and Settings*username*\Cookies\	C:\Documents and Settings\Administrator\Cookies\
Windows NT	C:\Windows\Cookies\	C:\Windows\Profiles*username*\Cookies\

< < < TIP

To view cookie folders in Windows, you have to show hidden files and folders. In Windows Vista, you do this by opening the Control Panel, selecting Appearance and Personalization, and selecting Show Hidden Files and Folders (under Folder Options). When the Folder Options dialog box appears, click the View tab and then check the Show Hidden Files and Folders option.

There is no harm in deleting any and all cookie files from these locations (if you don't mind deleting your website preferences and passwords, of course.) In fact, keeping your cookie folder clean is important to securing your privacy. Unless you periodically delete your cookies (either manually or automatically), traces of your web browsing continue to exist on your hard disk—for anyone with interest to see.

Browsing the Web, Anonymously

Cookies aren't the only way to track which websites you visit. When you're on the web, your computer's IP address always travels with you.

Here's how you get tracked. When you enter a page's URL into your web browser, you send out a request to view that page. That request is enclosed in a small data packet, sent from your PC to the host site. Unfortunately, every data packet sent from your computer includes your IP address as part of its header code.

Any website can use special traffic monitoring software to pull your IP address from the header information. The same software can also track what browser you're using, what pages you visit at the site, and what website you last visited. This is how tech-savvy criminal investigators can monitor who (or, more precisely, which computers) have visited a particular site—or, conversely, which sites have been visited by a specific computer.

IP address tracking seems to blow the concept of anonymous web browsing out of the water. Except, of course, for the fact that all grand plans can be foiled, if you work hard enough.

In other words, there *is* a way to browse the web anonymously. All you have to do is funnel all the web pages you visit through an *anonymizer* website.

How an Anonymizer Site Works

Here's how it works. You essentially surf the web through the anonymizer site, going to that site first and then routing all your pages from there. When you send a page request through the anonymizer, it strips off the header of each data packet, thus making your request anonymous. The requested page is then fed through the anonymizer back to your web browser. With no IP address to track, there's no way for any other site or authority to trace your activity back to your individual computer or ISP.

When you enter a URL at an anonymizer site, the page you request is appended to the anonymizer's URL, like this: http://www.anonymizer.com/http://www.molehillgroup.com/. And after you've accessed a particular site through an anonymizer, all the subsequent links you click are accessed in the same indirect fashion.

Finding a Web Anonymizer

There are several anonymizer sites on the web. All work in pretty much the same fashion; some of these sites are free, while others require registration or subscription.

The most popular anonymizers include:

- AnonService.com (www.anonservice.com)

- Anonymize.Net (www.anonymize.net)

- Anonymizer.com (www.anonymizer.com)

- Change IP Country (anonymizer.nntime.com)

- IDsecure (www.idzap.com)

- Somebody (www.somebody.net)

- Surfola.com (www.surfola.com)

- Ultimate Anonymity (www.ultimate-anonymity.com)

Some of these services go the extra step and create a completely new online identity for you. When you register, you are assigned a new IP address through a virtual private network (VPN); whenever you connect through their service, you're identified by the new, anonymous address—not your old address. This lets you get more use out of the sites you visit, as you have an actual identity that you can use for site preferences, and so on.

Using an Anonymizer as a Full-Time Proxy Server

Another way to use an anonymizer is to use it as a permanent proxy server in your web browser. When an anonymizer site is used as a proxy, your IP address is never revealed to any of the sites you browse—and you don't have to directly access the anonymizer site.

> > > **NOTE**

A proxy server functions as a kind of super firewall to your system, hiding your computer from the rest of the Internet. (Learn more about proxies and firewalls in Chapter 23, "Defending Your Personal Computer from Attack.")

To set up an anonymizer as a proxy server in Internet Explorer 7, follow these steps: Click the Tools button and select Internet Options. When the Internet Options dialog box appears, select the Connections tab, then click the LAN Settings button. When the Local Area Network (LAN) Settings dialog box appears, as shown in Figure 16.4, check the Use a Proxy Server for Your LAN option. Enter the anonymizer's URL in the Address field, enter 80 in the Port box, and then click OK. You should now be able to surf via your chosen anonymizer as you would normally.

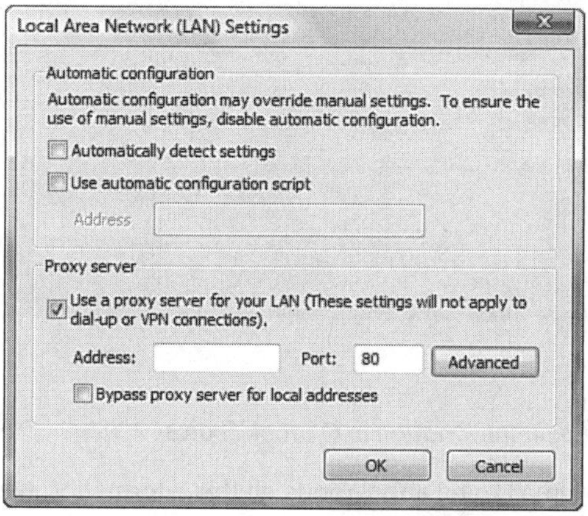

Figure 16.4
Configuring Internet Explorer 7 to use an anonymizer as a proxy server.

CAUTION!!!

You probably can't use an anonymizer as a proxy server if you're using file-sharing sites, as the software used by these sites require different connection settings when you connect through a proxy.

Sending Email, Anonymously

Web surfing isn't the only Internet activity that can be easily traced. Email is a particularly non-anonymous activity; not only do you provide visible proof of your identity (in the From: field of your message), but the hidden code behind the message—called the *header*—contains your email address, the address of your ISP's outgoing email server, and other similar information. This data is sent automatically whenever you send an email, and is easily read by anyone on the receiving end.

For example, to view header information for messages in Microsoft Outlook 2007, open the message, select the Message tab, and then click the corner right arrow in the Options section. This displays the Message Options dialog box, shown in Figure 16.5; the header information is displayed in the Internet Headers section of the dialog box.

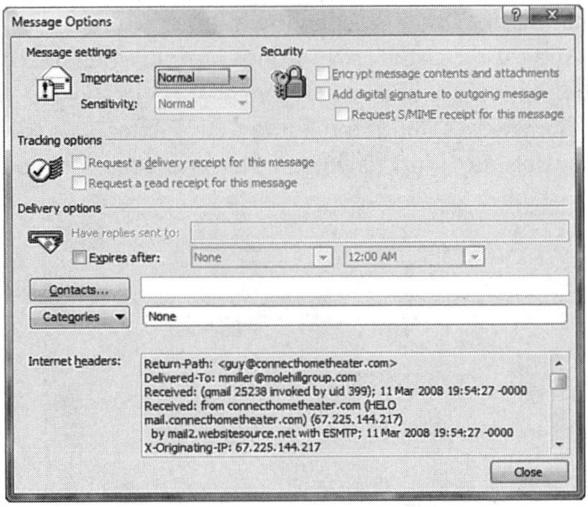

Figure 16.5
Viewing email message header information in Outlook Express 2007.

Here's the thing. For your email to be anonymous, all this information needs to be stripped from your message header. The easiest way to do this is to use a web-based service called a *remailer*.

How Remailers Work

A remailer functions as a middleman in the email operation. When you send your email to the remailer, it strips out your header information and then remails the message to the intended recipient(s). Because your original header information is no longer present, the email you send can't be traced back to you.

Some remailers operate with any standard POP email program, such as Microsoft Outlook and Windows Mail; you use your email program to compose and send the message (to the remailer), then the remailer does the rest. Other remailers are entirely web-based, requiring you to compose your messages on their site, much as you would if using Gmail, Hotmail, or any other web-based email service.

All remailers are fairly effective at what they do; some even take an extra step and add encryption to all outgoing messages. As with anonymizers, some remailers are free and some are subscription-based. Note, however, that because the goal of a remailer is to ensure your anonymity, recipients of your emails won't know how to respond to you—unless you include your email address in the body of the email, of course, which works against the anonymity goal.

Finding a Remailer Service

Some of the most popular anonymous email services include:

- Anonymize.Net (www.anonymize.net)
- Anonymous Speech (www.anonymousspeech.com)
- HushMail.com (www.hushmail.com)
- SecureNym (www.securenym.net)
- Somebody (www.somebody.net)
- TheAnonymousEmail.com (www.theanonymousemail.com)
- Ultimate Anonymity (www.ultimate-anonymity.com)
- W3 Anonymous Remailer (www.gilc.org/speech/anonymous/remailer.html)

Is It Safe?

It's a fact: Any high-tech detective can easily find out which websites you've visited and emails you've sent. This isn't the type of fabricated science you often see on *CSI* and other TV crime shows; it's simple information technology applied to real world activities.

That said, it is possible to hide your tracks when you're browsing and emailing online. You'll experience some reduced functionality, however, especially with those websites that use cookies to serve up personalized information; you'll also find yourself doing a bit more work to get from place to place and send email messages. It requires foresight and diligence, but it can be done.

Here are the simple steps you must take if you want to cover your tracks online:

- Turn off cookies in your web browser

- Delete all existing cookie files from your hard disk

- Delete your browser's cache (temporary files) and history

- Use an anonymizer site for all your web browsing

- Use a remailer for all your email

- Make sure you don't accidentally include your email address in your outgoing email messages and replies

> **> NOTE**
>
> Some web browsers, such as Firefox, offer the option to automatically delete cookies, cache, and other private info every time you close the browser.

Follow these steps, and it will be almost impossible for someone to track your online activities.

Protecting Yourself—and Your Children—from Online Predators

Imagine your inbox being spammed with a spate of nasty emails. Imagine someone posting expletive-ridden comments to your personal blog or MySpace page. Imagine someone forging your name to posts at your favorite discussion forums and groups. Imagine someone sending defamatory emails to your employer and compatriots, using your name. Imagine someone you met and rejected online telling you he knows where you live—and is coming to get you.

These scenarios can all happen to you—and your children. Online stalkers and predators abound, using the medium of the Internet to taunt, harass, stalk, and sometimes threaten physical harm to you and the ones you love. It's not a game; online stalking does exist, and it's a serious issue.

Protecting Yourself from Cyberstalkers

Stalking is a serious issue. Someone physically stalking you not only invades your privacy, but also harasses and intimidates you—and, in many instances, makes you fearful of physical harm.

In the Internet age, stalking isn't limited to the physical world. Stalking can also occur online, where it is known as *cyberstalking*. At its most benign, cyberstalking involves unwanted online communication, and can be annoying; at its worst, cyberstalking can take on a physical dimension and result in real-world harm.

How big a problem is cyberstalking—and what can you do about it? Read on to learn more.

What Is Cyberstalking?

Cyberstalking is a form of repeated harassment using the technologies of the Internet. Whereas real-world stalking involves physically following a person from place to place, or making repeated phone calls to that person, cyberstalking is an abuse of Internet-related communications and websites.

A person who becomes a cyberstalker has progressed beyond simple and occasional email communication into multiple, repeated, and obsessive online communications. We're talking about sending dozens of unwanted email messages or instant message invitations, perhaps bordering on the threatening or obscene, or obsessively responding to a person's blog or message board posts.

In reality, cyberstalking can describe a number of different online activities. These include, but are not limited to, the following:

- Sending unwanted advances to the victim via email or instant messaging
- Making direct threats to the victim via email, instant messaging, or posts to blogs and online forums
- Provoking online attacks against the victim by others
- Posting false profiles of the victim online
- Following the victim to one website to another to another
- Creating websites that target the victim
- Hacking into the victim's website or blog
- Posting fake dating or sex listings on personals websites
- Posting real or Photoshopped pornographic images of the victim on various online forums, or distributing such images via email
- Identity theft—for the express purpose of posing as the victim online
- Posing as the victim to attack others on various blogs and online message forums
- Sending inflammatory messages to the victim's family or employer—often when posing as the victim

> > > **N O T E**

According to a 2002 cyberstalking study by WiredSafety.org, the most common medium for online harassment is email (18%), followed by bulletin boards and newsgroups (16%) and then chat and instant messaging (11%).

In other words, cyberstalking involves a repeated pattern of online harassment. Many cyberstalkers have a grudge against the victim, posting negative comments, false information, and trying to damage his or her reputation. Other cyberstalkers are more like deranged fans or aggressive suitors, following the victim from site to site like a love-sick puppy dog or creating "fan" websites. Still other cyberstalkers are creepy obsessive-compulsives, gathering as much information as they can from the victim's online activities. Still others are out to harm the victim, either virtually (via identity theft and the like) or physically (by meeting with the victim offline). This last type of cyberstalker is the scariest, as their online stalking evolves into physical stalking and sometimes violence.

> > > **N O T E**

> When cyberstalking moves from the online world to the physical world, the perpetrator becomes an online predator. Learn more in the "Escalating the Danger: When Cyberstalkers Become Online Predators" section, later in this chapter.

Who Are the Cyberstalkers?

Who are these disturbed individuals who stalk their victims online? The group that calls itself Working to Halt Online Abuse (WHOA) looked at a large number of cyberstalking cases in 2006, and discovered that 36.5% of cyberstalkers are male, while 27.5% are female; in the remaining cases, the gender of the harasser was unknown.

In addition, WHOA reports that 48.5% of cyberstalkers had a previous relationship with their victims. In 47% of those cases, the victim was the ex-spouse or ex-lover of the harasser; in 37% of those cases, the victim had a casual relationship or was a friend of the cyberstalker.

What Motivates a Cyberstalker?

Why does someone become a cyberstalker? In most instances, it's someone reacting to a perceived slight—even if the victim isn't aware of said slight.

Here are some of the most common factors that motivate online stalkers:

- The stalker is a real or imagined potential or former lover of the victim, who feels rejected or jilted

- The stalker himself feels victimized by the subject, for real or imagined actions or omissions, and is seeking revenge

- The stalker is acting out of bigotry, prejudice, intolerance, or other type of hate; he may have had no previous personal interaction with the victim

- The stalker feels as if he has to teach the victim a lesson or enforce the perceived "cyber-rules" of a particular website or online community

- The stalker is a "fan" of the victim, who in the stalker's eyes is a type of cyber-celebrity

- The stalker has no previous knowledge of or interaction with the victim; the stalking is a totally random act, with the victim effectively being in the wrong place at the wrong time

Where Do Cyberstalkers Stalk?

Just where to cyberstalkers haunt their victims? Just about anywhere online, as it turns out. Cyberstalkers can harass their victims in chat rooms, message forums, blogs, virtual worlds, and the like, as well as via private email and instant messaging.

According to WHOA, 31% of cyberstalking cases start with email, and 17% start with instant messaging. A further 16.5% start with message boards, forums, newsgroups, and the like, while 8% start on some other type of website. Online chat is the starting point for 7.5% of cyber-stalking cases, whereas blogs and MySpace each account for 5% of all initial cyberstalking incidents. Surprisingly, only 1.5% of cyberstalking cases get their start on online dating sites.

In many instances, cyberstalkers don't limit themselves to a particular forum; they follow their victims around the Internet, much the way real-world stalkers follow their victims from physi-cal location to location. A cyberstalker might send his victim a threatening email, followed by a nasty posting at a community website, followed by a comment to the victim's blog or MySpace page, followed by harassing messages in an online chat room. Wherever the victim goes, so goes the cyberstalker.

Cyberstalkers use both technology and social engineering to find out more about the victim and discover new ways to harass. For example, a stalker might join a community forum and form relationships with others who are friendly with the victim to garner more information about the victim. Or the stalker may piece together postings made by the victim on various websites and blogs to form a surprisingly accurate picture of the victim's private life. Or, even more chilling, various spy programs can be used to expose the victim's personal information.

How does a cyberstalker find out where a victim hangs out online? It's part technology, part common sense. The stalker uses Google and other search engines to find out everything about the victim that's available online, including to what sites or blogs the victim has posted. The stalker also searches sites that the victim is likely to frequent, such as Facebook and MySpace. It's all about research—carried out by an obsessive personality.

Whom Do Cyberstalkers Stalk?

Although anyone can be the victim of a cyberstalker, some groups are more likely to be vic-tims than others. In fact, the profile of a cyberstalking victim mirrors that of stalking victims in the real world.

So who is most likely to be victimized by a cyberstalker? Here's the list of high-risk groups:

- Women—especially battered and abused women
- Minors (although they're likely to be stalked by other minors that they know)
- Newbies (people new to the Internet)
- Members of minority groups (who are typically more prone to be victims of hate crimes)
- Disabled and mentally challenged users (who are thought to be more easily victimized)

So the most typical victim is a female, aged 18–40, often involved in a real or imagined roman-tic or sexual relationship with the stalker. Next most common is a member of a minority group—gay, lesbian, African American, Asian, Hispanic, Muslim—who has somehow offended the sensibilities of the stalker.

Surprisingly, children and teenagers aren't overly prone to be victims of cyberstalking. And, if a child is being stalked online, it's likely to be by another youth—typically someone the child knows from school.

> > > **N O T E**

One youth stalking another is often a form of cyberbullying. Learn more about this trend in the "Defending Against Cyberbullies" section, later in this chapter.

For a more complete picture of cyberstalking victims, I refer you to Table 17.1, which details statistics compiled by WHOA in 2006.

Table 17.1   Cyberstalking Victim Statistics (WHOA, 2006)

Identifier	Percent of total
Gender	Female: 70%
	Male: 28.5%
Marital Status	Single: 46%
	Married: 29.5%
	Divorced: 10.5%
Age	18–30: 40%
	31–40: 29%
	41+: 28.5%
Race	Caucasian: 76.5%
	Hispanic: 15.4%
	Asian: 2.5%
	African American: 2.5%

Are Cyberstalkers Dangerous?

Cyberstalkers who only stalk online can be annoying and sometimes frightening, but as long as they restrict their activities to the Internet, they can't do you any physical harm. The truly dangerous cyberstalkers are those who move from the online world to the real world, where stalking can and sometimes does turn to violence and abuse.

WHOA reports that in 22% of cyberstalking cases, the stalker threatened violence against his victim. These threats become real when the cyberstalker progresses beyond the Internet and starts making telephone calls to the victim or physically follows the victim. Any stalker willing to up the ante with a physical presence should be considered potentially dangerous—as discussed in the "Escalating the Danger: When Cyberstalkers Become Online Predators" section, later in this chapter.

How Do You Defend Against Cyberstalkers?

The first step to protecting yourself against cyberstalkers is to, as much as possible, hide your identity online. If the cyberstalker doesn't know who you are, he can't stalk you.

Take Preventative Measures

To help create a safe and relatively anonymous identity online, here are some preventative measures you should take:

- Don't share personal information online—especially with strangers in chat rooms and message forums.
- Don't fill out public profiles on websites and blogs—or if you do, make sure the profile doesn't contain any personal information about you (your real name, location, and so on).
- Use a gender-neutral screen name and email address.
- Avoid making a provocative statement with your screen name and email address; don't deliberately invite controversy.
- When using online dating sites, create a separate email address used only for that site; don't use your general email address when registering or to receive replies and messages.
- Don't flirt with other users online; avoid sexually suggestive comments.
- Don't start arguments online; don't flame other users.

The goal here is to hide your identity—especially your gender or, if you're a member of an oppressed minority, your minority status. In addition, you want to avoid controversy—which means toning down the inflammatory and suggestive comments. Extreme comments attract cyberstalkers!

Confronting Cyberstalkers

Even if you take heed of all these precautions, you can still become the victim of an obsessive cyberstalker. What do you do if you think you're being cyberstalked? Here are tips on what to do when you're being harassed online:

- The first thing to do is to directly confront the cyberstalker. At the first sign of harassment, tell him in very direct terms to leave you alone—to quit harassing you and not to contact you again.

- If the harassment continues, do not reply to any further messages from the stalker. That means no replies to email, instant messages, or chat requests. It doesn't matter if the stalker is taunting you, threatening you, or trying to be nice—ignore him completely. This puts you in charge of the situation.

- If you find yourself being stalked in a particular chat room, start by ignoring the harassing messages; you can also configure the chat software to ignore or block all messages from the stalker. If the stalking continues, change your ID in that chat room; if the stalker figures out your new ID, consider abandoning that chat room.

- If you're being stalked via instant messaging, put the stalker on your ignore/block list. If the harassment continues, change your username and identity—including all aspects of the profile. You want to create a new identity that your harasser won't recognize as the old you.

- If you're being stalked via email, configure your email program to block all messages from the stalker. If the harassment continues, contact the stalker's ISP and make a complaint. Include copies of threatening emails to confirm your point.

< < < T I P

The harasser's ISP is typically found in the domain name part of his email address. For example, if the stalker has the email address bob@aol.com, you know his ISP is America Online, otherwise known as AOL.com. Forward your complaint to abuse@domain.name or postmaster@domain.name.

- Report the stalker to your ISP, and ask the ISP to trace the identity of the stalker.

- Enable logging in your instant messenger program and chat client, then save all log files that contain messages from the stalker—they may be necessary evidence sometime in the future.

- Along the same vein, keep all emails from the stalker, as well as any replies you've made.

- Avoid chat rooms, message forums, and blogs frequented by the harasser.

- If the stalker makes threatening comments or appears to know where you live or work, report the incident to your local law enforcement authorities.

- If you are physically approached by the stalker, immediately move to protect yourself, then contact your local police.

In other words, it's better to avoid the stalker than it is to confront him.

Escalating the Danger: When Cyberstalkers Become Online Predators

The real risk from cyberstalkers comes when they move from online to offline. Threatening emails and harassing instant messages can't really hurt you, but a stalker who meets you in the real world can do true physical harm.

To this end, a cyberstalker who harasses you physically becomes what many call an online predator. Don't kid yourself; these people are dangerous.

Who Are the Online Predators?

Cyberstalkers tend to be more bark than bite, but online predators are the real deal; many are capable of sexual abuse and physical violence.

So who are these online predators? The typical predator is male, somewhat introverted, often sadistic. Their behavior can be controlling and is often violent; these predators are both morally and sexually indiscriminate. Most are actively looking for victims.

Who Attracts Online Predators?

The victims of online sexual predators tend to be female, of any age, although younger males are also occasional victims. Sexual predators often target adolescent girls and boys of uncertain sexual orientation; youths with histories of sexual abuse and patterns of risk-taking are especially at risk.

The unifying factor here is vulnerability; predators pick victims based on their ability to influence and control the victim. Predators seldom stalk strong victims; perceived weakness, of some sort, is key.

A similar pattern exists for victims of hate group predators—those predators who, because of hatred or prejudice, want to inflict physical harm on members of the offending group. Here, the only qualifying factor is membership in a minority group; victims can be gay, lesbian, African-American, Muslim, or any type of minority. Victims of this type of predator are chosen more randomly than are victims of sexual predators.

How Do Online Predators Work?

Online predators are seldom initially violent. In fact, most predators seduce their victims through the use of attention, affection, and kindness. The predator, at first, is the victim's best friend; sometimes gifts are exchanged. Predators spend considerable amounts of time and energy to convince their victims that they can be trusted.

This is especially the case with those preying on children and teenagers. Children, more than anything, want a sympathetic ear to listen to their perceived problems, and this is what the predator provides. Younger victims seldom see predators as threatening, even when evidence exists to that end; to the victim, the predator might be his or her only friend in the whole world.

For a dedicated sexual predator, the game is long term. The predator gradually introduces sexual content and situations into his conversations; the victim, if even aware, views this change as a natural progression. It's a seduction; over time, the predator seeks to establish a sexual relationship with the victim.

For those predators driven by hate or prejudice, it's a shorter process. The goal here is to isolate the victim physically so that an attack can be made. This type of predator is less patient; he wants the immediate gratification of violence.

How Do You Defend Against Online Predators?

If you believe that an incident of cyberstalking is likely to turn physical, don't delay; you must act immediately to ward off the potential danger. Here are some of the things you should do:

- Do not reply to the stalker, no matter how threatening or cajoling the emails or messages.

- Do not agree to meet the predator in person.

- If it appears that the predator knows where you live or work, or if the predator threatens physical violence, call the police immediately.

- If you feel physically threatened, don't leave your house by yourself; arrange for one or more friends to accompany you until the threat subsides.

The key to preventing physical incidents is to minimize your availability. Don't encourage the predator, and don't leave yourself physically vulnerable. In this sort of situation, it's okay to ask for help.

Protecting Your Children from Online Stalkers and Predators

It's one thing to find yourself a victim of a cyberstalker or online predator; most adults can handle themselves in this sort of situation. But what do you do if your child is a potential victim? That's a much scarier proposition.

How Big Is the Threat?

Parents worry—a lot—about the safety of their children online. Are those fears justified?

The best answer to that question is: A little—but not as much as you think.

The incidence of Internet-based sexual abuse of or physical attacks on children and teenagers isn't nearly as high as what the fear-mongering media might have you believe. It's in the nature of parents to be somewhat paranoid and protective when their children are concerned, and the media plays to those fears; witness the big ratings for the "To Catch a Predator" segments on NBC's prime-time *Dateline* show. But the reality is that most online predators are quite open about their intentions, most so-called victims are well aware of what they're getting into, and today's youth are surprisingly savvy about the potential dangers lurking online—and know how to deal with them.

Janis Wolak is a sociologist at the Crimes Against Children Research Center at the University of New Hampshire. In early 2008, the center released a landmark study about the incidence of online sex predators, and here's what she said about the results:

> There's been some overreaction to the new technology, especially when it comes to the danger that strangers represent. Actually, Internet-related sex crimes are a pretty small proportion of sex crimes that adolescents suffer.

Let's compare the so-called common wisdom about online predators versus the reality discovered by the center's study. Table 17.2 does the comparison.

Table 17.2   Online Sex Predators—Common Wisdom Versus Reality

Common Wisdom	Reality
Online predators are driving up child sex crime rates.	Sexual assaults on teenagers decreased 52% from 1993 to 2005—the same years that saw the rise of the Internet.
Online predators are pedophiles.	Most online predators don't target prepubescent children, as pedophiles do. Instead, they target adolescents, who have more access to computers, more privacy, and more interest in sex and romance.
Online predators represent a new dimension in child sexual abuse.	Although the means of contact (the Internet) may be new, most of Internet-linked offenses are essentially statutory rape—nonviolent, unforced sex between an adult and a consenting minor.
Online predators trick or abduct their victims.	Most victims willingly meet online offenders face-to-face, going to these meetings expecting to have sex. In fact, nearly three-quarters of these underage victims have sex with their Internet partners more than once.
Online predators meet their victims by posing online as other teens.	The vast majority of online predators do not hide their age or intentions; only 5% pose online as teenagers.

The reality is much different than the common wisdom. Although online sexual predators may be more visible today, thanks to media oversaturation, their numbers are no larger. And there's nothing inherent about the Internet that makes sexual predation more likely or more common; it's just the most recent way for opportunistic predators to find vulnerable victims.

How Do Predators Connect with Their Victims?

Knowing that online predators are less common than you might think, it's important to realize that they do exist, and do prey on children and teenagers. That said, how do they woo their victims?

Predators can find victims in many different places on the Internet. Youth-oriented chat rooms are always fertile ground; many predators today troll the personal pages on MySpace and Facebook for potential victims. So-called virtual worlds and multiplayer online games are also frequently used.

The initial contact is most often via a simple conversation, typically in a chat room or via instant messaging. Sometimes the contact is via email, although that's a slower form of communication less used by today's youth; email is often used for follow-up communication, however.

Often, the initial communication involves the adult offering sympathy to the youth. The predator tries to be the youth's friend, the rare sympathetic adult in world full of adults who don't understand what the youth is going through. In this fashion, the predator worms his way into the victim's affections.

Sometimes the initial contact involves the predator sharing sexually explicit pictures or content with the potential victim. Adolescents are particularly curious about sex, and this is a way to draw their attention.

The predator, of course, doesn't view his behavior as preying on the victim. He views it more as a seduction, and himself more a loving partner than an exploitive attacker or pedophile. But however it's viewed, this type of luring behavior is illegal, and should be guarded against.

What Children Are Most at Risk?

One of the interesting findings of the University of New Hampshire survey is that most children and teenagers online are quite aware of the potential dangers and know how to protect themselves. They know instinctively when they're talking to adults online (dangerous or not) and, more often than not, simply avoid those conversations. Most youths don't want adults on their MySpace friends list; this distrust of their elders serves as a natural protective mechanism against online predators.

The average youth, then, knows that there are adult predators online, and simply ignores any contact from them. Not all children, however, are so aware; some youths are at a higher risk of abuse than others.

What are the characteristics of a youth who is at higher risk for online predation? Here are some of the key factors:

- Emotionally deprived; starving for attention and affection

- Isolated or lonely

- Rebellious; may be estranged from their parents

- Curious, especially about adult matters

- Confused regarding sexual identity

- Intrigued by subcultures outside of their parents' world

- Easily tricked by people older and more experienced

- New to the online world and unfamiliar with netiquette and procedures; may not know when they're being propositioned, or how to judge with whom they're talking

A more holistic picture is of a lonely child, isolated from his parents and other authority figures, starving for affection and vulnerable to someone pretending to be his friend.

How Do You Know Whether Your Child Is Targeted by an Online Predator?

Chances are, your children spend a lot of time online. I know that my stepson appears to be constantly online, engaging in a mix of instant messaging, Friendster page checking, fantasy sports trading, and online gaming. Somewhere in there he finds time to do his homework, or at least he says he does.

The thing is, when your child is online more than he's off, how do you know what he's doing—and, more important, how can you tell whether he's being targeted by an online predator? Although it's impossible to know for sure (unless you want to hover over his shoulder as he types, that is), some clues can lead you to question what's really going on:

- Your child spends inordinate amounts of time online—particularly in online chat rooms. Now, this may not be a perfect indicator; as I mentioned previously, most kids today spend a lot of time online. That said, be a little concerned if your child leaves the dinner table early to use his computer, or misses scheduled appointments or social interactions to go online. In such instances, it's okay to ask just what the kid is doing online—just to be safe.

- Your child turns off her computer monitor or quickly switches programs when you enter the room. What is she hiding? It could be a communication from her newfound adult friend. Ask to see what your child is doing—and don't take no for an answer.

- You find pornography on the child's computer. Yes, it's relatively easy for any teenager to stumble over porn sites in the course of everyday surfing, and spam laced with adult images can hit any inbox. But many predators use sexual images and content to lure their prey, so if you find dirty pictures or suggestive messages on the youth's computer, it should raise a red flag.

- You find suggestive pictures of your child on the computer, or stored in a digital camera. Many predators convince their victims to send them pictures, as a sign of their devotion or commitment.

- Your child receives phone calls from people you don't know—especially people who sound older. Along the same lines, watch out for your child *making* calls to people outside his immediate circle of friends, particularly long-distance calls. This is a sure sign of a predator escalating a relationship from online to something more physical.

- Your child receives gifts or packages in the mail from strangers. This is another escalation; the predator is trying to ingratiate himself by buying your child gifts and such. Some brazen predators even send plane tickets to their victims, to encourage them to visit the predator in his home city.

- Your child becomes withdrawn from family and friends. As your child becomes a teenager, it's common for him to become less friendly with family members. But he still should maintain solid friendships with his peers. If he withdraws both from you and from his former friends, that's a sign he's found a new friend—possibly in the form of an online predator.

In other words, look for behavior that is inconsistent with past behavior. Any change in behavior should raise a question mark in your mind.

How Can You Protect Your Children from Online Predators?

Protecting your children from online predators is not an easy task. You can't control what your children do 24/7; you have to give them some autonomy, and with that autonomy comes the freedom to make bad decisions.

That said, there are some steps you can take to protect your children online. Here are some of the most effective things you can do:

- Take an interest in your children's online pals, just as you (should) do with friends that your kids bring home to visit.

- Talk to your children about the dangers of getting together with someone they meet online.

- Provide your children with online pseudonyms, so they don't have to use their real names online. Their online screen names should be neutral in terms of revealing gender or age.

- Forbid your children to physically meet anyone they talk to online. (This includes talking to them on the phone.)

- If you do allow your children to set up a real-world meeting, accompany them to the meeting and introduce yourself to the new friend.

- Make sure your children know that people aren't always who they pretend to be online; explain that some people view online chatting as a kind of game, where they can assume different identities.

- Set reasonable rules and guidelines for your kids' computer use; consider limiting the number of minutes/hours they can spend online each day.

- Monitor your children's Internet activities; ask them to keep a log of all websites they visit; oversee any chat and instant messaging sessions in which they participate; check out any files they download; even consider sharing an email account (especially with younger children) so that you can oversee their messages.

- Instruct your children not to respond to messages that are suggestive, obscene, belligerent, or threatening, or that make them feel uncomfortable in any way; encourage your children to tell you if they receive any such messages, and then report the senders to your ISP.

- Don't let your children send pictures of themselves over the Internet; don't let them receive pictures from others. The same goes for posting personal photos on MySpace and Facebook; younger children, especially, should be discouraged from doing this.

- Caution your children about providing personal information (including passwords!) to strangers.

- Discourage your children from posting their phone numbers and other personal information on MySpace and Facebook pages.

- Instruct your children to add only people as MySpace and Facebook friends that they know in real life; they should reject friend requests from total strangers.

- On any social networking site, set your children's privacy settings so that people can be added as a friend only if your child approves it, and so that people can view your child's profile only if they have been approved as a friend.

- As much as your children won't like it, you should occasionally check out their MySpace and Facebook pages; look not only for any personal information they may have posted online, but also for signs of inappropriate or suspicious behavior.

- Teach your children not to respond if they receive offensive or suggestive email or instant messages.

- Install filtering software that prevents your children from giving out a name, address, and phone number online.

- Use the Internet with your children; make going online a family activity.

- Consider moving your children's PC into a public room (such as a living room or den), rather than a private bedroom.

- If you have serious concerns that your children might be targeted, consider installing tracking or keylogging software on their PC, as discussed in Chapter 18, "Engaging in Your Own Surveillance: Tracking Your Children's Online Activity."

- If you think that one of your children, or one of your children's friends, is in any danger, immediately contact the authorities.

Above all, teach your children that Internet access is not a right; it should be a privilege earned by your children, and kept only when their use of it matches your expectations.

Defending Against Cyberbullies

It used to be that the bullies bothered you only on the playground; after you got home, you were safe from attack.

Not anymore.

Thanks to the Internet, bullies can now continue their intimidating behavior practically 24 hours a day. Bullies now send harassing messages via email and instant messaging, and prey on their victims in Internet chat rooms and social networking sites.

What Is Cyberbullying?

This sort of online harassment by their peers is called *cyberbullying* or *e-bullying*. It's just like normal bullying, except it takes place on the Internet. And it's just as serious as physical bullying; youths have committed suicide after being victims of cyberbullying incidents.

Cyberbullying can include any or all of the following:

- Harassing instant messages or text messages via cell phone

- Harassing comments on blogs

- Stealing passwords to log onto sites posing as your child

- Creating "hate" websites that put down your child

- Sending embarrassing pictures (real or fake) via email or cell phones

- Harassing a child in online games and virtual worlds

- Leaving hateful comments on a child's blog or MySpace/Facebook page

> > > **N O T E**

Whatever the behavior, cyberbullying is a real threat. A 2005 survey by the National Children's Home charity found that 20% of children between 11 and 19 had been bullied via electronic means.

How Can You Defend Against Cyberbullies?

One of the advantages of monitoring your children's Internet activities is that you can become aware of any potential cyberbullying. If you suspect your child is a victim of a cyberbully, the first thing to do is contact authorities at your child's school. You'd be surprised how effective a call from the teacher or principal can be in stopping this sort of behavior.

You may also want to confront the bully's parents, just as you would those of a normal school-yard bully. In some instances, especially with older youths, having your child confront the bully himself might be advisable. (That said, your child shouldn't respond to the bully's online messages; the contact should be in person, along the lines of "Leave me alone, stop harassing me.")

Along these lines, the National Crime Prevention Council offers the following five tips to prevent cyberbullying:

- Do not give out personal information online, whether in instant message profiles, chat rooms, blogs, or personal websites.

- Never tell anyone your password, even friends.

- If someone sends a mean or threatening message, don't respond. Save it or print it out and show it to an adult.

- Never open emails (or read text messages or instant messages) from someone you don't know or from someone you know is a bully.

- Help peers who are harassed online by not joining in.

Beyond that, the normal precautions regarding any type of cyberstalking apply. Change your child's online ID, have your child start visiting different sites, and in general try to defuse the situation before a more explosive—and potentially physical—conflict occurs.

Is It Safe?

Here's the deal. Cyberbullying and cyberstalking exist, and neither are very pleasant things by which to be victimized. But the incidence of each is less than you think, and the actual physical risk from either is close to nil.

So you probably don't need to worry much about being stalked online—until it happens to you. Then you need to know how to respond, what steps to take to shut down or cut off contact from the harasser. You should also know the rudimentary steps to take to avoid being stalked—including that always-practical maxim, don't go around picking fights.

That's because much of what we refer to as cyberstalking is really just "Internet rage," or flame wars that result from ill-thought-out comments on blogs and message boards. Many people adopt a different persona when they're online, changing from their normal passive-aggressive selves to more aggressive Internet posters. There's a lot of hate on the web, thanks to these flamers hiding behind online pseudonyms and fake identities.

If you're verbally attacked on an online forum, the best course of action is to turn the other cheek. Ignore the post, rather than kindling the flame war. If you respond in kind to a hateful comment, it just inspires further comments (from the original poster, as well as latecomers to the game). If you let the issue drop, the flame war dies down and eventually goes away. That's a far more civilized outcome.

Fortunately, few flame wars develop into physical fistfights; at worst, a flamer might escalate his behavior into full-blown cyberstalking, taking his fight to other websites. But most flamers want nothing more than attention; deprive the flamer of this and he goes quietly into the night—or to another forum where he can pick another fight.

Serious cyberstalkers, although rare, still deserve your attention. These troublemakers don't stop when they're ignored; they keep on harassing you, no matter how much you try to avoid them. Fortunately, it's unlikely that you'll be a victim of cyberstalking, but if you are, know how to respond.

It's even less likely that you will be a victim of a dangerous online predator. Such predators do exist, but their numbers are small. Again, you need to know how to defend yourself if you become a victim, but you shouldn't worry needlessly about such an occurrence.

Likewise, there are fewer predators preying on your children than the media might lead you to believe. And, unlike what you see on "To Catch a Predator," these sexual predators are relatively upfront about their intentions; if your children use common sense and are reasonably well adjusted, they'll know to avoid these opportunistic offenders.

Bottom line: Know how to protect yourself in case a situation arises, but don't be overly concerned about it actually happening to you.

Engaging in Your Own Surveillance: Tracking Your Children's Online Activity

The Internet contains an almost limitless supply of information on its billions of web pages; likewise, the Internet's social networks, blogs, and forums provide an opportunity to communicate and form communities with new friends from all around the globe. But with all this valuable information and interaction comes some degree of offensive content and inappropriate communication—or at least offensive to and inappropriate for the youngest members of your family.

Even if just a small percentage of the Internet is unsuitable for children, that still leaves millions of individual pages and profiles that feature sexual, violent, and hateful content. How do you protect your children from the bad stuff on the web—while still allowing access to all the good stuff?

To protect your children, you have to turn the surveillance issue on its head; you have to be become Big Brother to monitor your children's online activities. This may be a noxious affront to civil liberties to some, but to others it's a necessary evil. Someone, after all, has to protect your children from inappropriate activity and interactions online.

How do you monitor or control what your children are doing online? There are lots of different approaches—most of which mirror the tactics that large companies use to monitor their employees' online activities.

Using Content Filtering Software

If you can't trust your children to always click away from inappropriate web content (and you can't; children are always too curious for their own good), you can choose instead to block access to that inappropriate content. This is done by installing content-filtering software on your kids' PCs.

How Content Filtering Works

Content-filtering software blocks access to those sites and pages that contain adult-oriented content, working from either a list of inappropriate sites or a list of inappropriate topics (or both). You can use the software's built-in list of inappropriate sites and content, or add your own list of sites and keywords to avoid.

When your child tries to access a blocked site or a page that contains questionable content, access is blocked and a warning message displayed, instead. With content-monitoring software installed on your children's computer, they can't access the really bad stuff on the web.

Choosing a Content Filtering Program

The most popular filtering programs include the following:

- Cyber Sentinel (www.cybersentinel.com)
- CyberPatrol (www.cyberpatrol.com)
- Cybersitter (www.cybersitter.com)
- FilterPak (www.centipedenetworks.com)
- MaxProtect (www.max.com)
- McAfee Parental Controls (www.mcafee.com)
- Net Nanny (www.netnanny.com)
- NetMop (www.netmop.com)
- Safe Eyes (www.internetsafety.com)
- WiseChoice (www.wisechoice.net)

Prices for these programs run from around $30 to $60. In addition, many of the big Internet security suites (such as those from McAfee and Norton/Symantec) offer built-in content filtering modules.

> > > **N O T E**

Many content filtering programs also filter or block access to inappropriate Internet chat, instant messaging, newsgroups, and email.

Setting Up Parental Controls in Windows Vista

If your family computer is running Microsoft Windows Vista, you have content filtering built into the operating system, thanks to the new Parental Controls feature. Parental Controls let you determine how your children use your computer—you can set time limits for when they can use the PC, which websites they can visit, which PC games they can play (based on game ratings), and which specific programs they can and cannot use. You can even have Vista create activity reports for each chosen user.

To activate and configure the various Parental Controls, open the Control Panel and select Set Up Parental Controls for Any User (in the User Accounts and Family Safety section). When the next screen appears, select the user that you want to monitor.

When you see the screen shown in Figure 18.1, do any or all of the following:

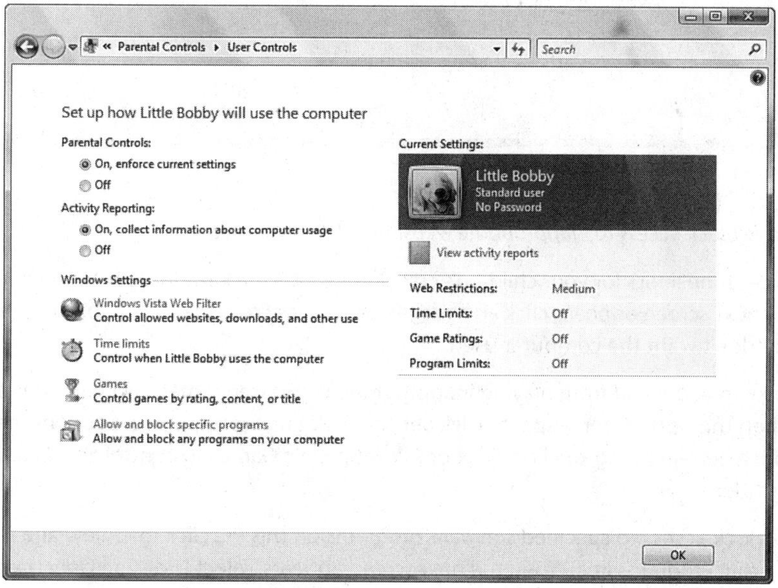

Figure 18.1

Controlling your children's computer usage with Windows Vista Parental Controls.

- To turn on Parental Controls, select On in the Parental Controls section.

- To create a log that details the computer usage for this user, select On in the Activity Reporting section.

- To block access to inappropriate websites, click the Windows Vista Web Filter link. When the next screen appears, as shown in Figure 18.2, click Block Some Websites or Content. Then, in the Block Web Content Automatically section, choose a web restriction level—High, Medium, or Custom. And, if you want to block potentially harmful file downloads, check the Block File Downloads option.

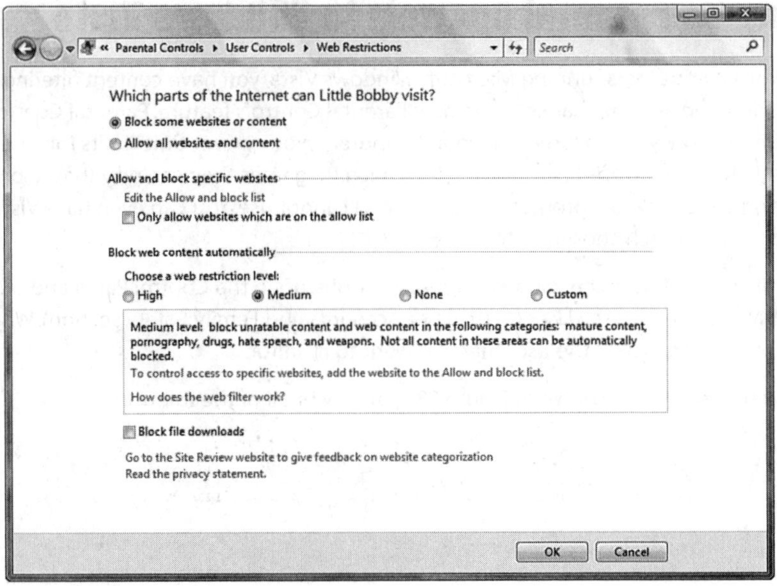

Figure 18.2
Preparing to block access to inappropriate websites in Windows Vista.

- To set time limits for your children's computer usage, click the Time Limits link. When the next screen appears, click and drag your cursor across the blocks for those hours you don't want the computer used.

- To keep your child from playing inappropriate computer games, click the Games link. When the next screen appears, click Set Game Ratings to allow access to only games with a certain rating, or click Block or Allow Specific Games to control access to individual titles.

- To block access to specified software programs on this PC, click the Allow and Block Specific Programs link. When the next screen appears, select User Can Only Use the Programs I Allow, and then check those programs that are okay to use.

< < < TIP

How strict should you set Vista's web restrictions? The Medium level blocks mature content, pornography, drugs, hate speech, and weapons. The High level blocks all content except websites specifically approved for children. You might want to start blocking at the Medium level, watch the activity logs to see what kinds of sites your kids are visiting, and then move the restrictions to High if necessary.

Encouraging Kid-Safe Searching

If you don't want to go to all the trouble of using content filtering software or setting up Vista's Parental Controls, you can at least steer your children to some of the safer sites on the web. The best of these sites offer kid-safe searching so that all inappropriate sites are filtered out of the search results.

The best of these kids-safe search and directory sites include

- AltaVista—AV Family Filter (www.altavista.com; go to the Settings page and click the Family Filter link)

- Ask for Kids (www.askforkids.com)

- Fact Monster (www.factmonster.com)

- Google SafeSearch (www.google.com; go to the Preferences page then choose a SafeSearch Filtering option)

- KidsClick! (www.kidsclick.org)

- KOL: Kids Online (kids.aol.com)

- Live Search SafeSearch (search.live.com; go to the Search Settings page then choose a SafeSearch filtering option)

- Yahoo! Kids (kids.yahoo.com)

< < < T I P

Kids-safe search sites are often good to use as the start page for your children's browser because they are launching pads to guaranteed safe content.

It's also important to train your kids to find acceptable and avoid unacceptable content themselves. You'd be surprised how responsible most kids are—and how most kids really don't want to be bothered with all the unacceptable and irrelevant content on the web.

Monitoring Your Children's Online Activities

Just as your employer can employ various technologies to monitor and control employee Internet usage, you can use these same technologies to monitor and control your children's online activities. Yes, it's a little bit of Big Brother in the home, but it may be worth it to ensure that your children are kept safe from the most unsavory aspects of the Internet.

C A U T I O N !!!

If you discover that your child is involved in an inappropriate online relationship that you suspect is of a sexual nature, report it to your local law enforcement officials and to the Center for Missing and Exploited Children; its tipline to report predatory online behavior is located at www.cybertipline.com.

Remote Monitoring Software

One of the most common ways to keep track of what your children are doing online is to use a remote monitoring program. This type of program lets you see on your PC what your child is doing on his computer; your screen shows the contents of his screen, in real time. In addition, most of these programs also create logs of activity on the controlled computer for you to review at your leisure.

Some of the more popular remote monitoring programs include

- CyberSieve (www.cybersieve.com)

- Golden Eye (www.monitoring-spy-software.com)

- Sentry Remote (www.sentryparentalcontrols.com)

- SnoopStick (www.snoopstick.com)

- WinSpy (www.win-spy.com)

For example, SnoopStick comes on what looks like a USB memory stick. Insert the stick into a USB port on your children's PC and it installs the secret monitoring software; your children will never know the program is loaded. Next, remove the stick from your children's computer and insert it into your PC. You can now monitor your children's online activities over any network or Internet connection—or even disable your children's Internet access, via remote control.

Activity Monitoring Software

Remote monitoring software requires constant attention on your part. A better solution for many parents is an activity monitoring program. This type of software creates a detailed log of your children's online activities—which websites they visit, what emails they send, even complete transcripts of all chat and instant messaging conversations. Some programs even capture actual screenshots at a predetermined interval, so you can see what your children are seeing onscreen. You can then view the log or screenshots at your own convenience.

> > > **N O T E**
>
> Some activity monitoring programs can be configured to send you an immediate cell phone or email alert if your child visits a questionable website or uses inappropriate language in email or instant messaging.

The most popular activity monitoring programs include

- 007 Spy Software (www.e-spy-software.com)

- eBlaster (www.eblaster.com)

- Guardian Monitor Family Edition (www.guardiansoftware.com)

- IamBigBrother (www.iambigbrother.com)

- Invisible Keylogger (www.invisiblekeylogger.com)

- KeyLogger Pro (www.keyloggerpro.com)

- SpectorPro (www.eblaster.com)

- SpyAgent (www.spytech-web.com)

- SpyBuddy (www.exploreanywhere.com)

- Spysure Online (www.spysureonline.com)

Is It Safe?

Is the Internet safe for your children? Mostly yes—if you do your job as a parent.

Here's the thing. You may feel like a creep, secretly monitoring your children's Internet activities, but what other recourse have you? After all, there is both good and bad content on the Internet. If all content can be freely accessed, how can you otherwise keep that bad content away from your children?

One solution, of course, is to ask the government to censor the Internet. Fortunately or unfortunately, depending on where you stand on civil liberties, it's extremely difficult for any single country to censor the entire web—which leaves it up to individual users to keep potentially harmful material away from their impressionable young children.

> > **N O T E**

When I say it's difficult to censor the entire Internet, I don't mean that it's impossible; anything is possible given enough time and resources. Hence China's fairly successful efforts to censor the web, achievable only because they have huge numbers of cheap laborers: They do it via brute force.

Just as it's practically impossible to execute censorship of the web, it's probably not possible to completely shield every child from every inappropriate web page. Dedicated content pushers have a knack of finding ways around whatever content blocks are enacted—and determined kids can always find the stuff you don't want them to find.

So, although you can employ content filtering software and remote monitoring programs, both of which work well *to a point*, the most important thing you can do as a parent is to create an environment that encourages appropriate use of the Internet—and discourages deliberate searching for inappropriate content. Technology is great, but nothing replaces traditional parental supervision. At the end of the day, you have to take responsibility for your children's online activities. Provide the guidance they need to make the Internet a fun and educational place to visit—and your entire family will be better for it.

Computer Viruses and Spyware: How Big a Problem?

or obvious reasons, many of my friends and family call on me as their unofficial technical support when something goes wrong with their computers. Not a month goes by that I don't have someone call me up about a computer that's running slowly, or not at all. A cursory examination, followed by a few simple questions, typically confirms the usual suspect: The computer has been infected by a virus or spyware program. In most cases the computer can be cleaned and put back in good working condition, but it's annoying to find so many computers being infected by those two things that are most easily guarded against.

This section of *Is It Safe?* addresses the dynamic duo behind so many computer problems—viruses and spyware. They're similar but not identical in how they work, how they invade a computer, and the type of damage they cause; most users see not the technological differences but the similarities, which is understandable.

So what are viruses and spyware—and how big a threat do they represent? Read on for a basic overview and threat assessment.

Understanding Computer Viruses

A computer virus is a malicious software program designed to do damage to your computer system by deleting files or even taking over your PC to launch attacks on other systems. A virus attacks your computer when you launch an infected software program, launching a "payload" that often is catastrophic.

Computer viruses represent one of the largest threats to both home and business computer users today; tens of millions of computers are infected by computer viruses every year. It's a simple fact—you must protect your computer against virus infection, or risk the consequences.

A Short—But Costly—History of Computer Viruses

If it seems to you that computer viruses have been around as long as personal computers have, you're right. That's true; in fact, the concept of the computer virus predates the personal computer by several decades.

Technically, the first computer virus was conceived in 1949, well before computers became commonplace. In that year, computer pioneer John von Neumann wrote a paper titled "Theory and Organization of Complicated Automata." In this paper, von Neumann postulated that a computer program could be self-replicating—and thus predicted today's self-replicating virus programs.

The theories of von Neumann came to life in the 1950s at Bell Labs. Programmers there developed a game called "Core Wars," where two players would unleash software "organisms" into the mainframe computer, and watch as the competing programs would vie for control of the machine—just as viruses do today.

ARPANET, the forerunner to today's Internet, saw the first network-born virus in the early 1970s. The so-called Creeper virus was propagated via the TENEX operating system and made use of any connected model to dial out to and infect remote computers. This virus wasn't particularly harmful; it merely displayed the message "I'M THE CREEPER: CATCH ME IF YOU CAN" on infected machines.

In the real world, computer viruses came to the fore in the early 1980s, coincident with the rise of the very first personal computers. These early viruses were typically spread by users sharing programs and documents on floppy disks; a shared floppy was the perfect medium for spreading virus files.

For example, the first virus to infect consumer computers was propagated across Apple II computers via floppy disks in 1982. The virus went by the name of Elk Cloner, and didn't do any real damage; all it did was display a short and somewhat nonsensical rhyme onscreen:

Elk Cloner: The program with a personality

It will get on all your disks

It will infiltrate your chips

Yes it's Cloner!

It will stick to you like glue

It will modify RAM too

Send in the Cloner!

> > > **NOTE**

The phrase "computer virus" was coined in 1983 by computer scientist Fred Cohen to describe self-replicating computer programs. The phrase was suggested by Cohen's teacher, Leonard Len Adleman—who himself designed and demonstrated the first experimental virus on a VAX 11/750 computer.

In 1986, the Brain virus became the first documented file infector virus for MS-DOS computers. (You remember MS-DOS, don't you—the character-based operating system that preceded Microsoft Windows?) That same year, the first PC-based Trojan horse was released, disguised as the then-popular shareware program, PC Write.

At this point, viruses tended to be geographically isolated; they were spread only as far as physical disks could be distributed. That changed with the increasing popularity of the computer bulletin board service (BBS), which helped to spread viruses around the world. BBSs were the online precursors to the Internet; users could use their low-speed modems to dial into public and private BBSs, both to exchange messages and to download files. As any Monday-morning quarterback could predict, there were viruses hiding amongst the standard utilities and applications that users downloaded, thus facilitating the spread of those viruses.

> > > **NOTE**

It didn't help that virus writers created their own BBSs, for the express purpose of exchanging virus code and learning new tricks. The first virus exchange BBS, housed on a computer in Bulgaria, went live in 1990.

Computer viruses hit the big time in 1992, when the Michelangelo virus hit. Michelangelo was one of the first viruses to spread worldwide, and garnered much media attention. Fortunately, its bark was worse than its bite, and little actual damage occurred.

The year 1996 saw the first virus designed specifically for Windows, as well as the first macro viruses for Word and Excel files. That year also saw the first virus for the Linux operating system.

By 1999, viruses had become almost mainstream. The Melissa virus, released that year, was a combination macro virus and worm that spread itself by emailing contacts in a user's Outlook or Outlook Express address book. Melissa did untold amounts of damage to computers and company networks around the world, and was followed (in 2000) by the IloveYou worm (also known as the "Love Bug"), which shut down tens of thousands of corporate email systems.

Since then, viruses have continued to proliferate and mutate, with attacks growing in intensity over the years—as witnessed by the Storm Worm virus, which infected more than 1 million computers in 2007. This worm created a botnet of zombie computers that was used to attack various host sites on the web, including sites maintained by several anti-spyware vendors.

How Computer Viruses Work

A computer virus is, in many ways, similar to the types of biological viruses that attack human bodies.

A biological virus isn't truly a living entity; as biologists will tell you, a virus is nothing more than a fragment of DNA sheathed in a protective jacket. It reproduces by injecting its DNA into a host cell. The DNA then uses the host cell's normal mechanisms to reproduce itself.

A computer virus is like a biological virus in that it also isn't alive, and it must piggyback on a host (another program or document) to propagate.

Many viruses are hidden in the code of legitimate software programs—programs that have been infected, that is. These viruses are called *file infector viruses*, and when the host program is launched, the code for the virus is executed and the virus loads itself into your computer's memory. From there, the virus code searches for other programs on your system that it can infect; if it finds one, it adds its code to the new program, which, now infected, can be used to infect other computers.

If all a virus did was copy itself to additional programs and computers, there would be little harm done, save for having all our programs get slightly larger (thanks to the added virus code). Unfortunately, most viruses not only replicate themselves, they also perform other operations—many of which are wholly destructive. A virus might, for example, delete certain files on your computer. It might overwrite the boot sector of your hard disk, making the disk inaccessible. It might write messages on your screen, or cause your system to emit rude noises. It might also hijack your email program and use the program to send itself to all your friends and colleagues, thus replicating itself to a large number of PCs.

Viruses that replicate themselves via email or over a computer network cause the subsidiary problem of increasing the amount of Internet and network traffic. These fast-replicating viruses—called *worms*—can completely overload a company's network, shutting down servers and forcing tens of thousands of users offline. Although no individual machines might be damaged, this type of communications disruption can be quite costly.

As you might suspect, most viruses are designed to deliver their payload when they're first executed. However, some viruses don't attack until specifically prompted, typically on a predetermined date or day of the week. They stay on your system, hidden from sight like a sleeper agent, until they're awakened on a specific date; then they go about the work they were programmed to do.

Other viruses open a back door to your system that can then be exploited by the virus writer. These types of backdoor viruses turn your machine into a so-called *zombie computer*, which the hacker operates via remote control to perform all manner of nefarious tasks. Hijacked computers of this sort are responsible for a large number of computer attacks and spam campaigns.

In short, viruses are nasty little bits of computer code, designed to inflict as much damage as possible, and to spread to as many computers as possible—a particularly vicious combination.

> > > **NOTE**

Viruses and malware aren't limited to computers. For example, so-called *mobile viruses* are designed to attack mobile phones, especially those smart phones typified by Apple's iPhone.

How to Catch a Virus

Viruses are spread by contact with other computers, or data copied from other computers. So whenever you share data with another computer or computer user, you risk exposing your computer to potential viruses.

There are many ways you can share data and many ways a virus can be transmitted:

- Opening an infected file attached to an email message or instant message
- Launching an infected program file downloaded from the Internet
- Sharing a data CD, USB memory drive, or floppy disk that contains an infected file
- Sharing over a network a computer file that contains an infected file

Of all these methods, the most common means of virus infection is via email—with instant messaging close behind. Whenever you open a file attached to an email message or instant message, you stand a good chance of infecting your computer system with a virus—even if the file was sent by someone you know and trust. That's because many viruses "spoof" the sender's name, thus making you think the file is from a friend or colleague. The bottom line is that no email or instant message attachment is safe unless you were expressly expecting it—and even then, an expected file attachment could still be infected with a virus, without the sender knowing it.

Almost as risky is the act of downloading files from so-called file-sharing sites or peer-to-peer (P2P) networks. This is the type of infection I see most often when troubleshooting teenagers' PCs; the teen downloads what he thinks are music files from a file-sharing site, and in the process infects his computer with one or more viruses. It's an extremely common occurrence.

Understanding Different Types of Computer Viruses

Not every piece of malicious software is a virus, even though they're often lumped together in the virus category. Technically, a computer virus is a piece of software that surreptitiously attaches itself to other programs, and then does something unexpected. There are other programs—such as Trojan horses and worms—that do similar damage, but don't embed themselves within other program code. These programs aren't technically viruses, but they pose the same danger to computer systems everywhere. For that reason, all these programs—virus and non-virus, alike—are typically lumped together and referred to, in common parlance, as viruses. We'll follow that convention here.

> > > **NOTE**

Malicious software programs are commonly referred to as *malware*.

That's not to say that all malicious programs work the same way, or pack the same potential punch. They don't. So it helps to know a little bit about each type of virus, to help better protect against them. We'll start by examining some of the older, more established types of viruses, and then move forward to discuss today's newest and most dangerous types of malware.

File Infector Viruses

The most "traditional" form of computer virus is the *file infector virus*, sometimes called a *parasitic* virus, which hides within the code of another program. The infected program can be a business application, a utility, or even a game—just as long as it's an executable program, typically with an EXE, COM, SYS, BAT, or PIF extension.

When an infected program is launched, the virus code is copied into your computer's memory, typically before the program code is loaded. By loading itself into memory separately from the host program, the virus can continue to run, in your system's memory, even after the host program is closed down.

Prior to the advent of the Internet and coincident creation of macro viruses, file infector viruses accounted for probably 85% of all virus infections. Today that number is much lower, because the other types of viruses are much easier to spread. (Virus writers tend to go for the low-hanging fruit....)

Boot-Sector Viruses

That part of a hard disk, floppy disk, or bootable CD that is read into memory and executed when your computer first boots up is called the boot sector. A *boot sector virus* resides in the boot sector of these bootable disks; after it is loaded, the virus can then infect any other disk used by the computer, including the PC's hard disk.

Before the days hard disks became common, most boot-sector viruses were spread by floppy disk. Because removable disks are less widely used today, boot-sector viruses have become much less prevalent than they were in the early 1990s.

> > > **NOTE**

> A *multipartite virus* combines the abilities of file infector and boot-sector viruses, and is able to infect either files or boot sectors.

Macro Viruses

So-called *macro viruses* are created with the macro code used by many of today's software applications. The most common macro code, used in all Microsoft applications, is called Visual Basic for Applications (VBA). VBA code can be added to a Word document to create custom menus and perform automatic operations; unfortunately, VBA code can also be used to modify files and send unwanted email messages, which is where the virus writers come in.

What makes macro viruses potentially more dangerous than file infector or boot-sector viruses is that macro viruses can be attached to document files, such as Word documents and Excel spreadsheets. Older virus types had to be embedded in executable programs, which made them relatively easy to find and stop. But when any Word or Excel document you open could contain a macro virus, the world is suddenly a much more dangerous place.

The widespread, relatively nonchalant sharing of data files contributed to a huge rise in macro virus attacks. Even users who are extra-vigilant about the programs they download often don't think twice about opening a Word or Excel document they receive from another user. Because data files are shared so freely, macro viruses are able to spread rapidly from one machine to another—and run, automatically, whenever the infected document is opened.

Script Viruses

Script viruses are based on common scripting languages, typically used on websites and in some computer applications. There are many different scripting languages, including Java, JavaScript, Visual Basic Script, and ActiveX; these languages are used to create everything from web pages to auto-run routines in the Windows operating system. These scripting languages are typically easier to learn than traditional programming languages, which is why virus writers have adopted these languages for their malicious endeavors.

Viruses created with these scripting languages can be quite destructive. They can also spread very quickly because the script code can be inserted into web pages, Word documents, and Excel spreadsheets, attached to email messages, and even secretly embedded in email messages. For that reason, many of today's most common viruses are script viruses.

Trojan Horses

A *Trojan horse* isn't technically a computer virus. Instead, it's a program that claims to do one thing but then does something totally different.

A typical Trojan horse has a filename that appears to be some type of harmless file; it looks innocuous enough to be safe to open. But when you run the file, it's actually a virus program that proceeds to inflict its damage on your system. It delivers its payload through deception, just like the fabled Trojan horse of yore.

Trojan horses are often propagated via email. These email Trojans spread as innocent-looking attachments to email messages; when you click to open the attachment, you launch the Trojan program.

And here's the thing—Trojan horses are, far and away, the most encountered type of malware today. According to the Kaspersky Labs' *Security Bulletin 2007*, 85% of all malware incidents in can be attributed to Trojans and related threats. In contrast, viruses and worms together accounted for only 5% of reported incidents.

Rootkits

A *rootkit* is a particular type of Trojan horse designed to take control of a computer's operating system. Rootkits obscure their presence on the host system by evading standard system security methods. Intruders use rootkits to gain backdoor access to a computer system without detection, then using that computer for various unauthorized activities.

{ P E R S O N A L   E X P E R I E N C E }

One of the most famous examples of a rootkit Trojan was the one that Sony BMG deliberately included on millions of commercial music CDs in 2005. (See the full list of affected CDs here: cp.sonybmg.com/xcp/english/titles.html.) When you played one of these CDs on a personal computer, it surreptitiously installed a program that could allow a hacker to gain access to and control the PC. Sony included the rootkit as part of an aggressive copy protection scheme, which itself played havoc with users' CD players and computers, and restricted users to making just three digital copies of each CD. I myself unknowingly purchased one of these tainted CDs, a copy of Burt Bacharach's album *At This Time*; rootkit issues aside, it wouldn't let me rip a lossless version of the CD to my Media Center PC's hard disk. I returned the CD for my money back, before I knew of the rootkit issues. Other users weren't so lucky, ending up with infected and potentially corrupted PCs. Sony ended up offering to swap all the infected CDs for clean ones and even offered up a (somewhat lame) rootkit-removal tool, but only after several states threatened class-action lawsuits and the U.S. Department of Homeland Security warned that it might seek regulation against the music industry if they continued to embed this type of dangerous software in their products. Certainly not a shining example of consumer-friendly marketing on Sony's behalf!

Botnet Trojans

A *botnet* is a collection of software robots, or "bots," that run automatically on hijacked zombie computers. The computers are hijacked when they're infected with a special kind of Trojan, called a botnet Trojan, which is designed specifically to allow remote control of a large mass of computers. The network of botnet computers is then used for various purposes, typically to send spam or conduct denial of service attacks on targeted websites.

> > > NOTE

Some virus experts refer to botnet Trojans as *malware 2.0*—the next generation of malware that targets multiple computers for a single task.

Zombie computers working together as botnets are thought to be responsible for most of the spam sent today. As an example, Internet security company Marshal reports that in February 2008, six botnets accounted for more than 85% of all spam sent over the Internet. As detailed in Figure 19.1, the Srixbi botnet alone sent out more than a third of all spam messages. That's a lot of spam coming from a single network of remote controlled computers.

How big are these networks of zombie computers? The largest botnets consist of tens of thousands of controlled computers. The Mega-D botnet, as an example, is thought to contain approximately 35,000 hijacked PCs, while the Storm botnet has more than 85,000 individual bots.

Interestingly, most botnet Trojans include reporting and control features. It's common for a hijacked computer to provide feedback and statistics to the control computer or server regarding which email addresses in a spam attack were good and which were bad. The entire operation is quite sophisticated—especially considering the owners of these hijacked computers aren't at all aware that their machines are being used.

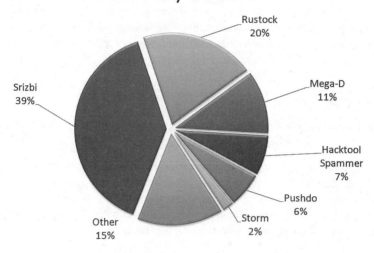

Spam Received by Botnet Type February 2008

Figure 19.1
Six botnets accounted for 85% of all spam in February, 2008, according to security firm Marshal (www.marshal.com).

> > > **NOTE**

> Different botnets tend to specialize in specific types of spam. For example, the Mega-D botnet is known for spam messages about male enhancement products under the guise of "herbal" products such as VPXL and Megadik from Express Herbals, Herbal King, and similar companies.

Worms

A *worm*, like a Trojan horse, isn't technically a computer virus. Instead, it's a program that scans a company's network or the Internet for another computer that has a specific security hole. It copies itself to the new machine (through the security hole), and then starts replicating itself there. Worms replicate themselves very quickly; a network infected with a worm can be brought to its knees within a matter of hours.

> > > **NOTE**

> Worms don't even have to be delivered via conventional programs. So-called "fileless" worms exist only in system memory, making them harder to identify than conventional file-hosted worms.

Email Viruses

An email virus is a program that is distributed as an attachment to an email message. These viruses are typically separate programs (Trojan horses, primarily) that do their damage when they're manually executed by the user. These viruses masquerade as JPG images, Word documents, and other common attachments, but are really executable files in disguise. Many email viruses hijack your email program and send themselves out to all the contacts in your address book.

Chat and Instant Messaging Viruses

Most chat rooms and instant messaging services let users send files to one another; it's this capability that has contributed to the spread of so-called "instant" viruses.

Just as some users are accustomed to automatically opening all attachments to their incoming email messages, many users are also accustomed to accepting any files sent to them when they're chatting. Unfortunately, a significant percentage of files sent via chat or IM are virus files, often Trojan horses masquerading as photographs or helpful utilities. Downloading and then opening one of these files begins the infection process.

Social Networking Viruses

The growth of social networks, such as MySpace and Facebook, has led to a corresponding growth in malware propagated over such networks. These are typically script viruses or worms that attempt to appropriate users' personal information, which is then used to hijack their accounts or initiate identity theft.

As an example, in December of 2006 MySpace shut down hundreds of personal pages after they were struck by a Javascript-based worm. The worm converted legitimate links to fraudulent links that took users to a phishing website that attempted to obtain their personal information. A similar worm hit Google's Orkut social networking site late in 2007, affecting close to a half-million users.

> > > **N O T E**

> This type of social networking virus uses a technique called *cross-site scripting*, or XSS. A virus of this type
> takes advantage of a vulnerability in some sites that allows the injection of replacement code into the web
> pages maintained by the site's users.

Understanding Spyware

Similar to computer viruses is the growing problem of *spyware*. Spyware is a type of program that installs itself on your computer, typically without your knowledge or consent, and then surreptitiously sends information about the way you use your PC to some interested third party.

> > > **N O T E**

Spyware hasn't been around nearly as long as computer viruses. In fact, the term "spyware" originally referred to a type of hardware used for espionage purposes. The first reference to spyware software was in 2000, by Gregor Freund, the founder of Zone Labs.

Having spyware on your system is nasty, almost as bad as being infected with a computer virus; the added load of spyware programs in your system's memory inevitably leads to sluggish performance, at the very least. Some spyware programs do more than just slow down your system, instead hijacking your computer and launching pop-up windows and advertisements when you visit certain web pages. If there's spyware on your computer, you definitely want to get rid of it.

> > > **N O T E**

Unfortunately, most anti-virus programs won't catch spyware because spyware isn't a virus. To track down and uninstall these programs, then, you need to run a separate anti-spyware utility.

What Spyware Is

Spyware and viruses are similar but technically different. Like a Trojan horse, spyware typically gets installed in the background when you're installing another program. Unlike a virus, however, spyware doesn't replicate itself; after it's installed, its job is to spy on your system, not to spread itself to other computers.

Some industry experts describe spyware as a program that has the following attributes:

- It installs without your permission, or with your permission based on misleading information
- Maintains a presence on your computer on terms to which you never agreed
- Interfaces with a third-party computer with which you have not requested a relationship
- Transmits data from your computer to the third-party computer, using a system over which you have no control
- Typically does not come with an uninstall routine

> > > **N O T E**

Some adware programs (spyware distributed for advertising purposes) do come with uninstall routines, or can be uninstalled via Windows' "uninstall software" utility.

In other words, spyware is a software program you didn't request from someone you don't know, which does stuff you have no control over. Doesn't sound like something you'd want on your home or work computer, does it?

How Spyware Works

A spyware program is a stealth program. It runs in the background, hidden from view, and monitors your computer and Internet usage. That could mean performing some or all of the following operations:

- Recording the addresses of each web page you visit
- Recording the recipient addresses of each email you send
- Recording the sender addresses of each email you receive
- Recording the contents of each email you send or receive
- Recording the contents of all the instant messages you send or receive—along with the usernames and addresses of your IM partners
- Recording the entire contents of each chat room you visit—and logging the usernames and addresses of other channel members
- Recording every keystroke you type with your computer keyboard—including usernames, passwords, and other personal information
- Recording all your Windows-related activities, including the movement and operation of your mouse

The information recorded by the spyware is typically saved to a log file. That log file, at a predetermined time, is transmitted (via the Internet) to a central source. That source can then aggregate your information for marketing purposes, use the information to target personalized communications or advertisements, or steal any confidential data for illegal purposes.

> > > **N O T E**
>
> There are many different uses for the information that spyware captures, and they're not all malicious. For example, large corporations often use spyware to monitor the computer and Internet usage of their employees; parents frequently use spyware to monitor their children's computer and Internet usage; and advertising and marketing companies sometimes use spyware to assemble marketing data—and to serve personalized ads to individual users.

How to Become Infected with Spyware

Spyware can get onto your computer in many of the same ways that viruses infect your PC. Typical means of transmission include email attachments, misleading links on websites, and files downloaded from the Internet.

From my experience, some of the biggest sources of spyware are peer-to-peer music-trading networks. I'm not talking legitimate online music stores, such as Apple's iTunes Store, which are almost totally free of viruses and spyware. Instead, it's the rogue file-trading networks, such as Blubster, iMesh, Kazaa, LimeWire, and Morpheus that are risky. In many instances, spyware is actually attached to the file-trading software you have to download to use the network; when you install the software, the spyware is also installed. (And, believe it or not, you can't remove the spyware without also removing the host software—which causes some users to keep the spyware!)

{ P E R S O N A L   E X P E R I E N C E }

Because noncommercial music sharing networks are so rife with spyware, I advise all my friends to block their teenage sons and daughters from using these file trading networks. The legality of file sharing aside, it's tiring to keep removing the same spyware from the same computers used by the same teenagers. It's practically a given that a user of LimeWire or similar network will end up with spyware on his PC. Why submit yourself to this risk?

Here's the thing that's tricky. Many software distributors present their malicious programs as helpful utilities. For example, you may be prompted to download what is advertised as a web accelerator utility, only to find that you're downloading spyware instead. In this regard, spyware is a bit like a Trojan horse, but using social engineering as the way into your system.

Another way to have spyware installed on your system is to be tricked into doing it. You go to a website, perhaps one mentioned in a spam email message, and click on a link there. What you see next looks like a standard Windows dialog box, asking you whether you want to scan your system for spyware, or optimize your Internet browsing, or something similar. In reality, the "dialog box" is just a pop-up window designed to look like the real deal, and when you click the Yes button, you're authorizing the installation of spyware on your system. In some instances, clicking No also installs the software, so you're damned if you do and damned if you don't.

Finally, some spyware is installed through known security holes in the Internet Explorer browser. When you navigate to a web page controlled by the software author (again, typically from a link in a spam email message), the page contains hidden code that exploits the browser weakness and automatically downloads the spyware.

> > > **N O T E**

This behind-the-scenes installation of spyware on a specially coded website is called a *drive-by download*.

Adware: A Special Kind of Spyware

There's a particular type of spyware that has a certain legitimacy. This spyware is used by advertisers and marketers, and is called *adware*.

Like other types of spyware, adware is typically placed on your PC when you install some other legitimate software, piggybacking on the main installation. (Although, technically, you have to agree to the adware installation; the agreement is typically buried in the boilerplate terms of service agreement you agree to to install the main software.) After it is installed, the adware works like spyware, monitoring your various activities and reporting back to the host advertiser or marketing firm. The host firm can then use the collected data in a marketing-related fashion—totally unbeknownst to you, of course.

For example, adware might monitor your web surfing habits and report to the advertiser which sites you visit. The adware might pop up a window and ask for your demographic data, which it also reports back to the host. The adware might even use your personal data to generate its own targeted banner ads, and display those ads on top of the normal banner ads when you visit other websites.

> > > **N O T E**

> Many adware programs use a technology called a browser helper object (BHO). This small add-in program attaches itself to the Internet Explorer browser and tracks websites visited. This information is then routed back to the adware company.

Adware is the type of spyware you most often encounter when you download software from P2P file-sharing networks; the adware is typically bundled as part of the network's client software. The P2P network generates revenue from the adware company, whereas the adware company generates revenues by serving you personalized ads or by selling the data it collects.

Beware: Fake Anti-Spyware Programs!

Remember how I said that some spyware programs masquerade as helpful system utilities, the better to trick you into installing them? Well, there's a new breed of spyware programs that pose as anti-spyware programs! That's right, you're coaxed into installing what you think is a program to get rid of spyware, when instead you're installing yet another piece of spyware instead.

> > > **N O T E**

> This type of fake anti-spyware program is referred to as *rogue software*.

Most of these programs are installed via fake Windows dialog boxes or pop-up advertisements or warnings. You're warned that spyware has been detected on your system, and encouraged to download this free program to help get rid of it. Woe be you if you agree; all you get is yet another piece of spyware gunking up the works.

Just to make sure you aren't tricked into installing one of these rogue programs, here's a list of most of the known fake anti-spyware programs you might encounter:

- AntiVirus Gold
- AV System Care
- BetterAntivirus

- ContraVirus
- Disk Knight
- errorsafe
- MagicAntiSpy
- MalwareAlarm
- PAL Spyware Remover
- PCSecuresystem
- Pest Trap
- PSGuard
- SecurePCcleaner
- Spy Ranger
- Spy Sherrif
- Spy Wiper
- SpyAxe
- Spydawn
- Spylocked
- SpyShredder
- Spyware Quake
- SpywareStrike
- System Doctor
- SysProtect
- TrustedAntivirus
- Registrycleanerxp.com
- UltimateCleaner
- Virus Protect Pro
- WinAntiVirus Pro
- WinFixer
- WorldAntiSpy
- Your Privacy Guard

That's a pretty long list—longer than the list of legitimate anti-spyware programs discussed in Chapter 21. And, as you might suspect, many of these rogue programs install the same spyware—they're just different names for the same offenders. Beware!

Examples of Spyware and Adware

Before we examine the size of the spyware problem, let's look at examples of some of the most common spyware and adware floating around the Internet today.

For example, CoolWebSearch is an adware program typically installed via drive-by download. After it is installed, it redirects search queries to its own so-called search engine, replaces your designated homepage with the www.coolwebsearch.com page, randomly directs you to sites that install other spyware programs, and displays pop-up windows that redirect to pornography sites. (And to make matters worse, it's extremely difficult to extricate from your hard disk!)

Another common adware program is Zango, formerly known as 180 Solutions. It's typically installed when you download certain games from the Internet; it piggybacks on the game installation and installs its own toolbar (known as the Hotbar) in the Internet Explorer browser. The toolbar is pretty much useless; it serves to host the adware that displays pop-up ads, replaces normal web page banner ads with ads from its advertisers, and transmits detailed information about your web activities to its advertising partners.

> > > **N O T E**

> Zango also distributes the Zango Cash Toolbar, which is another toolbar-based adware program, this one automatically installed when you play one of the many Zango videos (that look suspiciously like YouTube videos) embedded on MySpace pages.

Then there's Internet Optimizer, also known as DyFuCa. When this spyware is installed and you accidentally enter an incorrect URL into Internet Explorer, instead of displaying the default IE error page, the browser instead is redirected to advertising pages.

As you can see, none of these programs are particularly malicious, but they all install without your express consent and in some fashion cause Internet Explorer to perform differently from what you may intend. They're all badware, and should not be welcome on your system.

Sizing the Problem

You've no doubt read about various computer viruses making their way around the Internet; you may even have known someone who was the victim of a virus or spyware infection. With all these malicious programs out there, what's the risk of your computers becoming infected?

How Big Is the Virus Threat?

Given that a single computer virus can infect millions of individual computers, the threat of virus infection is real and significant. The United States Department of Justice estimated that

34% of all computers in 2005 were infected with computer viruses. Assuming that there were approximately 500 million computers in use worldwide at that time, this means that more than 150 million computers were victims of virus attacks. That's a big number.

The threat is even greater for the corporate world, where a single infected computer can spread the virus among the entire corporate network. The 2007 CSI Survey found that 52% of responding firms had been hit by viruses the preceding year, making viruses the number-two overall threat (behind insider abuse of Internet access). And organizations don't get hit just once; Computer Economics says that the typical organization experiences five malware events per year. This figure rises to 10 events per year for organizations with over 5,000 desktop computers.

And here's the kicker: Every computer infected costs money to get up and running again. We're talking real money, measured in terms of downtime, lost data, and the cost of disinfection and repair. According to Computer Economics' *2007 Malware Report*, the worldwide cost attributed to malware infection totaled $13.3 billion in 2006. (Figure 19.2 details the financial impact of these attacks over a ten-year period.) The only good news is that the damage is starting to decrease, thanks to the impact of anti-spyware technology.

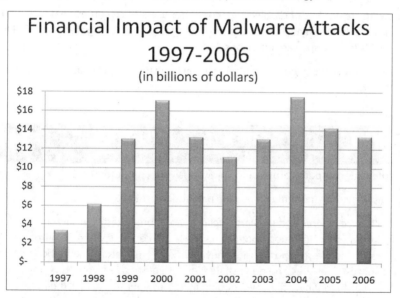

Figure 19.2
The cost of malware infection, as reported by Computer Economics (www.computereconomics.com).

{ P E R S O N A L   E X P E R I E N C E }

For years now, the common wisdom has been that Apple computers are less prone to virus attack than Windows-based computers. That may have been true in the past, but is less true now. It's not because the Apple OS is inherently more secure than Windows; either operating system can be easily exploited. It's more an issue of effort versus reward. In years past, the installed base of Apple computers was simply too small to interest virus writers. But as Apple has increased both its market and number of users, the Macintosh has become a more appealing target. Hence the rise in Mac-based viruses in recent years—although the majority of new viruses continue to be targeted at Windows-based computers.

How Big Is the Spyware Threat?

If you thought the virus threat was big, consider the incidence of spyware infection.

A 2005 study by America Online and the National Cyber-Security Alliance found that 61% of users' PCs were infected by some form of spyware. Of these users, 92% reported they did not know of the presence of this spyware.

Even more startling, Webroot Software estimates that 9 out of 10 computers connected to the Internet are infected with spyware. And PCSecurityNews.com states that an infected PC has, on average, 24.4 spyware programs surreptitiously installed. That's a lot of spyware!

All this spyware creates lots of problems for computer users. Microsoft estimates that 50% of all PC crashes are due to spyware. Dell confirms the problem, reporting that 20% of all technical support calls involve spyware infections.

So, like the virus problem, spyware represents a real issue for computer users—and one with practical consequences.

Is It Safe?

In a world rife with computer viruses and spyware, is your computer safe?

The short answer is, no—not unless you take precautions, that is.

Given the incidence of virus and spyware infection, an unprotected computer is a computer at high risk for some sort of infection. Your risk decreases, of course, if you refrain from risky behavior. If you avoid file-sharing websites, never click on email attachments, don't download files from suspicious websites, and don't share files with other users, your risk is minimized. On the other hand, indiscriminate file downloading increases your risk; in fact, the more interaction you have with other computers (over a network, on the Internet, or via any sort of removable media), the higher your risk for infection.

Let's face it. The only way your computer will be completely safe is if it's completely isolated. That means not connecting it to a network or the Internet, and never sharing files of any sort with other users. For most of us that sort of isolation is simply impractical, which means we have some risk of virus and spyware infection.

Fortunately, you can reduce your risk of infection by minimizing your risky behavior and by using a combination of anti-virus and anti-spyware utilities. To learn more about reducing your risks, read on to Chapter 20, "Defending Against Computer Viruses," and Chapter 21, "Avoiding Spyware."

Defending Against Computer Viruses

After reading the previous chapter, you should be convinced that the threat represented by computer viruses is a real one, and that your PC may be at risk of contracting a potentially destructive infection. What can you do to reduce your risk, and prevent future attacks?

Fortunately, there's a lot you can do to protect your system. And, if you follow all the advice in this chapter, you can greatly reduce your risk of being infected by most known types of viruses.

How Do You Know Whether Your Computer Is Infected?

Here's the big question: How do you know whether your computer system has been infected with a virus?

In general, whenever your computer starts acting different from normal, it's possible that you have a virus. For example, you might see strange messages or graphics displayed on your computer screen or find that normally well-behaved programs are acting erratically. You might discover that certain files have gone missing from your hard disk or that your system is acting sluggish—or failing to start at all. You might even find that your friends are receiving emails from you that you never sent, or that you're getting returned emails from people you've never heard of (a sure sign that your computer has been hijacked to send out reams of spam messages).

If your computer exhibits one or more of these symptoms—especially if you've just downloaded a file from the Internet or received a suspicious email message—the prognosis is not good. Your computer is probably infected.

> > > **N O T E**

If you experience some or all of these symptoms but find you don't have a virus on your system, it's possible that you have spyware installed, instead. Learn more in Chapter 21, "Avoiding Spyware."

Preventing Virus Attacks with Safe Computing

Here's the good news. Even though viruses are infecting millions of computers daily, you can take some simple steps to reduce your risk of infection. In fact, most virus protection is simple common sense; a little effort on your part will have major impact on the security of your system.

That said, the only sure-fire way to shield your system from computer viruses is to completely cut off all contact with other computers. That means no Internet connection, no sharing files via CD or USB memory drive, no connecting to a home or office network. In today's connected world, however, none of these things is practical.

So know this: Because you're not going to completely quit doing any of these activities, you'll never be 100% safe from the threat of computer viruses. There are, however, some steps you can take to reduce your risk. Let's look at a few.

Don't Open Email Attachments

Most virus infections today are spread via email. The virus is typically encased in a file attached to an email message; when you click to view or open the file, you launch the virus—and your computer is automatically infected.

To that end, the best way to reduce your risk of virus infection is to never open email attachments. Never. Especially from people you don't know.

But you also shouldn't open attachments from people you *do* know, if you aren't expecting them. That's because some viruses can hijack the address book on an infected PC, thus sending out infected email that the owner isn't even aware of.

So any email attachment is suspect, unless you were explicitly expecting it from a trusted user. Click on any other attachment, and chances are your computer will be infected.

C A U T I O N

If you remember nothing else from this chapter, remember this: *Never open an unexpected file attachment.* Period!

Don't Open Files Sent via Instant Messaging

The previous advice goes for any files sent to you via instant messaging. IM is a growing source of virus infection, if only because users (especially younger ones) are naturally trusting of other users.

This becomes more of a problem as you grow your friends or buddies list; if you have a hundred friends, it's difficult to know whether an incoming message comes from a friend or from a stranger. And even if the IM purports to come from a friend, it could come from someone posing as your friend, or from your friend's computer that has already been hijacked by the virus.

Bottom line: Don't accept any files sent to you via instant messaging. If a trusted friend really wants to send you a file, ask him to email it to you—and then use normal caution before opening it.

Don't Click IM or Chat Links

While we're on the subject of instant messaging, here's another bit of common sense that can greatly reduce your risk of virus infection. If a someone you don't know sends you a link to another site while you're instant messaging or in a chat room, don't click it! Nine times out of ten, this link either directly downloads a virus file to your PC or takes you to a website that has plenty of surreptitiously-infected files to download. In any case, ignore the unsolicited links and you'll be a lot safer.

Don't Execute Files Found in Newsgroups or Message Boards

Email and instant messaging are not the only channels for downloading virus infected files. You can find plenty of infected files in web message boards, blogs, and USENET newsgroups. For this reason, resist downloading programs you find in these channels; although many are safe, some are not.

Don't Download Files from Suspect Websites

There are lots of websites out there that hold infected files. The owners of these sites are just waiting for naïve users to download the files, so that their PCs can become infected.

For this reason, you should avoid downloading files from sites with which you're not familiar. Instead, download files only from reliable file archive websites, such as Download.com (www.download.com) and Tucows (www.tucows.com), or from known sites that offer software for sale, such as Apple.com and Microsoft.com. These sites scan all their files for viruses before they're available for downloading. It's the only safe way to download files from the Internet.

Limit Your Sharing of Removable Media

In the old days (before the Internet, anyway), the most common way for your computer to get infected was through files shared through some form of removable media. Back in the day, this meant floppy disks or Zip disks; today, the preferred media are more likely to be data CDs or DVDs, or files stored on portable USB storage devices.

The logic is simple. Any file you receive has the potential to carry a computer virus. It doesn't matter what that file looks like (its filename and extension) or who gave it to you, the bottom line is that you don't know where that file came from. If you run that file on your system—either from the storage device or after you've saved it to your computer's hard disk—any malicious code contained within can infect and potentially trash your system.

To that end, same advice applies now as it did twenty years ago: You should share disks, memory sticks, and files only with users you know and trust. (And make sure you scan the files in question with an anti-virus program before you open them on your computer.)

Or, to be completely safe, don't accept *any* files given to you on any portable storage medium.

Display and Check File Extensions

Certain types of files can carry virus infections; certain types of files can't. You need to know which files are potentially dangerous and which aren't, which you can by consulting the file type data in Table 20.1.

Table 20.1   Types of Files that Can and Can't Carry Computer Viruses

Safe File Types	Unsafe File Types
BMP	BAT
GIF	COM
JPG	DOC
MP3	DOT
MPEG	EXE
PDF	INF
QT	JS
TIF	REG
TXT	SCR
WAV	SYS
WMA	VB
	VBE
	VBS
	XLS
	XLW

CAUTION!!!

You should also avoid Zip files, as they can contain compressed files of any type—including executable files.

Of course, to guard against the riskier file types, you need to see what types of files you're dealing with. Unfortunately, since Windows 95, the Windows operating system's default configuration turns off the display of file extensions. When you look at a list of files in My Computer or My Documents, all you see is the main part of the filename, *not* the extension; you'll see something like **my picture file**, but not know whether it's **my picture file.jpg**, **my picture file.doc**, or **my picture file.exe**.

The solution to this dilemma is to reconfigure Windows to display file extensions—which you can do via the Folder Options applet (View tab) in the Windows Control Panel. Then, and only then, can you carefully examine the extension of any file before you open it.

> > > NOTE

One of the more common Trojan activities is to disguise a bad file type as a safe file type. There are many ways to do this, but the most common is the double-dot, or double-extension, exploit. This is accomplished by adding a .jpg or .txt to the first part of the filename, before the real extension. You end up with a name like **thisfile.jpg.exe**, which, if you're not fully alert, might appear to be a safe file. This exploit is further exacerbated by the inclusion of spaces after the middle extension, like this:

thisfile.jpg   .exe.

In some instances, the last part of the filename—the *real* extension—gets pushed off the screen, so you don't see it and you think you're opening a safe file.

Use Anti-Virus Software

In addition to all the safe computing practices just discussed, you need to protect your system with a good anti-virus program. This is so important that I devote the following section to the topic—so read on to learn more.

Protecting Your System with Anti-Virus Software

If you're serious about protecting your computer against viruses, worms, and Trojan horses, it's essential that you install and use an anti-virus software program. Anti-virus programs vigilantly guard your system for any viruses that might arrive via file download or email attachment, scan all the files on your system for hint of infection, and either clean or delete any files that have been found to be infected.

If your computer is connected to any network or the Internet, or if you share files with any other users, you must install an anti-virus program on your system. To not do so is to expose your computer to an unacceptable level of risk.

How Anti-Virus Programs Work

Most anti-virus programs perform several different types of checks on the files found on your computer's hard disk—and on files you try to copy to your hard disk. These checks are typically done on some sort of schedule, either daily or weekly, and whenever a new file is introduced to your system.

What kinds of scans does a typical anti-virus program perform? Here's the short list:

- **Signature scanning**—This is the most common type of anti-virus scan. With signature scanning, the program compares the files on your system against the code signatures of known viruses. (The code signatures are stored in the program's virus definition database, which must be kept up to date on a regular basis.)

- **Heuristic scanning**—Signature scanning is great for finding known viruses; but what do you do about new viruses that haven't yet made it into the program's virus definition database? This is where heuristic scanning comes in; it's a way to scan for new and unknown viruses, before they become well known, by looking for certain instructions or commands that are not found in normal application programs.

- **Real-time scanning**—Often called "dynamic system monitoring," this simply means that the anti-virus program is always turned on, working in the background to catch any infected file that may be copied or downloaded to your system. Real-time scanning checks all new files as they arrive, whether they come from data CDs, email attachments, instant messaging, or network or Internet downloads.

- **Email scanning**—Speaking of email, most anti-virus programs make a point of dynamically scanning all files attached to email messages—the better to catch those viruses and worms disguised as email attachments.

- **Script scanning**—This type of scan specifically looks for script viruses, whether written in ActiveX, JavaScript, or a similar language.

- **Macro scanning**—This type of scanning moves beyond executable and script files to examine document files (from Word, Excel, and similar programs) for macro viruses.

Choosing an Anti-Virus Program

A bevy of anti-virus programs is on the market today. Most programs are targeted at the home or small business market, although many programs and services also exist that are better suited for larger organizations and corporations.

As noted, most of these programs work in a similar fashion, detecting known viruses and protecting your system against new, unknown viruses. These programs check your system for viruses each time your system is booted and can be configured to check any programs you download from the Internet. They're also used to disinfect your system if it becomes infected with a virus.

The most popular anti-virus programs for the home and small business include the following:

- AVG Anti-Virus (www.grisoft.com)
- CA Anti-Virus (www.ca.com)
- ESET NOD32 Anti-virus (www.eset.com)
- F-PROT Anti-virus (www.f-prot.com)
- F-Secure Anti-Virus (www.f-secure.com)
- Kaspersky Anti-Virus (www.kaspersky.com)
- McAfee VirusScan Plus (www.mcafee.com)
- Norman Anti-virus & Antispyware (www.norman.com)
- Norton Anti-virus (www.symantec.com)
- Panda Anti-virus (www.pandasecurity.com)
- Trend Micro Anti-virus plus AntiSpyware (www.trendmicro.com)
- Vexira Anti-virus (www.centralcommand.com)
- Windows Live OneCare (onecare.live.com)

< < < T I P

Some of these programs combine virus and spyware protection. Other options to consider are the full-blown "security suites" offered by many of the same companies, which combine virus protection with other forms of Internet security.

All these programs do a good job—although their prices vary somewhat. Some programs are sold for a one-time price but require additional subscriptions (beyond the first year) to receive updated definitions; others are sold on a yearly subscription basis. For example, AVG Anti-Virus is available in a free edition (free.grisoft.com) that offers basic protection that's perfect for most home users; Norton Anti-virus offers more functionality but costs $39.99 for a one-year subscription; and Windows Live OneCare costs $49.95 per year—although you can use it on up to three different PCs, which makes it a real bargain for multiple-PC households.

{PERSONAL EXPERIENCE}

Which of these programs do I personally recommend? Well, I'll buck the trend and not recommend the industry leading programs, Norton Anti-virus and McAfee VirusScan Plus; both of these programs have caused problems with various computers of mine over the years, typically by interfering with normal program operation. In essence, I find these two programs overly intrusive. The two programs I'm currently using (on different computers) are AVG Anti-Virus Free Edition, a lean and mean yet effective little program, and Windows Live OneCare, which I find quite cost-effective for small network use. I've yet to experience significant compatibility problems with either of these two programs—and they both do the virus-catching job as advertised.

Examining Corporate Anti-Virus Programs

In addition to these consumer products, there are many products tailored to the large corporate market. Like their consumer cousins, all these programs feature aggressive virus scanning and detection; in addition, many of these programs also include other Internet security features, such as email spam control and content filtering.

The most popular of these enterprise anti-virus products include the following:

- AVG Anti-Virus Network Edition (www.grisoft.com)
- CA Anti-Virus for the Enterprise (www.ca.com)
- ESET NOD32 Anti-virus Business Edition (www.eset.com)
- F-PROT AVES (www.f-prot.com)
- F-Secure Anti-Virus Enterprise Suite (www.f-secure.com)
- InterScan VirusWall (www.trendmicro.com)
- Kaspersky Enterprise Space Security (www.kaspersky.com)
- McAfee VirusScan Enterprise (www.mcafee.com)
- Norman Virus Control Business Edition (www.norman.com)
- Panda Security for Business (www.pandasecurity.com)
- Sophos Endpoint Security Control (www.sophos.com)
- Symantec Endpoint Protection (www.symantec.com)

Prices on these programs vary according to features offered and number of computers covered. Pricing is often on a "per seat" basis.

Using an Anti-Virus Program

Most anti-virus programs work in a familiar fashion—and are easy enough to figure out on their own. When you install the program, you typically configure it to run automatically, in the background, whenever your computer is turned on. Running in this fashion, the program scans any file you try to copy or download to your hard disk; any USB memory drives, floppy disks, or data CDs you insert in your system; and any files attached to email messages, instant messages, and the like. If a virus is found, the file isn't copied or downloaded, and you are alerted to the problem.

In addition to this automatic background scanning, all anti-virus programs also include full scans of files currently on your hard disk; this type of all-system scan finds any bad files that got through the first line of defense, and alerts you to the problem. You can perform this type of scan manually, or schedule scans on a regular basis. I recommend running automatic scans at least weekly, if not daily.

< < < **T I P**

> Running automatic scans during the overnight hours, when you're not otherwise using your PC, is always a good approach.

You also want to configure your anti-virus program to scan all incoming email messages and instant messages for infected attachments. If you have your anti-virus software scanning your attachments, it becomes safer to open those attachments that pass muster (although still not recommended, in general). If an attachment is found to contain a virus, your anti-virus program blocks the download of the file and alerts you of the infected message. The infected file never makes it to your hard disk, and your system remains safe.

Keeping Your Anti-Virus Program Up to Date

Every anti-virus program includes a built-in database of virus definitions. You need to configure your program to periodically go online and download the latest virus definitions. Downloading once a week is a good idea; wait much longer than that, and you're likely to miss the definition for any "hot" virus circulating that week.

Most anti-virus software companies provide some number of definition updates free of charge, but then charge you for new updates, typically on a subscription basis. That's why purchasing these programs isn't a one-time thing; you have to keep paying to keep the programs up to date. (But it's necessary—and worth it.)

CAUTION!!!

Your anti-virus software is next to useless if you don't update it at least weekly. An outdated anti-virus program isn't capable of recognizing—and protecting against—the very latest computer viruses.

< < < TIP

It's also important to keep your operating system updated on a regular basis. For example, Microsoft constantly updates Windows to patch holes that can be exploited by viruses and other malware; without these patches, your system is at risk.

Recovering from a Virus Infection

If you discover that your computer has been infected with some sort of virus, the most common initial reaction is panic, often followed by despair. Although this type of reaction is understandable, it's important to know that catching a virus isn't the end of the world. Most virus infections can be successfully recovered from, with minimal effort on your part. You don't, as a friend of mine once thought, have to throw away your PC and buy a new one; with today's anti-virus tools, you can remove the virus from your system and recover most infected files with relative ease.

Preparing for Disaster

The ease and degree of recovery from a virus infection depends, of course, on the amount of disaster preparation you've done ahead of time. The more prepared you are, the less affected you'll be by most virus attacks. So before you get infected for the first time, you have to plan for what you'll do in the event of said infection.

Preparing for a virus infection is remarkably similar to preparing for any type of computer disaster, like a hard disk crash or total system failure. You want to have the proper tools on hand to get your system up and running again, and you want to have backups of any important data you could lose during the disaster.

In practice, that means following these disaster prevention steps:

1. Install anti-virus software on your system, and keep the installation CD and instruction booklet handy for future reference. If you downloaded the anti-virus program from the Internet, check the program's Help file to see whether the option exists to manually create such an emergency rescue CD.

2. Use your anti-virus software to create an emergency CD.

> > > N O T E

Many anti-virus programs enable the creation of an emergency rescue disk or CD, which can be used to dis-infect your system in the event of a catastrophic virus infection. Refer to your program's manual or help sys-tem for specific instructions on how to create this disk.

3. If your computer came with a Windows installation CD, keep it handy. If, on the other hand, your computer came with a full system restore CD (which restores your computer to condition it was at time of purchase), keep that handy, instead.

4. Keep the installation CDs for all your programs handy. Or, if you downloaded any of these programs direct from the Internet, keep the download information handy—so that you can re-download the programs without having to purchase them again.

5. Make a regular backup of your key document files, and keep the backup copies handy. (And, if you're using an external hard drive backup, don't keep the drive connected to your PC; it has less chance of being infected if it's not constantly connected.)

6. On Windows computers, create a regular System Restore Point (described later in this chapter), so that you can restore your system to an earlier working condition.

With these tools at your fingertips, you'll be ready to perform all the emergency operations necessary if and when your system falls victim to a virus attack.

Responding to an Infection—If Your System Is Still Running

If you think your system has been infected by a virus, here's the first and most essential thing to do:

DON'T PANIC!

That's right, the first action to take, if you think your system has been infected, is no action at all. Don't pound the keyboard, don't delete any files, don't run any software. And don't pull your hair out!

Just sit back, take a deep breath, and calm yourself down.

Then, after you're nice and calm, you can figure out what to do next—which mainly depends on what symptoms your system is exhibiting.

If your computer is still up and running—albeit slowly, or exhibiting some unusual behavior—you're in relatively good shape. Excellent shape, actually.

In this situation, all you have to do is use your anti-virus program to scan your system to see whether it really is infected, and then (if the news is bad), remove the infection.

Just follow these general steps:

1. Use your anti-virus software to run a manual scan of your system.

2. If infected files are found, make note of the type of infection, then try to clean or disin-fect those files.

3. If an infected file can't be cleaned, delete the file.

4. Reboot your system.

5. Go online to your anti-virus software's website and search for information about the type of virus identified during the scan; follow any additional instructions given on the site for completing the removal of that specific virus. (For example, you may be instructed to delete or edit certain entries in the Windows Registry.)

6. If you were forced to delete any document files, restore those files from a backup copy.

That's it. Most virus infections—those that don't crash your system, that is—can be dealt with simply and easily by your anti-virus software. Just run the software and follow all instructions, then look for additional information online.

> > > **NOTE**

For some viruses, a specific "fix file" may be available from your anti-virus programs website. These programs are specifically designed to remove a particular virus from your system, and supplement the normal virus-removal operation of your anti-virus software.

Responding to an Infection—If Your System Isn't Running

If a virus causes your computer to lock up or not start, then you have bigger problems. You'll need to get your system up and running again first, and then go through the necessary virus removal techniques. You'll also need to restore any files damaged during the infection—and you'll probably have some damaged files.

{ PERSONAL EXPERIENCE }

If you're not comfortable with troubleshooting technical problems, you may want to call in a friend or colleague who likes to tinker with PCs to track down and remove the virus from your PC. To that end, computer repair firms do a big business in virus cleaning; you can always take your computer to Best Buy's Geek Squad or Circuit City's Firedog staff to have your computer disinfected and put back in working order. In fact, this is the course of action I recommend for any non-technical friend or family member with a PC that is either slowed down or nonfunctional. Trying to lead a non-technical person through the troubleshooting process is frustrating at best and impractical in many cases. Better to have a pro do the work; that's what they get paid for.

Here are the general steps you need to take to get your computer back in working condition:

1. Turn off your computer.

2. Insert your anti-virus emergency rescue CD, if you have one, into your computer's CD drive.

3. Turn on your computer and opt to boot from the CD drive. (Some computers boot automatically from the CD if a bootable CD is present; others need to be configured, as such from the PC's startup menu.)

4. If your computer starts, follow the instructions in your anti-virus software manual to run an emergency scan operation. (With some anti-virus software, this emergency scan starts automatically when you boot from the emergency rescue disk.)

5. If your computer doesn't start with the anti-virus emergency rescue CD, turn off your computer, insert the Windows installation/startup CD (if you have it) in your computer's CD drive, then restart your computer. When your computer finishes booting, remove the Windows CD, replace it with the anti-virus emergency rescue CD, and proceed with the emergency scan operation.

> > > **N O T E**

Most new computers today no longer come with a Windows installation or startup CD. This is a cost-saving measure on the part of the hardware manufacturer, who can save a few pennies by not including this CD. Unfortunately, it makes your life tougher if you ever get infected with a virus or have major computer problems, almost necessitating a trip to the computer repair shop, which has its own Windows startup CDs it can use.

6. The emergency scan operation attempts to clean any infected files it finds. If it can't clean a file, it denies further access to the bad file.

7. When the emergency scan operation is finished, note any messages or information displayed onscreen, then remove the emergency rescue disk from your computer's CD drive and turn off your computer.

8. Make sure that the CD drive is empty, then restart your computer.

9. When your system finishes booting, launch the normal version of your anti-virus software and run a full-system scan.

10. If additional infected files are found, make note of the type of infection, then try to clean or disinfect those files; if an infected file can't be cleaned, delete the file.

11. Go online to your anti-virus software's website and search for information about the type of virus identified during the two scans; follow any additional instructions given on the site for completing the removal of that specific virus.

12. If you were forced to delete any document files, restore those files from a backup copy.

There are, unfortunately, a few possible kinks in this procedure. First, your anti-virus program may not come with an emergency rescue CD or let you manually create such a CD. If this is the case, consult with your anti-virus program's instruction manual or website on how to proceed.

Second, you may not have a Windows installation/startup CD, in that most new PCs no longer come with such media. If this is the case, you can try booting Windows into Safe mode (by pressing the designated key during the initial boot process) and then running your normal anti-virus program from there. If this isn't possible, you may be forced to take your PC to a repair shop to get it started properly.

Finally, you may not be able to restart your system normally after performing the emergency scan. This can happen if the emergency scan doesn't detect the infection, if the scan can't repair the infected files, or if key system files are irreparably damaged by the infection. If this happens to you, you have several possible courses of action you can take, in ascending order of magnitude:

- Use someone else's computer to access your anti-virus program's website and search for an alternative solution, if available.

- Restart your system from the Windows installation/startup CD, and use Windows System Restore to restore your system to a previous Restore Point. (See "Using Windows System Restore," later in this chapter, for detailed instructions.)

- Restart your system from the Windows installation/startup CD, and then reinstall the entire Windows operating system. (This is a fairly drastic and time-consuming measure.)

- Restart your system from the Windows installation/startup CD, reformat your computer's hard drive, reinstall the entire Windows operating system, reinstall all your software applications, and then restore all your document files from backup copies. (This is also a drastic measure, and one that will completely delete everything on the drive—including all your software programs and document files.)

It goes without saying that by the time you get to the last option, you've reached the point of last resort. It's probably worth consulting with a more experienced user or technical support person before you reach this point—there may be other, less extreme, options available that you haven't yet thought of.

Cleaning a Virus from Your System

Cleaning a virus from your system is normally as easy as running a system scan with your anti-virus software, and choosing the "clean" option when an infected file is found. This type of file cleaning, however, doesn't always work—and there are sometimes other options available.

Understanding File Cleaning Options

When you run a virus scan, your anti-virus software looks for any and all infected files on your hard drive. When an infected file is found, you're typically presented with three options:

- Clean/disinfect/repair

- Quarantine

- Delete

Just what are these options—and which should you choose?

Clean/Disinfect/Repair

The option to clean (or disinfect or repair—they're all different names for the same action) an infected file looks to be straightforward. When you select this option, your anti-virus software attempts to remove the virus code from the infected file. If the virus is "neat" about what it does, the infected code is easily identifiable and easily removed. All the anti-virus program has to do is cut the virus code out of the infected file, then save the altered file under its original filename. If all goes well, the cleaned file is identical to the original, uninfected file, and everything works fine.

Problems arise if the virus code *isn't* neat, and is jumbled in with the file's original code. This makes it difficult, if not impossible, to isolate and surgically extract the virus code without damaging the original file.

> > > **N O T E**

Other problems arise if the insertion of the virus code caused some of the file's original code to get chopped off. This can happen if the original file is supposed to be a certain size, and the virus code pushes the original code past the cut-off point. If any of the original code is lost, the "cleaned" file won't function properly.

Still, if you have the choice, you want to try to clean (or "disinfect") an infected file. If the file can't be successfully cleaned, then you turn to one of the remaining options.

Quarantine

The word "quarantine" is confusing to many users, even though it certainly sounds like it has something to do with viruses. In terms of computer viruses, when you select the quarantine option, you choose to isolate the infected file so that it can't be accessed by you or your computer system. This is done by moving the file to a special folder, to which normal access is blocked. The file is thus isolated, so it can't do further harm to your system.

Why should you choose to quarantine a file, rather than simply delete it? There are two possible reasons for choosing this option:

- You think the file has been infected by a relatively new virus. If this is the case, current cleaning techniques might not work, but as the anti-virus community learns more about the virus, more effective techniques might be developed. So you keep the infected file "on ice" until your anti-virus software is updated and the file can be better cleaned.

- You want to send a copy of the file to your anti-virus software company for more thorough analysis. This is a good idea if you've been infected by a new virus, or a new strain of an existing virus. The anti-virus software company can use the infected file to update its virus definition database, and thus help protect other users from the virus infecting your system.

If you have no intention of sending the infected file to the anti-virus software company, and doubt the file can ever be cleaned, then skip this option and just delete the thing.

< < < TIP

In my humble opinion, the only reason you might want to quarantine rather than delete a file is if the file contains unduplicable information and you have hope that some future development will enable you to save the information in the file. Otherwise, a quarantined file is next to useless; you might as well delete it and be done with it.

Delete

When you choose to delete an infected file, you remove it from your hard disk, simple as that. When a file is deleted, it can do no further harm, and it won't take up any valuable disk space.

Plus, deleting an infected file has a satisfying finality to it that might be the only pleasure you get out of this entire exercise.

Cleaning Specific Viruses

Some of the more common viruses have inspired anti-virus software companies to create virus-specific fixes. These fixes typically come in the form of a small software program that you download to your system and then run. The fix program then searches for and cleans any files infected by the particular virus, as well as makes any additional changes to your system— removing the virus' settings from the Windows Registry, for example.

These fix programs are great if you don't have any other anti-virus software installed on your system, and if you know you've been infected with a particular virus. In most cases, however, your regular anti-virus program does exactly the same job as the fix program—so running the program would be a duplication of effort.

Restoring Your System

Just cleaning a virus from your system might not be enough. If a virus damaged files to the extent that they had to be quarantined or deleted, you need to somehow restore those no-longer-usable files to your hard disk.

This task is made easier if you had the foresight to create backup copies of your data files. It's also easier if you're running any version of Windows distributed in the last ten years or so (since Windows Me), all of which include the nifty System Restore utility.

Before you try to restore any files, however, you need to know *what* files to restore. This is an easy task, if you take the time to write down the names of any files that your anti-virus software has to quarantine or delete. (Your anti-virus program should display the name of each infected file it finds; get out your pen and pencil and write down the names as they appear onscreen.)

After you know which files you need to restore, then you have to figure out what restoration methods to use:

- If the unusable files are document files—Word DOC files, Excel XLS or XLW worksheets, or even JPG picture files—you'll probably need to restore these files from the backup copies you (I hope) made.

- If the files are application files (typically EXE files for a particular software program), then you'll probably need to reinstall that entire piece of software.

- If the files are Windows system files (with a variety of extensions, including COM, DLL, DRV, EXE, and SYS), then you'll either need to use Windows System Restore to revert to a previously saved version, reinstall that particular file from your Windows installation CD, or reinstall the entire Windows operating system from your Windows installation CD.

Obviously, you should start with the easiest method first.

Restoring Backup Files

If you have the prescience to make a backup of your key data files on a regular basis, you can use your backup utility of choice (either Windows Backup or the utility included with your external hard drive) to restore the backup copies to your hard disk. Just follow the instructions in the backup utility to choose and restore specific files from a given backup set.

> > > **N O T E**

> Depending on when you made your backup, the backup copies you restore could be older than the files that were deleted. That might not be ideal, but it's better than having no backup at all.

Using Windows System Restore

In most cases, you make backup copies of your document files only—*not* of every file on your system. That's because when you count all the operating system and program files, there are just too many files to bother with. (And, besides, these files aren't constantly changing, as your document files are.)

If you're a Windows user, you have access to a handy utility called System Restore. This utility automatically restores key system files to the state in which they were before your problems, virus or otherwise, cropped up.

The way it works is that System Restore creates a "mirror" of key system files and settings (called a *restore point*) on a regular basis, whenever you install a new piece of software, or whenever you manually decide to do so. When something goes wrong on your system (like a virus eats some important system files, or resets essential settings), you can revert to a restore point from before the problem occurred, and very quickly put your system back in working order.

> > > **NOTE**

Be sure to close all programs before you use System Restore because Windows needs to be restarted when the process is complete.

If you're using Windows Vista, for example, follow these steps to use System Restore to return your system to a previous state:

1. Select Start, All Programs, Accessories, System Tools, System Restore.

2. When the System Restore window appears, as shown in Figure 20.1, click Recommended Restore to accept the recommend restore point.

3. To restore to a different point in time, click Choose a Different Restore Point and click Next.

4. If you opted to choose a different restore point, click a date from the list, then click Next.

5. When the confirmation screen appears, click Finish to begin the restore process.

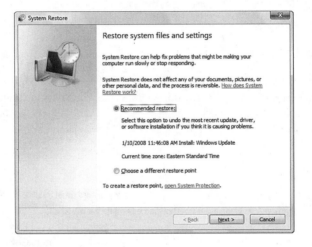

Figure 20.1
Restoring your system with Windows Vista's System Restore utility.

System Restore now goes to work, restoring your system files and settings to the way they were at the selected point in time. Note that this is a somewhat slow process, which could take a half hour or more to complete.

Reinstalling System Files

Unfortunately, System Restore doesn't restore *every* system file on your hard disk. This means that you still may need to manually install some Windows system files—if you can.

Some older versions of Windows let you browse the installation CD and search for individual files. If you can find the file you want, you can copy it from the installation CD to your hard drive.

Other versions of Windows let you browse the installation CD, but store all the system files (pre-installation) in compressed CAB-format files. Although you *can* extract single files from CAB files, you have to know which CAB file contains the file you want, and then use a CAB-extraction utility to pull out the individual file—which isn't a job for casual or inexperienced computer users.

Windows XP and Vista go one step further and make it pretty much impossible to browse the installation CD. This means that if you want to reinstall a single system file in Windows XP or Vista, you have to reinstall the entire operating system.

Fortunately, reinstalling Windows should restore all damaged or deleted system files, without harming any application or data files. Just insert your Windows installation CD and follow the instructions to affect a full installation.

> > > **N O T E**

> In some extreme instances—typically caused by destructive boot sector viruses—you may be forced to start from scratch and reformat your hard disk. If this happens to you, you'll lose all programs and data currently stored on the hard disk, and have to reinstall Windows and all the other programs you use.

Reinstalling Application Files

If a virus has damaged the files of a particular application, you probably won't be able to run that application at all—until you've replaced the damaged or deleted files, that is. With most applications, that means reinstalling the complete program from scratch. Get out your original application installation CD (or access the program's download site, if you downloaded it from the web) and follow the specific installation and setup instructions.

> > > **N O T E**

> Some programs may require you to delete the existing version of the program before you try installing it again. You can do this with Windows' Add or Remove Programs utility, accessible from the Windows Control Panel. After the uninstallation is complete, you can then install a fresh version of the program from the program's installation CD.

Is It Safe?

Can you completely protect your home or work PCs from computer viruses? No, not unless you completely isolate your system from all other computers and computer users—which means no file swapping, no networks, and no Internet. As I said earlier in this chapter, that's pretty much impractical in today's connected day and age.

So complete protection isn't possible. But pretty good protection is, assuming you use common sense in how you use your computer, and install (and keep up to date) one of the major anti-virus programs. In fact, common sense is probably more effective than an anti-virus program; if you follow safe computing practices, you may never download a virus to your computer for the anti-virus program to catch. When it comes to computer viruses, an ounce of prevention is definitely more valuable than a pound of cure.

Just remember that any file sent to you that you weren't expecting could contain a virus. Also be suspicious of links in unsolicited emails (and not only because of viruses; phishing is also a big issue in this regard), and of any website outside of the major download archives that offers files of any sort for free download—including and especially music swapping sites. Avoid these types of files and links and you'll significantly reduce your risk of virus infection.

Add a good anti-virus program to the mix, for safety's sake, and your risk factor will get close to that zero mark. You'll never be 100% safe, but the combination of smart computing and an anti-virus program provides a high degree of protection for most home and office users.

Avoiding Spyware

As you learned in Chapter 19, "Computer Viruses and Spyware: How Big a Problem," spyware is malicious software that installs itself on your computer system without your approval, and then sends your personal data back to some sort of central service. Adware is a special type of spyware that uses this collected data to serve up advertisements based on the personal data it spied on.

Although spyware is a lot like a computer virus, in that it invades your computer without invitation or approval, it's different enough not to be recognized by many anti-virus programs. To guard your system against spyware, then, you need to take discrete action in addition to what you do to avoid computer viruses. Spyware stands alone.

How do you avoid downloading spyware to your system—or remove it, after it's been installed? It's all about practicing smart computing and then using one or more anti-spyware programs. The combination should reduce your risk of falling victim to a spyware infection—and keeping your computer clean from the effects of such infection.

Do You Have Spyware on Your System?

Before we discuss avoiding new instances of spyware, let's take a moment to see whether you already have spyware installed on your computer system. It's certainly possible, especially if you visit file swapping websites.

Most spyware infections are recognizable by how they affect your system's performance. Put simply, spyware tends to slow down operations on most computers—and sometimes worse. Some spyware programs can cause Internet Explorer to freeze or not work properly; others may actually cause your computer to crash. So if your computer is acting slowly or suspiciously, the usual suspect is some sort of spyware infection.

In particular, take notice if your computer exhibits any or all of the following behaviors—all symptomatic of a spyware infection:

- Your computer runs slowly. Spyware is just another software program, and the more programs you have running at one time, the slower your computer runs. Spyware can be especially draining, making its presence known via sluggish system performance.

- You experience other unusual problems with Windows, including system freezes and crashes. These are caused by spyware programs behaving badly around other legitimate programs.

- Your computer has a mind of its own. Spyware doesn't just run in the background; it also performs a variety of operations that make it look as if your computer is being remote controlled. If your computer sends emails to people in your address book without your knowledge or permission, or shows a lot of hard disk activity or Internet access when you're not actively using it, all that activity could be a symptom of the spyware doing its thing in the background.

- Your computer's hard disk and/or network activities lights constantly blink or stay lit. This indicates a lot of hard drive activity or Internet access. Unless you yourself are causing this activity, it's likely due to spyware doing what it does best—reporting back to the mother ship, without your explicit approval.

- You get a lot of returned or bounced back emails. Many spyware programs take control of your email program and use it to mail out loads of spam—without your knowledge or permission. A raft of returned emails that you don't remember sending could be the aftereffect of a spyware-induced spam attack.

> > > NOTE

Some spyware programs don't control your email program per se, but instead "borrow" your address book to send spam from another computer to users in your address book.

- You find that your web browser's home page has been changed to another site, without your approval. This is a common trick of many spyware programs, to force you to view a particular website.

- You see a strange new toolbar in your web browser. Many spyware programs install such toolbars for their "sponsor" sites.

- When you perform a web search, you end up at some strange site. Again, a favorite trick of spyware developers is to send you to a site of their choosing whenever you perform a search.

- If you try to go to a website that doesn't exist, instead of seeing the browser's typical "404 error" page, you see the page for a previously unknown website.

- Your find that your anti-virus and firewall programs have been turned off, without your knowledge. Again, this is how spyware programs try to stay "alive" on your PC.

- You get a lot of unexpected pop-up windows onscreen. Spyware likes to open pop-up windows, so if you see a lot of the things, you know the cause. (For example, some adware displays pop-up advertisements every few minutes, like clockwork.)

- Windows displays strange icons in your taskbar or new shortcuts on your desktop. These are signs that a new spyware program has been installed on your computer.

- You see one or more strange new sites in the Favorites section of your web browser. These favorites are typically put there when a spyware program has been installed on your PC.

- You find new programs in the Add or Remove Software utility in the Windows Control Panel. Almost all programs installed on your computer should be able to be uninstalled via this utility, so new programs listed there are most certainly spyware.

- When you try to start your favorite anti-spyware program, it doesn't launch. Many spyware programs block access to their nemesis anti-spyware programs.

- You receive frequent alerts from your firewall program about some unknown program or process trying to access the Internet. This one's easy; the offending program is the spyware program.

- The Java console appears in the Windows task bar even though you haven't recently run any Java software. Obviously, the spyware program is the one that ran Java.

- If you're using a dial-up Internet connection, you get a phone bill with numerous 1-900 calls you didn't make. Some older spyware programs contained an "auto dial" component that directed the infected computer to dial said numbers, thus racking up fees paid to the "sponsor" company.

- You appear to be the victim of identity theft. Spyware, by definition, is software that collects your personal data and then sends it back to the spyware companies or their surrogates for use in identity theft and other such crimes. If you're checking your credit card regularly and find some irregularities, it's possible that those irregularities were caused by the data breach resulting from the data purloined by the spyware program.

As you can see, many of these symptoms are similar to what you might expect from a computer virus infection. Other symptoms are wholly unique to the world of spyware. In any instance, if your computer exhibits one or more of these symptoms, it's time to run an anti-spyware program—which is discussed later in this chapter.

> > > **N O T E**

A single spyware program on your computer is unlikely to affect system performance. Unfortunately, how-ever, the most at-risk computers tend to be infected with multiple spyware programs; it's the combination of all these programs running at the same time that can make your computer slow to a crawl.

Avoiding Spyware-Infested Websites and Programs

The best way to avoid a spyware infestation is to defeat the spyware at the source—by not installing it in the first place. If you know where you're likely to find spyware programs, you can avoid those sites, and thus avoid installing spyware on your system.

That said, you should know that you may inadvertently agree to install some adware pro-grams. That's because the installation of these programs is often optional when you install the host program with which the adware is bundled; if you look closely, you'll see that you're given the option *not* to install these so-called "companion programs" when you install the host pro-gram. Check (or uncheck) the proper box on the installation screen, and you avoid installing the adware.

> > > **N O T E**

Some of the biggest offending sites for piggyback adware are file-sharing and illegal music download sites, such as Kazaa and LimeWire. In many instances, adware is piggybacked onto the official file sharing soft-ware you have to download to use the site; you may or may not have the option of declining the installa-tion of the adware.

Other adware programs, however, are *not* optional components; they install automatically when you install the host program. If you know that a particular program includes piggyback adware, and you don't have the option not to install the adware, then you can always opt not to install the main software itself. Why, in the end, do you want to deal with a company that allows other companies to secretly exploit its users?

Of course, much spyware is installed entirely without your knowledge or approval. In most instances, you're tricked into clicking a link in an email or on a website that automatically installs the spyware. And some of these links are trickier than others.

Particularly annoying are those sites that display a window that looks like a standard Windows dialog box. When you click the Cancel button to close the dialog box, you instead install a spy-ware program. (Better to click the "X" in the top-right corner of the window, which should close the window without downloading any spyware.)

Also effective are sites that display what appears to be a pop-up window advertising an anti-spyware program. The ad says something along the lines of "your system may be infected—click here to remove all spyware from your system." Instead of removing spyware, the program you install is itself a spyware program, and your system is newly infected.

The takeaway here is to be careful what links you click and what sites you download from. The only truly safe download sites are reputable sites like Tucows.com and Download.com; most other sites offering free downloads also feature piggyback adware and spyware as part of the package. And when you do download a file, read the user agreement first—you may be able to opt out of installing piggyback adware. In other words—look before you click!

Using Anti-Spyware Programs

If you're like most users, however, you've already installed some spyware on your computer. It's good to get diligent about downloading in the future, but what do you do about any spyware programs already installed on your system today?

Fortunately, several companies offer anti-spyware programs that scan your system for known spyware. These programs work much the same way that anti-virus programs detect and remove computer viruses. Anti-spyware programs are designed to identify any and all spyware programs lurking on your computer, and also uninstall the offending programs and remove their entries from the Windows Registry.

Know, however, that spyware is different enough from a computer virus that most anti-virus programs don't detect spyware—and vice versa. Although there are some exceptions (some of the major anti-virus programs have added anti-spyware components), you probably need to install an anti-spyware program *in addition to* an anti-virus program.

Choosing an Anti-Spyware Program

The most popular anti-spyware programs today include the following:

- Ad-Aware (www.lavasoftusa.com)
- CounterSpy (www.sunbelt-software.com)
- ParetoLogic Anti-Spyware (www.paretologic.com/products/paretologicas/)
- Spybot Search & Destroy (www.safer-networking.org)
- Spyware Doctor (www.pctools.com/spyware-doctor/)
- Webroot Spy Sweeper (www.webroot.com)
- Windows Defender (www.microsoft.com/athome/security/spyware/software/)
- ZoneAlarm Anti-Spyware (www.zonelabs.com)

Most of these are low-cost (under-$30) programs, and many of them are free. In addition to these standalone programs, some of the major Internet security suites, such as Norton Internet Security and the McAfee Internet Security Suite, include anti-spyware modules. Many of these companies also offer enterprise versions of their programs, specifically designed for use in larger organizations.

{PERSONAL EXPERIENCE}

I particularly like Windows Defender, which is included as part of the Windows Vista operating system or available for free download from Microsoft's website. That said, there is so much spyware circulating today that I find that no single one of these programs will catch it all. To that end, I typically use *two* anti-spyware programs, one after another. This approach, while somewhat duplicative, does a much better job of rooting out all the offending spyware on my system.

How Anti-Spyware Programs Work

Spyware, after it is installed on your system, runs in the background, hidden from view, and spies on all your computer-related activities. To determine whether a program is spyware, most anti-spyware programs check to see whether a program performs some or all of the following activities:

- Runs processes on your computer without notifying you
- Collects or communicates your personal information and behavior without your consent
- Attempts to circumvent the security features on your computer
- Undermines your computer's performance

In addition, most anti-spyware programs check for all programs listed in the company's database of malicious software. So if a program is recognized as spyware, it is flagged by the anti-spyware program.

Like an anti-virus program, an anti-spyware program can be configured to either manually or periodically scan your system for infection. If a spyware program is found, it is automatically quarantined or uninstalled from your system.

< < < TIP

Another way to cleanse your system of spyware and adware programs is to manually search your computer for such programs, and then use Windows' Add or Remove Programs utility to manually remove the programs. To this purpose, you can find lists of known spyware programs at SpywareGuide (www.spywareguide.com/product_list_full.php) and StopBadware.org (www.stopbadware.org).

In addition, several of these programs provide real-time protection against the download and installation of new spyware programs. This works much like the similar function in anti-virus programs; all new files and incoming network/Internet traffic is scanned for spyware signatures, with all offending programs blocked from being installed.

And, as most anti-spyware programs in part depend on a database of known spyware programs, it's important to keep this database of spyware definitions up-to-date. You'll need to configure your program to update its list of definitions on a regular basis—weekly at the least, daily if possible.

Removing Stubborn Spyware Programs

An anti-spyware program should do a decent job of finding and deleting most spyware programs. Some spyware, however, is more stubborn, resisting the anti-spyware programs' simple removal techniques.

Savvy spyware authors devise their programs to work in pairs—that is, to either run two instances of the program, or to launch two similar (but differently named) executable files. When an anti-spyware program terminates or removes one running process, the other one re-creates and reinstalls the killed program.

Similarly, some spyware detects any attempt to remove its key in the Windows Registry, immediately adding the deleted keys. This keeps the program on your system, even if you think you've deleted it.

Most of these stubborn spyware programs can be more effectively deleted by booting your system into Safe mode. When running in Safe mode, your anti-spyware program stands a better chance of avoiding the re-infestation techniques and deleting all remnants of the offending program.

So if you think you've deleted a spyware program only to see it crop back up almost immediately, you need to reboot your computer and enter Safe Mode on the restart. When the text-based startup screen displays (just before the Windows welcome screen appears), press the F8 key on your keyboard, and then select Safe Mode from the resulting startup menu. Then, when you're running in Safe mode, launch your anti-spyware program and try once again to delete the offending program; you should have more success.

> > > **N O T E**

Safe mode is a special mode of operation, typically used for troubleshooting startup problems, that loads Windows in a minimal configuration. This minimal configuration runs Windows as cleanly as possible, with a low-resolution display and without any unnecessary device drivers or software.

Securing Your Web Browser

Many spyware programs take advantage of technologies included in the Internet Explorer web browser, as well as known security holes and exploits in the browser. To that end, some experts recommend reducing your spyware risk by switching from Internet Explorer to a less-exploited browser, such as Mozilla Firefox. Although no web browser is completely secure, it is true that most spyware authors target Internet Explorer because of its huge installed base. Using a different browser reduces your risk to some degree.

If you're a dyed-in-the-wool IE user, you can still reduce your risk by turning off some of the most exploited technologies in the browser, such as cookies, ActiveX, Java, and other scripts and plug-ins. I'll show you how.

Setting Security Levels by Zone

Assuming that you're using Internet Explorer 7 or later, start by clicking the Tools button and selecting Internet Options. (On previous versions of IE, click the Tools menu and select Internet Options.) When the Internet Options dialog box appears, select the Security tab, shown in Figure 21.1. This tab lists the various security zones used by Internet Explorer. The key is to set a high level of protection for each zone, thus blocking most spyware offenders.

Figure 21.1
Setting security levels for Internet Explorer's zones.

Start with the Internet zone, which is the zone that IE uses by default for all new websites visited. Click the Internet icon and then drag the Security Level slider to High; this disables ActiveX, Active scripting, and Java, which makes your browser much more secure.

> > > **N O T E**

You can configure even more options for this or any other zone by clicking the Custom Level button. This displays the Security Settings dialog box, which lets you disable all ActiveX controls, enable prompting before a file is downloaded, disable script controls, and the like.

Of the other zones, the Trusted Sites zone is the one that most warrants your attention. This is a list of sites that you explicitly trust; you can add sites to this zone by clicking the Sites button and adding a site's URL to the list. I recommend setting the security level for the Trusted Sites zone to Medium-High.

Turning Off Cookies

Because many spyware programs use cookies to track your online behavior (and then report that behavior back to the mother ship), additional protection from spyware comes from disabling IE's Cookies function. You do this from the Privacy tab in the Internet Options dialog box, shown in Figure 21.2.

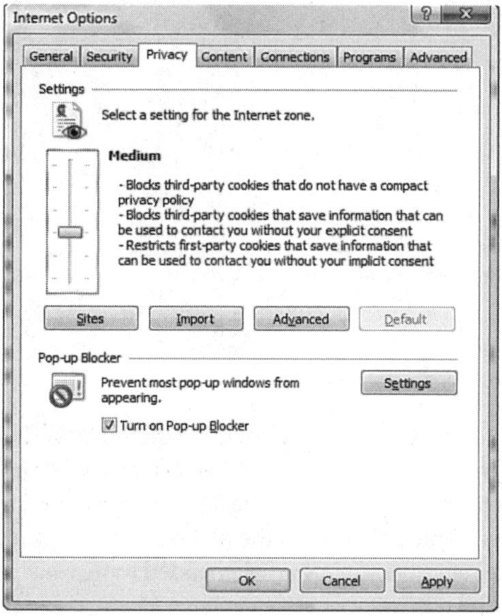

Figure 21.2
Managing cookies in Internet Explorer.

> > > **N O T E**

Learn more about cookies in Chapter 16, "Covering Your Tracks Online."

By default, IE's cookie management is set to the Medium setting, which doesn't block a lot of cookies. You can move the setting to High, which blocks all cookies that save information that can be used to contact you without your consent, but even that isn't enough for some people.

For the most protection, click the Advanced button and, when the Advanced Privacy Settings dialog box appears (shown in Figure 21.3), select Override Automatic Cookie Handling; you should also select Prompt for Both First-Party and Third-Party Cookies. This configures IE to prompt you each time a site tries to place a cookie on your machine. If the cookie is useful for access to a given site, you can okay the cookie; if it isn't, you can block it.

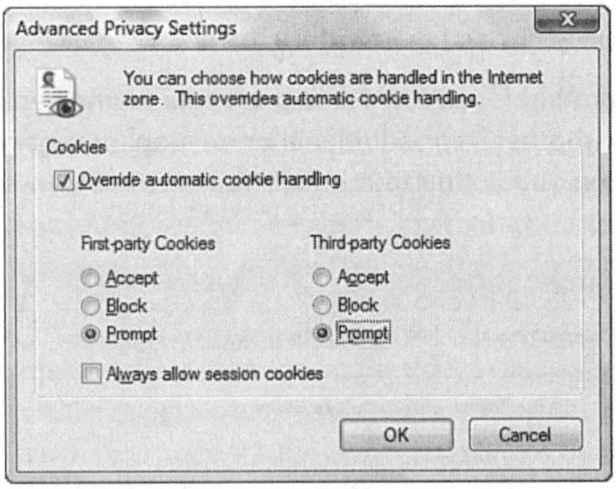

Figure 21.3
Configuring IE to prompt before installing any new cookies.

Deactivating Other Risky Features

Additional risky features can be turned off by selecting the Advanced tab in the Internet Options dialog box, shown in Figure 21.4. I recommend unchecking the Enable Third-Party Browser Extensions option, which blocks the installation of unwanted toolbars and Browser Helper Objects (BHOs). You should also check the Always Show Encoded Addresses option; this forces IE to display spoofed URLs in a special encoded form, which makes it less likely to confuse these URLs with the real URLs.

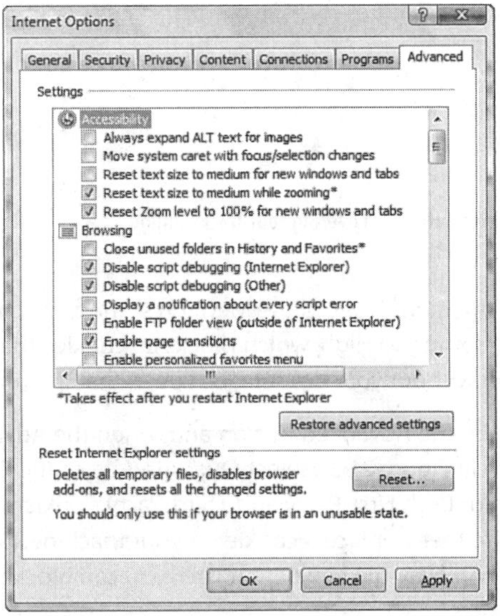

Figure 21.4
Configuring Advanced options in Internet Explorer.

Blocking Spyware Domains

After spyware is installed on your system, one way to keep it from functioning is to keep the program from reporting back to the host website. If you know the name of the server(s) that your adware contacts, you can use site blocking or filtering software to block access to the addresses of these servers, thus rendering the adware totally useless.

One way to do this is to route all outbound traffic to the ad server back to your own computer. This defeats all outbound communications from the adware. To do this, you have to edit (or, if it doesn't already exist, create) a file named **Hosts** (no file extension). On most recent Windows systems this file is in the Windows\system32\drivers\etc\ folder. Open this file and add the following lines:

```
127.0.0.1    adserver1.com
127.0.0.1    adserver2.com
```

And so on. The `127.0.0.1` references your computer; the `adserver1.com` should be the actual name of the adware server.

On Macintosh computers, the Hosts file is in the Preferences folder. The format of the file is similar, but slightly different:

```
adserver1.com    CNAME    127.0.0.1
adserver2.com    CNAME    127.0.0.1
```

Another way to do this is to add known spyware domains to the list of restricted sites in Internet Explorer. The best way to do this is to install the combination of the ZonedOut software program (www.funkytoad.com/content/view/15/33/) and the IE-SPYAD list (www.spywarewarrior.com/uiuc/resource.htm). You use ZonedOut to manage Internet Explorer's zones, and the IE-SPYAD list to add known spyware sites to the restricted sites zone. (In case it isn't clear, IE-SPYAD is a constantly updated list of sites and domains used by known spyware and adware companies.) This approach blocks spyware programs from using IE to contact their host sites, which keeps your private information private.

Is It Safe?

Spyware isn't nearly as damaging as computer viruses; spyware's intent isn't to take down your system, but rather to keep it up and running so it can report back to the mother ship all manner of personal information. To that end, you typically don't have to worry about spyware crashing your system—although it does often slow it down. No, the bigger concern is the information that the spyware reports back to its sponsoring company. Although this is often nothing more than a list of websites you visit (as is the case with most adware), it could be a lot worse.

All the more reason, then, to avoid spyware infestations when at all possible. Given the high rate of spyware infection, you might think this is a particularly difficult task. Fortunately, that isn't the case; it's just that most computer users don't behave in a particularly smart or safe fashion.

The easiest way to reduce your risk of spyware infection is to avoid those sites that are rife with spyware and adware—most notably, peer-to-peer file download and music sharing sites. I have to tell you, these sites are the bane of my existence; probably 90% of the spyware I encounter can be directly traced to these sites. Avoid this type of illegal file downloading and sharing, and your risk of installing spyware dramatically decreases.

Other types of sites can also distribute spyware, of course. You should, for example, avoid pornographic websites, as well as clicking the links in most spam emails (many of which link back to spyware download sites). In general, if you follow the tenets of safe computing discussed in Chapter 20, "Defending Against Computer Viruses," you'll also defend against spyware.

You can further reduce your risk by regularly scanning your system with a good anti-spyware program. As previously noted, I like Windows Defender, which is one of the few programs that run in the background to protect your system fulltime. Add a second anti-spyware program for even more protection, and you'll have a fairly low risk profile.

Let's look at this another way. If you practice safe computing and regularly run anti-spyware software, you can take your risk of infection to near zero. And that's a good thing.

On the other hand, if you or a family member (re: music-hungry teenager) are addicted to P2P music-sharing websites, you might as well resign yourself to dealing with a series of annoying and potentially harmful spyware infestations. Your risk increases dramatically if you frequent these spyware-riddled sites; just expect to be infected if you do a lot of illegal downloading. It would be better if you (or your teenager) forsook the P2P sites in favor of the much safer (and completely legal) commercial download sites, such as the iTunes Store, but I know how hard it can be to shake the free download habit.

So your risk can be either high or low, depending on your browsing and downloading behavior. It's totally in your hands—or, as I said, in the hands of any less safety-conscious teenagers in your household.

Computer Attacks: How Big a Problem?

I f you've read this far, you know about the many risks to your computer and to yourself in this digital world. You know about identity theft and data theft. You know about online fraud and click fraud. You know about email scams and spam. You know about online surveillance and online stalkers. You know about computer viruses and spyware.

What we haven't covered yet is perhaps the most dangerous problem you can encounter online. Maybe not the biggest risk, in terms of number of occurrences, but the thing that can literally destroy your entire computer system—or your company's network.

This ultimate threat to your system's safety and security comes when malicious individuals stage an attack on your computer or network. Attackers access your system via some sort of backdoor and then steal important data, delete files and folders, or use your computer to initiate additional attacks on other computers, networks, or websites. Particularly malevolent attackers can even flood your system with data requests and emails, overloading your system until it crashes or goes offline.

An Internet-based attack, then, is the thing that all computer users should fear. To that end, this chapter looks at what constitutes a computer attack, and how big your risk is of such an attack.

What Is a Computer Attack?

A computer attack is any operation executed with the intent to disrupt, deny, degrade, or destroy information on a computer or computer network. This type of attack typically takes place over the Internet, with the operation executed by a remote computer or a master computer controlling a network of hijacked zombie computers.

In most instances, computer attacks are directed at large computer networks or websites, typically by an individual with a grudge against the organization attacked. Malicious attacks against individual computers are more rare but not unheard of, again especially if the attacker has a grudge against the victim of the attack.

As defined, a computer attack can be designed to damage either the host computer or the data stored on that computer, or to steal the data stored on the computer. The intent of the attacker is clearly malicious; often no monetary benefit ensues to the attacker.

So if an attacker is of a mind to execute an attack on a particular computer system, just what sort of things can he do? If you think of a computer attack being something like a home invasion, you can see that the attacker has his choice of malicious activities. He can rob the victim, vandalize the property, assault or destroy the property, or hijack the property for his own (often criminal) use. Let's look at each of these types of attacks separately.

Robbery

Robbery is often a prime attack activity. In a computer attack, the robbery often takes the form of *data theft*, where the attacker steals valuable data stored on the system attacked— usernames, passwords, credit card numbers, back account numbers, and the like. With these numbers in hand, the attacker can then access all the compromised accounts and perform additional thefts, often resulting in an epidemic of identity theft.

> > > **N O T E**

We discussed data theft in more depth in Chapter 4, "Data Theft: How Big a Problem?"

Sometimes the robbery is more specific, a form of industrial espionage. Witness the attack in January 2008 on Dassault Systemes, a French software company. The hacker, codenamed ASTRA, gained entrance to one of the company's servers and thus the entire company network. After he was inside the network, he stole several confidential documents as well as a copy of the company's professional modeling software. The hacker then sold copies of the software over the Internet, costing the company in excess of $300 million in lost sales.

Vandalism

An attacker doesn't have to steal something to do damage. After he's inside a computer system, he can do all sorts of damage by deleting and altering valuable files—including the files that comprise the host's website.

Like real-world vandalism, computer vandalism can take many forms. To that end, we examine the three primary forms of computer vandalism separately: data destruction, data diddling, and website defacement.

Data Destruction

Data destruction is fairly straightforward. The attacker gains access to a computer system and starts deleting things. He deletes data files, program files, even the system files necessary to keep the host computer up and running. The damage comes from the missing files, which often can't easily be replaced.

< < < **T I P**

> A regular program of data backups can minimize the impact of data destruction—even though your system or network might need to be taken offline until the restore procedure can be completed.

Data Diddling

Data diddling is more insidious than data destruction. This type of vandalism occurs when the attacker enters a computer system and makes changes to selected files. He doesn't delete the files—he merely edits and corrupts the data in some fashion.

Imagine an attacker entering your company's employee database and making subtle changes to the employee salary field. When the next payday arrives, your employees notice that their paychecks aren't right—they're either paid a lot less or a lot more than they should be. It could take weeks, if not months, to straighten out the problem, all because the vandal diddled with your data.

Or how about an attacker targeting your customer database, so that your next customer mailing includes a variety of rude comments to your valued customers? Or maybe it's the financial files that get diddled—throwing off your next financial statements. Or maybe the product photos in your marketing database have been replaced with nude pictures of Jenna Jameson.

You get the idea. Data diddling can do tremendous damage, and it isn't always quickly—or easily—noticed. It might take some time for you to discover all the diddled data, and even then it's likely to be the results you notice, after the damage has been done.

Take the example of famed hacker Adrian Lamo and his attack on the *New York Times*. In February 2002 he gained entry to the newspaper's internal network, and began to modify critical files, including the company's confidential databases. To one such database, which listed the well-known experts in contact with the newspaper, he added his own name. (He also ran up a $300,000 bill on the Lexis-Nexis search tool, billed to the *Times*.) In this instance, no damage was done—although Lamo did serve time for the crime.

Website Defacement

One of the most visible forms of computer vandalism is website defacement. This is when an attacker invades your website and replaces existing web pages with new pages of his own design.

For example, an attacker might totally replace your page with a new, deliberately offensive, page. He might change key information on the page, to confuse or insult visitors. He might change the links on your page to point to different, possibly offensive, pages. He may even insert hostile Java applets or ActiveX controls into the page.

It's likely that you'll first notice a website defacement when a visitor emails you about the changes. Actually, the visitor will probably be *complaining* about the changes—likely offended by the new content. To deal with the problem, you'll need to take your website offline, then reconstruct all the pages from a backup copy.

Assault

You might want to call this one "pummeling into submission." These are attacks designed to crash a computer network or website, typically by inundating it with pings and emails and other forms of electronic requests. As the system receives more and more of these requests, it begins to slow down, then to crawl to a halt.

The most common type of assault is the *denial of service* attack—which we'll discuss later in this chapter. In this attack, hordes of hijacked computers are used to inundate the target site, for no reason other than to force the site to go offline.

Hijacking

The final form of attack might not do any damage to a computer system, but likely results in damage to someone else's network or website.

In a hijacking attack, the attacker surreptitiously installs backdoor software on your PC so that he can operate it via remote control. With your PC under his control, the attacker then uses it to initiate a larger attack on another system. By co-opting thousands of unsuspecting computers, the attacker is able to amplify an attack—and provide a safety layer between himself and the targeted websites.

> > > N O T E

An individual who initiates a computer attack is commonly referred to as a *hacker*—although that's actually a misuse of the term. Technically, a hacker is a person who enjoys exploring the details of computer systems and programming code. A hacker might "hack" his way into a protected computer system, but only to look around and expand his knowledge. In other words, hackers don't deliberately cause mischief—although damage can inadvertently result from a sloppy hack. That's in contrast to an individual who *maliciously* breaks into a computer system, who is more accurately called a *cracker*. Hackers don't cause damage; crackers do. And, believe it or not, there is very little overlap between the hacker and cracker communities; most hackers condemn the activities of crackers. So don't get confused by the terminology; hackers are (mostly) good guys, whereas it's crackers who cause most of the damage.

What Are the Different Methods Used for Computer Attacks?

It's an unfortunate fact of online life that there are many different ways for a determined cracker to attack a computer, network, or website. Attacks can be very low-tech (so-called social engineering attacks, such as impersonating a company employee in a phone call) or extremely high-tech (redirecting a website's URL to another server). And, depending on the motives of the attackers, they can exact tremendous damage. Let's look at some of the most common types of attacks.

Social Engineering Attacks

A social engineering attack is like an old-fashioned con game. The attacker uses human nature to fool the victim into allowing improper access, or revealing private information.

Social engineering attacks can come in a number of guises. For example, you may receive an email from some official-sounding source, asking you to verify your Internet password via return mail. When you do so, you send your password to the attacker, who can now access your account at will. This type of high-tech social engineering is called *phishing*, which was already discussed in several sections of this book.

> > > N O T E

Learn more about phishing in Chapter 11, "Avoiding Email Fraud and Phishing Scams."

Instant messaging and web-based chat rooms are two other popular channels for social engineering attacks. You may get a message from a stranger, supposedly sending you naked pictures or MP3 files or something else of interest or value; when you download the file, it contains a backdoor Trojan (or something worse). Or you may get the official-sounding message from a user with a fancy, authoritative title, asking you to change passwords or supply credit card information. If you go along with the con, you provide personal information to the attacker.

Of course, social engineering attacks don't have to be technical in nature. Smooth-talking con men have always been able to talk their way into just about any situation they want. Take the example of the would-be attacker who phones your company's switchboard or IT department, impersonating a real-life employee and asking for information such as the network's virtual private network (VPN), or that user's password. ("I forgot my password—can you believe it?") Once he has the required information, the attacker can gain access to the company's network—and do his dirty work.

It's surprising how often this sort of con actually works.

Valuable information can also be stolen by more traditional methods. For instance, many attackers retrieve passwords and other information by "dumpster diving," and looking for scraps of paper used to write down important numbers and then thrown in the trash. In addition, many employees write their passwords on Post-It notes and leave them affixed to their computer screens; a data thief in the parking lot with a pair of binoculars (or an attacker posing as part of the cleaning crew) can obtain a wealth of information thanks to these sloppy security habits. For that matter, many social engineering attacks start when a con artist poses as an employee and boldly walks into the building; he tells the person at the door he forgot his access card, and they let him in.

The discouraging thing is that it's virtually impossible to protect against these types of social engineering attacks. You can educate your family and colleagues until you're blue in the face, but some people will always be gullible enough to provide information that they shouldn't. All you can do is look out for yourself, and do your best to resist these types of official-sounding cons—and, as always, refuse any files sent over instant messaging or email and never, *never*, send private information unless you're sure you're talking to an honest-to-goodness officially authorized representative of the company at hand.

Impersonation Attacks

An impersonation attack occurs when an attacker steals the access rights of an authorized user. The attacker can then configure his computer to impersonate the other, authorized computer, and gain access to otherwise-closed systems.

Impersonation attacks work because the company's security apparatus thinks that it is dealing with the original computer. It's like stealing someone's ID, but on a more technical level; by all accounts, you *are* that person, and your actions are never questioned.

A typical impersonation attack starts when a cracker uses some sort of "sniffer" software to eavesdrop on an individual connecting to an ISP or company network. This software records the data flowing back and forth, which includes the user's username and password. This information at hand, the attacker can then log on to the ISP or network, using the stolen username and password, and then do anything and go anywhere permitted by the original user's access level.

After the damage has been done, the attacker can log off, with absolutely no fear of ever being caught. Even if the damage can be traced, it will be traced back to the user the attacker is impersonating, who (unknowingly) had his or her password stolen—*not* to the attacker himself.

For this reason, impersonation attacks are difficult to protect against. Perhaps the best defense is to require all users to frequently (once a week or so) change passwords. This way the risk for an impersonation attack is always limited in duration: It can last only until the impersonated password is officially changed.

> > > **N O T E**

> Anytime you're connected to a network (or to the Internet via a network), your presence can be detected by a "sniffer" program. Sniffers listen to network traffic and then examine what exactly comes across the network. Your online presence can also be detected with *port scanning* software—robot programs that examine computers connected to the Internet, looking for what services each computer is running. When an unprotected port is detected, that information is sent back to the attacker—who then knows which computers are vulnerable to attack, and can target his attacks accordingly.

Transitive Trust Attacks

This type of attack exploits the inherent trust in a host-to-host or network-to-network relationship. This type of trust typically enables computers outside the current network to access the network as though they were part of the network—without the typical passwords and protocols necessary for remote access. By breaking into this trusted relationship, the attacker can then access the network without a password.

For example, a network administrator can create a database of "trusted" host computers (typically other servers in a big company), so that users from those computers can log in without giving a password. If an attacker can edit that list of trusted computers to include his own computer, then he can gain access to the network without even needing a password.

Another way this works is via an administrator account—the type of account provided to network administrators that enables them access to configuration and control operations that normal users typically can't access. If an attacker can compromise one of these administrator accounts, he is automatically "trusted" by the system to perform all manner of file operations.

< < < **T I P**

> Transitive trust attacks can be limited in scope if internal firewalls are put into place between different parts of the network, or installed on individual PCs. This way an attacker gaining privileged access to the network would be thwarted when making any attempt to exploit those privileges.

Exploits

An exploit is an attack that takes advantage of a bug or hole in a piece of software or operating system. Unfortunately, in today's world of bloated, poorly programmed, and inadequately tested software, bugs and holes are the norm.

With hackers and crackers diligently looking for holes big enough to break in through, it's no surprise that attacks via exploits are increasingly common. Naturally, for an exploit to occur, there first has to be an identified security hole. But when the hole exists, it's there for any inspired cracker to exploit.

The best defense against computer exploits is to keep all your software updated with the latest security patches. In most cases, a manufacturer reacts to the discovery of a security hole with an immediate security patch. If you're aware of newly discovered holes, and up to date on your patching, you'll reduce your risk of being the victim of an exploit attack.

Infrastructure Attacks

An infrastructure-based attack exploits weaknesses in a technical protocol or particular infrastructure. It's like an exploit, except more widespread—it isn't limited to a particular piece of software; it's system-wide. And, with few exceptions, the security holes exploited in infrastructure attacks are not easily fixed; the weaknesses are inherent in the infrastructure.

There are many types of infrastructure attacks, most of which allow a cracker (with the proper tools) to gain access to your computer or network. Let's look at a few.

DNS Spoofing

DNS spoofing takes place when an attacker hijacks the name (actually, the DNS address) of an individual computer or web server. The attacker maps your computer's DNS name (**mycomputer.com**) to his own computer; any user referencing **mycomputer.com** is automatically routed to the attacker's computer, instead.

By using DNS spoofing, an attacker can also gain access to other servers and networks, via a transitive trust attack. If Network A grants trusted access to Server B, and an attacker spoofs Server B (by mapping Server B to Computer C), then Computer C can access Network A at will.

ICMP Bombing

The Internet Control Message Protocol (ICMP) is used by Internet routers to notify a host computer when a specified destination is unreachable. An attacker can effectively knock a computer off the Internet by "bombing" it with bogus ICMP messages. (This effect is similar to that of a denial of service attack, discussed later in this chapter.)

The best defense against an ICMP bombing is a strong firewall, configured to block all ICMP messages.

Source Routing

This is a sophisticated attack that uses ICMP bombing and DNS spoofing as interim steps in the larger attack. It takes advantage of an infrastructure quirk that requires source-routed traffic over the Internet to return via the route from which it came.

This type of attack starts with an ICMP attack on a trusted host on the target network. The initial attack knocks the host off the Internet, and enables the attacker's computer to take that computer's place—by setting its address to that of the bombed computer. The host computer now views all communications from the attacking computer as coming from the trusted host, coming over the expected source route. This enables the attacking computer to gain access to the target network and do whatever it wants.

A strong firewall is a good defense against this type of attack. Heavy-duty network firewalls block source-routed data and trigger alarms during a possible attack.

Racing Authentication

This is a fun little attack, where the attacker's goal is to "fill in the blank" faster than the victim he's trying to impersonate.

In this type of attack the attacker begins to log in to the target network at the same time as another user. The attacker uses the other user's username, and waits until the user has entered all but the last digit of his or her password. Then, before the user can enter the final digit, the attacker enters a single character, guessing at the proper response. If the attacker guesses correctly—and types fast enough—he enters the target network, while the slower-typing user gets locked out.

If the password is numeric-only, the attacker has a 1-in-10 chance of guessing correctly. (Not bad odds.) If the password is alphanumeric, however, the odds of guessing correctly diminish—which reinforces the security value of a password that combines letters, numbers, and special characters.

TCP Sequence Guessing

This type of attack enables a flow of attack data to infiltrate the target network. The technique hinges on the fact that connections over the Internet are numbered, in a semi-random, increasing-number sequence. The attacker intercepts the current connection to the target computer, and (using the appropriate software) guesses the number of the next possible sequence. If the attacker guesses correctly, a new connection to the target computer is established, and malicious data or instructions can then be transmitted.

As with most infrastructure attacks, a TCP sequence attack can be thwarted by a correctly configured network firewall—which should identify any attempts to guess at a connection sequence.

TCP Splicing

TCP splicing is the cracker equivalent to splicing into a coaxial cable to steal a cable television signal. With this type of attack, the attacker positions himself between two computers and waits for a legitimate connection to be established between the two. After the connection is established, the attacker splices into the connection, effectively hijacking the data stream and "becoming" one of the users. After he is connected in this fashion, the attacker can do anything the original user could do.

This type of attack, however, is limited by the effective use of application-level passwords on the target computer. Even though the attacker can imitate the original user, he doesn't know all that user's passwords—and thus can't access password-protected programs and data.

FTP Bouncing

Another common type of infrastructure attack is FTP bouncing, which is a form of session hijacking, which you'll read more about in a few pages. In this instance, an unwitting FTP server is used to send email to other computers, thus hiding the source of any email-based attack.

FTP bouncing occurs when an attacker finds an FTP server that has a writable upload area. The attacker uploads an email message to the server, and then uses another script or program to send the email from the FTP server to the target recipient(s). When the recipient receives the message, it appears to come from the FTP server—*not* from the attacker's normal email address.

FTP bouncing can be used to send a flood of spam to multiple recipients, or multiple messages to the same recipient (thus clogging the recipient's inbox with what is called an *email bomb*).

Anyone running an FTP server must carefully manage the server traffic to prevent this type of hijacking—or eliminate all write privileges for anonymous users. As to the ultimate recipients of the email bomb, there's not much you can do except delete the unsolicited—and unwanted—messages.

Wireless Attacks

Wireless computer networks present a unique set of infrastructure-related security concerns. With an increasing number of companies, households, and public hotspot using WiFi wireless networks, the risk of wireless intrusion is rising.

Although WiFi can use several types of encryption systems to protect against intrusion (WEP and WPA being the most prevalent), this feature is not always activated during a basic installation. (According to an informal survey by security firm i-sec, two-thirds of all WiFi networks don't have wireless security turned on.) Without this encryption, it's relatively easy for someone to crack into the network, no wires necessary.

This WiFi vulnerability isn't an issue just for crackers. If one of your neighbors has a wireless network without wireless security enabled, you may be able to access their network from your WiFi-equipped PC. Yes, there's a distance limitation (that's why crackers use an additional antenna, to boost the signals), but if you're in the neighborhood, any unsecured wireless network is fair game.

Denial of Service Attacks

A denial of service (DoS) attack floods a computer or network with data or messages, essentially overwhelming the system and preventing it from being used. This type of attack is perhaps the most destructive type of Internet-based attack, as it can completely shut down a target computer or website for several hours, or even days. It's also the most common form of network attack.

There are many ways to initiate a denial of service attack, including

- Using ICMP bombing (discussed earlier) to throw the router off the Internet
- Using email bombing to overwhelm the target's email server
- Flooding the target computer with garbage data packets to overwhelm its Internet bandwidth
- Repeatedly pinging the target computer to overwhelm its Internet bandwidth

Most DoS attackers utilize multiple remote-controlled zombie computers to better flood the target computer. A large-scale denial of service attack—technically called a *distributed denial of service* (DDoS) attack—can utilize thousands of zombie computers in a destructive botnet, all simultaneously flooding the target with junk data.

There is little one can do to protect against DoS attacks. After an attack begins, however, the way to shut it down is to block the attacking computers' access.

Session Hijacking

This type of attack doesn't affect the target computer, but rather uses it to perpetrate a further attack on another computer. Session hijacking occurs when an attacker gains remote control of an individual computer. Rather than inflict damage on that machine, the attacker uses it to participate in a denial of service attack, or execute some other form of Internet-based attack. Because the attack comes from a hijacked computer, it can't be traced back to the original attacker; the hijacked machine is nothing more than a zombie, doing its master's bidding.

> > > **NOTE**

Most session hijacking is enabled by the installation of backdoor Trojan software or spyware on the zombie machine. You can avoid session hijacking by taking the normal precautions against Trojan infection, as detailed in Chapter 20, "Defending Against Computer Viruses."

Data-Driven Attacks

A data-driven attack is a virus or Trojan attack. You receive a file—via email, instant messaging, or whatever—and then download and run the file. After it is launched, the file performs some sort of malicious action.

In a network environment, the most common data-driven attack is the backdoor Trojan. In a backdoor Trojan attack, the attacker somehow convinces you to download and run a program that opens a backdoor to your computer system. This backdoor enables the attacker to remotely access and control your computer—and, if you're on a network, to remotely access the entire network via your hijacked PC.

The best defense against a data-driven attack is to avoid receiving and running unrequested files, and to use an anti-virus program. Installing a firewall also helps to mitigate the effects of a backdoor Trojan by blocking an attacker's remote-control access.

Multistaged Attacks

Simple "head on" attacks are less effective than they used to be, thanks to beefed-up protection programs and security measures. For that reason, many newer attacks come in phases, the better to infiltrate today's security.

For example, a multistage attack might start with a low-profile compromise, like a Trojan, that is used to establish a beachhead to launch subsequent, more devastating attacks. The goal is to put a foot in the door, so to speak, and then sneak in other forms of attack.

Staged Download Attacks

Similar to a multistage attack is one involving a staged downloader. This type of threat involves a program that, when installed on a computer or network, downloads and installs other malicious code onto the computer. According to Symantec, 28 of the top 50 malicious code samples in 2007 were staged downloaders.

Computer Attacks and Cyberterrorism

When it comes to computer attacks, there's another, more worrisome threat—terrorists using a computer attack to bring down public or government networks or systems. The risk of this so-called *cyberterrorism* is rising, and could be a factor in future terrorist attacks.

What, exactly, is cyberterrorism? Security expert Dorothy Denning defines cyberterrorism as "politically motivated hacking operations intended to cause grave harm such as loss of life or severe economic damage." Similarly, the Federal Emergency Management Agency (FEMA) defines it as "unlawful attacks and threats of attack against computers, networks, and the information stored therein when done to intimidate or coerce a government or its people in furtherance of political or social objectives."

However you define it, cyberterrorism exists—and is a grave threat to the security of individuals, companies, and nations.

Cyberterrorism: A Real-World Example

How exactly would cyberterrorism work? One needs only to look at a real-world example to recognize its potential impact.

The Republic of Estonia is a small Baltic country, bordered by Finland to the north, Sweden to the west, Latvia to the south, and the big bear of Russia to the east. On April 27, 2007, officials in Estonia decided to move a Soviet-era war memorial that commemorated an unknown Russian soldier who died fighting the Nazis in WWII. The monumental move stirred up Estonia's ethnic Russian population—and led to a series of large and sustained distributed denial-of-service attacks.

The DDoS attacks were launched against several Estonian websites, including those of government ministries and the prime minister's Reform Party. In the early days of the attacks, sites that previously received about 1,000 visits a day were receiving 2,000 hits every second. This caused the repeated shutdown of several sites for several hours at a time. The attacks lasted for several weeks.

When the attacks failed to subside, NATO and the United States sent computer security experts to help Estonia deal with the situation. Analyzing the attacks, the experts deduced that the attacks were instigated by a loose federation of separate attackers. (Not the Russian government, as some initially suspected.) The attack wasn't criminal in nature, nor was it an early instance of cyberwarfare; instead, it was an attack by cyberterrorists on Estonia's digital infrastructure.

Detailing the Terrorist Threat

The situation in Estonia illustrates the nature of the threat, especially as countries become more dependent on the Internet. You can imagine how crippling a similar attack would be in our country; an almost uncountable number of systems, transactions, and communications rely on the security and stability of the Internet. If that stability is threatened, chaos could ensue.

How likely is it that cyberterrorists will target your personal computer or small network? Not very. But it is possible that these online criminals will target larger systems on which you depend—large ISPs, major email servers, even the Internet backbone itself. A major attack that shut down the Internet's most popular sites could disrupt communications and commerce across the civilized world.

The 2007 report, *Botnets, Cybercrime, and Cyberterrorism: Vulnerabilities and Policy Issues for Congress*, prepared by the Congressional Research Service, detailed several possible targets and effects of a cyberattack. For example, an attack on the computers in a credit card network could corrupt secure transaction data at online retail sites and flow that corrupted data into larger banking and commerce systems. Or an attack on the Supervisory Control and Data Acquisition (ACADA) systems used by critical infrastructure organizations could disrupt water, electricity, gas, and other utility services across a wide swath of the country; such an attack could result in power outages, air traffic disruptions, and the like.

However you look at it, a cyberattack has the potential to create economic damage that is far out of proportion to the cost of initiating the attack. That makes this type of attack particularly attractive to terrorist organizations that typically don't have significant financial backing.

> > > **N O T E**

>> A widespread cyberattack on the nation's infrastructure would likely require significant resources and long-term planning—perhaps up to 2 to 4 years in advance.

So what types of organizations would be most likely to launch a cyberattack on American institutions? Al Qaeda has shown a familiarity with a willingness to use technology to achieve its aims; even smaller organizations are potential attackers, especially as younger and more technologically savvy recruits join the ranks. And the threat isn't limited to rogue groups; terrorist-sponsoring nations, such as Iran, Cuba, North Korea, and Syria, are more than capable of carrying on this type of attack—as are larger countries, such as China and Russia. In short, cyberattacks could be a weapon not only for terrorist groups, but also for aggressive nations on the global front.

Of course, what's good for the goose may also be good for the gander. Not surprisingly, the United States Department of Defense has examined its own potential use of cyberterrorism tactics. DOD officials reportedly stated that the U.S. could confuse enemies by using cyberattacks to open floodgates, control traffic lights, or scramble the banking systems in other countries.

Is all this talk of cyberterrorism a science fiction fantasy? Just ask those officials in Estonia—this is a very real and very dangerous threat.

How Is a Computer Attack Executed?

How difficult is it to execute a computer attack over the Internet?

Unfortunately, it isn't that difficult at all. All you need is the right information, the right tools (in the form of cracker software), and a little technical know-how. It also helps if you've identified a computer system with inadequate security.

Steps to Attack

Let's say you wanted to initiate an attack on some computer system somewhere in the world. Just how would you go about it?

Believe it or not, there are plenty of websites that provide very explicit instructions for this type of malicious activity. But without getting into those kinds of specifics, we can go through the basic steps of an attack, as detailed here:

1. Choose a target.

2. Footprint the target—identify IP addresses, domain name servers, phone numbers, key personnel, and other information that might be useful in infiltrating the system.

3. Scan and map the target network to identify systems and devices.

4. Identify vulnerable services and systems resources.

5. Choose a part of the network—typically an individual computer—with a particular vulnerability.

6. Exploit the vulnerability, by whatever method appropriate.

7. Take control of the system and perform desired operations.

In short, you target a network or website, find its weakness, exploit that weakness to gain entrance, and then do your dirty work. With the right tools—cracker software, available at the aforementioned underground websites—this isn't difficult to do.

Examining a Real-World Attack

Let's look at how this works in the real world—by examining a real-world network attack. This particular attack occurred in February 2000, when, during a single 48-hour period, seven of the largest Internet sites fell victim to devastating attacks.

It started at 10:20 a.m. on February 7th, when Yahoo! was flooded with data requests from thousands of different computers. The flood of requests pushed Yahoo!'s system to overload and knocked it offline. Yahoo! stayed offline for three hours, until the attack subsided and the website could be brought back online.

The next day, at 10:30 a.m., Internet retailer Buy.com experienced a similar attack, which knocked it offline for several hours. At 3:20 p.m., another attack hit eBay, which went down for 90 minutes; CNN.com was hit at 4:00 p.m., and Amazon.com at 5:00 p.m., knocking both sites offline. The attacks continued into the morning of February 9th, with online trader E*Trade attacked at 5:00 a.m. and ZDNet at 6:45 a.m.

In reality, this attack started some time before February 7th. That's because the attacker had to "recruit" thousands of slave computers to do his dirty work. The attacker used a software program called a *port scanner* to troll the Internet for computers he could hijack—ideally, computers with high-speed connections to the Internet.

After the zombie machines were identified, the attacker sent them each a backdoor Trojan program. Not all the systems accepted the software, but a lot did. With the backdoor program installed on each machine, the attacker could then control them remotely—at his convenience.

It's likely that all this prep work took place weeks before the initial February 7th attack. In the meantime, the zombie computers all operated normally, with the backdoor software "sleeping" in the background, ready to take control when ordered to do so.

On the morning of February 7th, the attacker went to work. He sent instructions to each of the zombie computers, probably via some sort of batch file. (It's unlikely he sent individual instructions to thousands of different computers, manually.) These instructions commanded each zombie computer to send a series of data requests (called *pings*) to the Yahoo! site, the first victim on the attacker's hit list. Each computer sent hundreds and thousands of pings, one after another, as rapidly as they were capable. These pings, coming simultaneously from so many different machines, were more than the Yahoo! servers could handle. The result was a slowdown, then a shutdown, of the Yahoo! website, until the attack subsided.

> > > **N O T E**

> It goes without saying that all the attacker's instructions were suitably encrypted, so they couldn't be traced back to his personal machine. It's also likely that the instructions were filtered through multiple layers of machines, to further mask where the instructions originated.

It's worth noting that the amount of activity coming from the zombie computers probably couldn't continue for long without being noticed. That sort of constant repetitive outbound pinging would likely slow down the rest of the hijacked computer and jam up the computer's Internet connection—which would be noticed by the machine's owner. That's why attacks like these typically diminish over a matter of hours, as zombie after zombie is taken out of the loop.

As you probably surmised, this type of brute-force attack is an example of a well-executed denial of service attack. The attacker used a combination of techniques—Trojan horses and backdoor viruses, botnets of zombie computers, and the like—to carry out the attack. And the result was singularly devastating to some of the largest, most stable sites on the web.

How High Is Your Risk?

If Yahoo! and Amazon.com can be attacked, so can your company and even your personal home computer. But how high is your risk?

Your risk of attack depends a lot on who you are, and what you do. Obviously, large companies are more at risk than individuals—and the more high-profile the company, the higher the risk.

In essence, attackers like to go after large and visible targets. It's a matter of efficiency and effectiveness; why go through all the effort to mount a denial of service attack just to bring down a single home computer? The effort is better spent on a larger target, one that will bring more notoriety to the attacker.

To that end, large organizations are most at risk of all types of computer attacks. This is evidenced by the Computer Security Institute's *Computer Crime and Security Survey*, which reports that 25% of enterprise respondents in 2007 had been victims of denial of service attacks; 10% had had their websites defaced.

That's not to say, of course, that smaller companies and individuals are completely safe from attack. Crackers love to infiltrate individual systems and small networks to hijack the computers they use for larger attacks. Do you really want your personal computer turned into a zombie that is used to commit a larger computer crime? And, by the way, while your computer is being remote controlled, there's nothing to stop the attacker from stealing your bank account passwords and credit card data, placing you at risk for identity theft. No, the threat is real, even to individuals.

Of course, it goes without saying that computer attacks can be costly. Again according to the CSI survey, the average cost associated with a DoS attack in 2007 was $2.8 million. The average website defacement cost $725,000. This isn't small potatoes, folks.

Is It Safe?

Are you safe from computer attack? Not unless you take the proper precautions—even if you're just a lowly home user.

The primary concern for any home computer user is an attack on your system that results in data theft—having your financial or personal information stolen and used by cybercriminals. A secondary threat is having your computer hijacked into a botnet and used to send spam or attack other computers. Granted, the odds of either happening are small, but the danger is real. You only have to be hit once to feel the pain.

That said, if you're a typical home PC user, you shouldn't get paranoid about these types of Internet-based attacks. The simple fact is that home users are much less likely than businesses to the direct or indirect targets of a computer attack. Crackers typically pick big targets—and the PC sitting in your den just isn't that important or visible.

For businesses, large and small, the risk is much higher. You need to be concerned not only about data theft and corruption, but also website defacement and denial of service attacks. We examine all these dangers in the following chapters—and look at ways to reduce the risks.

Defending Your Home Network from Attack

As you learned in the previous chapter, a single home computer is an unlikely target for computer attack; what reason would a big-time cracker have to take down your PC? What attackers are interested in, however, are computers they can use to conduct other, more significant activities—such as attacking large networks and websites, or sending out tons of spam email messages. In this regard, your computer is a valued recruit in an army of zombie computers—just one of many, but an important part of the whole.

Of course, it's also possible that an individual with a specific goal in mind might like to infiltrate your personal computer or home network, malicious intent beforehand. Perhaps this individual wants to steal some confidential files or your personal financial data, or maybe he wants to delete key files and cause your system not to work. Or maybe it's just someone who wants to piggyback on your wireless Internet connection; even though no harm is intended, he's still stealing your Internet signal.

In any case, there is good reason to protect your personal computer and home network from attackers. Read on to learn how.

Evaluating Your Risk

Home computer users are at relatively low risk for computer attack. It's unlikely, for example, that your home computer will be the target of a devastating denial of service attack. Your risk increases, however, if you have more than one computer at home on a network, if you connect to the Internet over a broadband DSL or cable connection, or if you run your own website.

How can you evaluate your risk of computer attack? Let's look at the key factors that can increase your risk.

Who Uses Your Computer?

Here's a discomforting fact—the more people who use your computer, the higher your risk of attack.

Why is this? There are a number of reasons.

First, children (including and especially teenagers) are typically less diligent with security precautions than adults are. So if you have younger computer users in your household, your risk is higher.

For that matter, you're presumably more diligent than your spouse. (You're the one reading this book, right?) Unless your spouse is employed in the IT profession or happens to be a security expert, your risk increases whenever he or she is online.

Your risk is also higher if you have guests or friends who frequently use your computer—even if they're just checking email while they're away from home. After all, you don't know what sites your guests will visit, or what kinds of things they might download. Beware the unknown.

> > > **N O T E**

> Guests on your computer or wireless network also put you at risk for *internal* attacks—that is, your guests can be intruders. For this reason, make sure your data is password-protected before you allow your guests to log on.

So unless you're the only person using the sole computer in your household, your risk increases.

How Do You Connect to the Internet?

If you're behind the technology curve and connect to the Internet via a dial-up connection, your security risk is rather low. If you have a broadband connection, however, your risk increases considerably—even though the faster Internet connection might make that risk worth taking.

The reason an always-on connection is more risky than a dial-up connection is because the longer you're online, the more likely it is you'll be noticed by potential attackers. When you're connected 24/7, that's a lot more hours where a would-be attacker can use sniffer or scanner software to discover your presence.

What Do You Do Online?

Your online activities determine a large part of your security risk. The following activities are regarded as higher-risk activities, since they involve the transmittal of personal information:

- Downloading software
- Swapping MP3 and other music files via P2P file-swapping network
- Chatting or instant messaging
- Playing online games
- Shopping online
- Buying or selling on eBay and Craigslist
- Banking online (paying bills, checking account balances, and so on)
- Buying or selling stocks or mutual funds at an online investment firm

On the other hand, sending and receiving email and general web browsing (without entering personal information) are relatively safe activities, from a security standpoint. (These activities do put you at a higher risk for catching a computer virus, however.)

Do You Have a Home Network?

The more computers funneling through your Internet gateway, the bigger target you are for crackers. Crackers like big targets, because there is more potentially valuable stuff to get at— or to damage, if that's the intent.

A multiple-computer network also has more weak points than a single computer. Every user on the network is a potential security risk, with loose passwords and sloppy practices. The more people that are connected, the greater the chance that *someone* will screw up and do something that will allow the cracker access. A chain, after all, is only as strong as its weakest link.

The bottom line? The more computers you have connected through your Internet connection, the bigger the risk of attack.

Do You Have a Website or Blog?

Any public exposure you create also creates a more visible and attractive target for crackers. Putting a site on the web or hosting a blog is like flashing a business card in a busy coffeehouse; you announce your presence, and—for crackers—your vulnerability.

This is true even if it's just a personal web page. Although experienced crackers tend to pass up personal pages (too small a challenge), beginning crackers might appreciate the practice they can get, at your expense. Besides, most personal websites have very little security; they're an easy target.

In any case, any public exposure you have on the web increases your risk of attack—and websites and blogs increase your public exposure.

Recognizing an Attack

What are the signs that your computer or network is under attack, or being used to attack another computer? Here are some behaviors to look out for:

- An unusual amount of hard disk activity—especially when your PC isn't being used.
- An unusual amount of Internet access via your wireless router or modem—especially when you're not browsing the web or using email.
- Your Internet connection appears to slow down, taking longer to load web pages and download files.
- An unusual number of email messages appearing in your inbox—especially returned messages that you never personally sent.
- Missing or edited files on your hard disk.
- Unusual behavior—lots of pop-up windows, programs launching of their own accord, sluggish performance, and the like.

If you recognize any of these behaviors, it's possible that your computer has been or is being attacked.

Reducing Your Risk of Attack

Although you can't stop crackers from trying to attack your computer or home network, you can lessen the chances of an attack succeeding—and minimize any damage that might result from a successful attack.

Use Strong Passwords—and Lots of Them

The first step to security is to use passwords. Everywhere.

Start by reconfiguring your Windows account (and accounts for all others in your household) for password operation. You don't want your operating system to start unless the proper password is issued.

Next, password-protect any and all applications that offer this feature. Or, in the case of Word and Excel, password-protect individual documents—the most sensitive ones, at any rate.

Finally, make sure you use strong passwords to access your Internet account and your network. Don't keep the default password offered to you, or enter a bunch of blanks to create an empty password field. Crackers know all the standard default passwords, and are smart enough to try entering an empty password. You at least have to put forth the effort to create a unique password.

While you're at it, try to create a strong password—one that's relatively complex. You'd be amazed how effective a complicated password can be; if it's too hard to crack, a cracker will give up and move to an easier target.

< < < TIP

> Don't forget Microsoft's password strength checker, located at www.microsoft.com/protect/yourself/password/checker.mspx.

You see, most people choose a short password, one that's easy to remember, and then use the same password on multiple accounts. (Who wants to remember a dozen different passwords?) This, unfortunately, creates a significant security risk —especially when it comes to logging onto your computer, or your company's computer network.

The problem is, these short passwords are relatively easy to crack—and if you use the same password on multiple accounts, a single crack can gain the attacker multiple entrées. For example, a three-character alphabetic password (no numbers) can be cracked in less than eight minutes. Choosing a seven-character alphanumeric password (mixing letters, numbers, and a few special characters) can take up to two years to crack, using even the most sophisticated cracking software.

You should also make sure that your password isn't easy for a cracker to guess. That means don't use passwords based on your social security number, birth date, names of family members, names of your pets, birth dates of family members, and so on. The combination of letters and numbers in your password should be as near random as possible.

In addition, you should make sure that the password you use to log onto your computer or company network is used *only* for that single log-in. Don't use the same password for your home computer as you do your company network. Don't use the same password you use for your ATM, or to access your online banking account, or to log into your Internet service provider. Create separate passwords for each account, and keep them separate.

Finally, you should change your passwords on a regular basis. Every time you change your password, you eliminate any risk from a previously stolen password. A stolen password is useless if the password has been changed.

Turn Off File Sharing

Let's say an unauthorized user gains access to your system. If you're like most users, all the folders and files on your hard disk are open for anyone to access—which means the cracker will have a field day defacing and deleting your files, at will.

You can keep unauthorized users from accessing your private files and folders by disabling Windows' file- and print-sharing on your network computers. This keeps the contents of your system private, even to other users of your network.

< < < T I P

If file sharing is essential to your computer operation, then at least activate password-protected file shar-ing—where users have to enter a password to access any files shared across the network.

Keep Your Operating System and Software Updated

Because many computer attacks exploit bugs and security holes in the Windows operating system and in specific pieces of software, you want to make sure that you have the latest, greatest version of all your software—the version that includes all the latest security patches. In practice, this means that you need to be aware of all available software upgrades, and then download and install all security patches, as appropriate.

For Windows users, this means activating Windows Update on your computer to automatically download the latest Windows patches and fixes when available. For other Microsoft programs, monitor the Microsoft Security site (www.microsoft.com/security/); this is where you'll find all the latest downloadable security patches for everything that Microsoft distributes. Of course, for other software and operating systems, monitor the manufacturers' websites.

Be vigilant!

Keep Backup Copies

I've offered this advice elsewhere in this book, but it applies again here: Always make backup copies of your essential data. Whether you're running a single PC or a small home network, you need the assurance that your data won't be lost if you're the victim of a malicious attack. The only way to guarantee data permanence is to have a spare copy handy.

It doesn't matter what kind of backup device you use (although external hard drives are par-ticularly affordable these days) or what backup software you employ (the one that came with your backup drive, the one included in Windows Vista, or one you purchase or download else-where). What's important is that you perform a full backup of all your data on a regular basis—just in case an attacker deletes or destroys your valuable data.

Use Common Sense

It must be said: Common sense matters.

You can fend off a lot of attacks—especially those that use "social engineering" and phishing to obtain passwords and other private information—by using a generous amount of common sense. Don't let anyone talk you into divulging your passwords or credit card numbers. Don't reply to instant messages and emails asking you to supply private information, no matter how official-sounding the request. Don't accept files from anyone over instant messaging or in chat rooms—or open files you receive via IM or email. Don't leave your password taped to your computer monitor, or sitting out in the open on your desk.

In other words, be careful and be properly secretive. Don't let out any information that shouldn't be made public, and don't believe anything that strangers tell you. Keep your private information private, and be properly aware of all the dangers that exist online.

Protecting Your Computers with a Firewall

If even one computer in your household is connected to the Internet, you need constant protection from Internet-based attacks. The best way to protect against these attacks is with a *firewall*—a piece of software placed between your computer or network and the Internet. A firewall blocks unauthorized inbound traffic, thus insulating your system from any potential attack.

> > > **N O T E**

   While we talk about firewall software in this chapter, there is also firewall hardware—dedicated devices that isolate your network from Internet attack. Some wireless routers function as hardware firewalls.

How Firewalls Work

Simply put, a firewall is a piece of software or hardware that acts as a barrier between your computer or network and the Internet. A firewall functions like a guard on a door—it lets good visitors in and keeps bad visitors out. In the case of your computer system, good visitors are the normal email communications and web pages you visit; bad visitors are attackers trying to bomb or infiltrate your system.

How do firewalls tell the good visitors from the bad? There are a number of technologies employed, discussed next.

Traffic Filtering

The first thing a firewall does is inspect each data packet coming through your Internet connection and filter it, based on some predefined rules. The firewall passes or blocks each individual data packet, depending on whether or not it meets the criteria.

The rule set used by a firewall can filter traffic based on various combinations of factors. Typically, these rules look at some combination of the originating computer's IP address and the port being accessed on your computer to determine the validity of the incoming data. (A port is a specific access point into your system; different ports perform different functions.) In this fashion, most firewalls let you block access on a port-by-port basis, as well as explicitly block access from specific IP addresses and Internet domains.

> > > **N O T E**

Most firewall programs come with their own default rule sets to filter incoming traffic. You can typically add to or delete rules from this default set, based on your own criteria.

Matching Incoming and Outgoing Traffic

Most firewalls also employ a more advanced filtering processes that uses so-called *stateful packet inspection*. A stateful firewall works by matching incoming traffic with outgoing requests; any data not specifically requested is automatically blocked.

The concept is actually quite simple. As a user, just about everything you do on the Internet is the result of a proactive request on your end. When you want to read your email, you request that new messages be downloaded to your email program. When you want to download a file, you request the download from the website server to your hard disk. When you want to view a web page, you request that page to be displayed in your Web browser.

There is very little activity that isn't preceded by a request. A firewall program using stateful packet inspection automatically blocks any incoming traffic that wasn't explicitly requested by you. And, because any intrusion or attack is nature unrequested, this is a good way to defend your system.

Sniffing Packet Contents

Of course, a firewall can theoretically block incoming traffic based on any criteria—including the contents of each data packet that arrive at your system's front door. Along these lines, a firewall could be configured to "sniff" all incoming packets for the presence of certain words or phrases, and block access accordingly. Or a firewall could be configured to block all incoming file attachments, or attachments of a specific type. The more robust the firewall, the more filtering options possible.

What to Look for in a Firewall

When you're looking for a personal firewall for your home PC or small network, you need to consider several factors, including the following:

- **Balance between ease-of-use and configurability**—A firewall is no good if it's too confusing for you to use. You want a firewall program that's easy enough for you to use, but also configurable enough to meet your specific needs. If you're just a normal user with a broadband Internet connection, you should go with the easiest-to-use program you can find. On the other hand, if you're running a web server out of your home, then you'll need a firewall that lets you create your own custom configuration.

- **Port blocking and filtering**—A port is an access point into your computer system. Every network service, such as HTTP web transfers or SMTP email, has a dedicated port, identified by number. On a default Windows installation, your computer has more than

65,000 ports available—each of which is a potential source of entry into your machine, and thus a potential source of outside attack. A good firewall monitors attempted port access, and blocks all access that hasn't been previously approved by you.

< < < **T I P**

Although a firewall can be configured to block incoming traffic to all the ports on your system, that may not always be desirable. For example, if you're using your computer to run a web server, you need to allow remote computers to connect to your PC via port 80. Your firewall, then, can be configured to inspect every arriving packet and permit connections only to port 80; any computer trying to access your system via another port is denied.

- **User-defined rule sets**—When it comes to configuration, what you want to look for is the capability of creating your own self-defined rule sets for what gets past the firewall and what doesn't. Again, if you're just a casual home user, you probably won't need your own custom rule sets. But if you're running a network or a web server, you'll want to be able to set your own rules and filters.

- **Stateful packet inspection**—Stateful packet inspection keeps unsolicited communications (such as those in a denial of service attack or backdoor remote control) from reaching your PC. It's a very effective way to stop most intrusions and attacks, and—for many users—a must-have feature.

- **Block unauthorized outbound traffic**—Most firewall software today not only blocks unauthorized incoming traffic, but also blocks unauthorized *outbound* traffic—the kind of traffic typically resulting from a computer hijacked by a backdoor program. Outbound traffic blocking is necessary to keep your computer from being used in remote control attacks against other systems.

> > > **N O T E**

When you're examining firewall software, you can also look to see whether a particular program has been certified by ICSA Labs (www.icsalabs.com). This independent organization awards its PC Firewall Certification to all products that meet specified functionality.

Choosing a Software Firewall

Most personal firewall software is relatively inexpensive, easy to install, and operates in the background whenever you start your computer and connect to the Internet. The best of these programs not only block unauthorized access, but also create a log of all computers that try to attack your system—and alert you of any successful attempts.

The most popular personal firewalls include the following:

- CA Personal Firewall (www.ca.com)

- Comodo Firewall Pro (www.personalfirewall.comodo.com)

- eConceal Pro (www.mwti.net)

- Injoy Firewall (www.fx.dk/firewall/)

- Norman Personal Firewall (www.norman.com)

- Online Armor Personal Firewall (www.tallemu.com)

- Outpost Firewall PRO (www.agnitum.com/products/outpost/)

- PC Tools Firewall Plus (www.pctools.com/firewall/)

- Sunbelt Personal Firewall (www.sunbelt-software.com/Home-Home-Office/Sunbelt-Personal-Firewall/)

- SurfSecret Firewall (www.surfsecret.com)

- WebRoot Desktop Firewall (www.webroot.com)

- ZoneAlarm Pro (www.zonealarm.com)

Most of these programs are priced less than $50—some much less. In addition, many so-called Internet security suites, such as Windows Live OneCare and Norton Internet Security, also include firewalls as part of their overall functionality.

C A U T I O N ! ! !

If you install a third-party firewall program, you need to turn off the Windows Firewall; two firewall programs working at the same time can cause problems.

Using the Windows Firewall

If you're running Windows Vista or Windows XP, you already have a firewall program installed on your system. The Windows Firewall is activated by default, although you can always check to make sure that it's up and working properly. In Windows Vista, open the Control Panel and select Security, Windows Firewall. When the Windows Firewall window appears, as shown in Figure 23.1, you can turn the firewall on and off, choose to allow particular programs through the firewall, or click Change Settings to configure the firewall's settings.

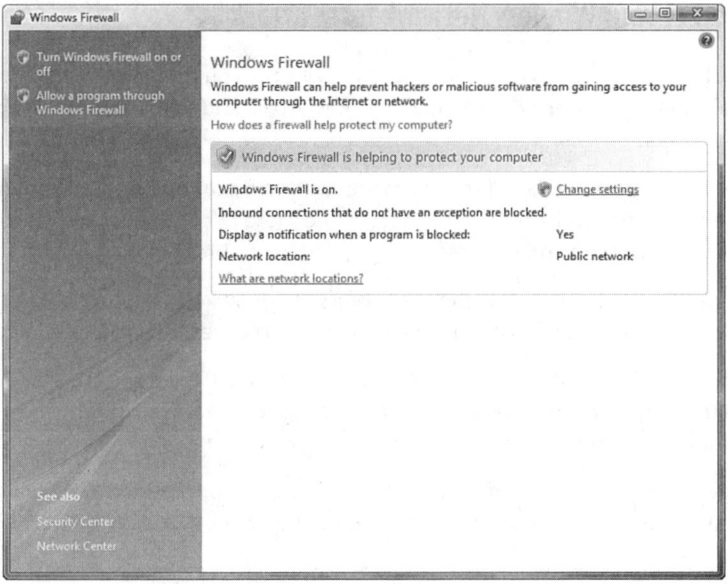

Figure 23.1
Checking the Windows Firewall settings in Windows Vista.

In Windows XP, open the Control Panel and go to the Windows Security Center. All of Windows security settings are visible there, including those for the Windows Firewall.

> > > **N O T E**

> For many users, the Windows Firewall is more than enough protection against computer attacks. That said, most of the third-party firewalls just listed are more robust and offer more protection than Windows' built-in firewall—although you pay for that added functionality.

Securing a Wireless Home Network

An increasing number of households today have multiple computers, connected together via a simple home network. In most instances, that network is a wireless one, using radio frequency (RF) technology to transmit data from one computer to another.

One of the issues with a wireless network is that all your data is just out there, broadcast over the air via radio waves, for anyone to grab. You see, when you connect your computer to a network or to the Internet, not only can your PC access other computers, but other computers can also access *your* PC. Unless you take precautions, attackers (whether other network users or individuals on the Internet) can access your PC and steal important data, delete files and folders, or use your computer (via remote control) to attack other computers.

How to Protect Your Wireless Network from Attack

If the threat of unwanted intrusion scares you, that's good—you should be scared. Fortunately, you can take a number of steps to reduce your risk of attack and to minimize the impact if an intrusion does occur.

The key to protecting a network is to create as many obstacles as possible for a potential cracker. Although no network can be 100% secure, the more effort an attacker has to make, the more likely he'll give up and try a network that's easier to break into.

So how can you protect against unauthorized access to your wireless network? By using a little common sense, along with enabling basic security procedures, including the following:

- Activate the wireless security technology built into your Wi-Fi router. This wireless security, in the form of encrypted or password access, should keep all but the most dedicated hackers from accessing your wireless network.

- Change the default password for your wireless router. (You'd be surprised how many wireless networks can be accessed by entering the default "PASSWORD" password.)

- Change the default network name (also called a *service set identifier*, or *SSID*) of your wireless access router.

- Disable broadcast SSID function on your wireless router (if possible), so that the name of your network isn't publicly broadcast to the world at large.

- Physically locate your wireless router toward the center of your home or office—not near the windows, where it can extend the range of your network well outside your building.

- Install and activate a firewall program on every PC on your home network to block attacks from outside your network.

- Install and regularly update anti-virus and anti-spyware utilities on each PC on your network.

- Periodically check for firmware updates for the wireless router and for each network adapter on the network; updates often include enhanced security features.

- Deactivate file sharing on your PCs, so attackers won't be able to access your personal files.

- If your network is not going to be used for an extended time, turn off the wireless router

- Make regular backup copies of your important data—just in case.

We discuss most of these steps in the following sections.

Different Types of Wireless Security

Wireless security works by encrypting all data transmitted over the network. Decrypting network data requires the use of a network key. This network key may be generated automatically by your network router or adapter, or you may have to specify the key by typing it yourself. The longer the network key, the greater the encryption—and the more secure your wireless network will be.

There are four primary types of wireless security in use today. Here are the protocols available, with the most secure listed first:

- **WPA2**—WPA stands for Wi-Fi Protected Access, and the new WPA2 standard offers the strongest level of security available today. With WPA2 (and the older WPA standard), network keys are automatically changed on a regular basis.

- **WPA**—This is the older, slightly less secure version of Wi-Fi Protected Access security, still a good choice for securing most small networks.

- **WEP 128-bit**—*WEP* stands for *Wired Equivalent Privacy*. There are two levels of WEP protection: the stronger 128-bit and the weaker 64-bit.

- **WEP 64-bit**—This is the weakest level of wireless protection available. If you have an older laptop PC or wireless adapter, you may have to use this level of protection instead of WEP 128-bit or WPA/WPA2.

> > > **N O T E**

   WPA2 is supported in Windows Vista—but not yet by all wireless routers.

You should choose the highest level of protection supported by all the equipment on your network—your wireless router, wireless adapters, and notebook PCs. If just one piece of equipment doesn't support a higher level of security, you have to switch to the next-lowest level; the security level you choose has to fit the lowest common denominator, as defined by the wireless equipment in use.

So if your wireless router and all your wireless adapters and notebook PCs support WPA or WPA2 encryption, you should switch to that method because it provides the strongest protection. Otherwise, choose either WEP 128-bit (preferred) or WEP 64-bit encryption.

Enabling Wireless Security

Securing a wireless network is more challenging than securing a wired network. When you're transmitting network signals via radio waves, anyone within range can receive your signals. You need to secure those signals to keep outsiders from listening or breaking in to your network.

C A U T I O N ! ! !

Without some form of wireless security, anyone with a wireless PC can tap into your wireless network. At the very least, they can steal bandwidth from your Internet connection. Worst case, they might be able to access the personal files stored on your PC.

To keep outsiders from tapping into your wireless network, you can assign to your network a fairly complex encryption code, called a *network key*, via your wireless router's configuration settings. To access your network, a computer must know the code—which, unless it's officially part of your network, it won't.

There are several ways to assign a network key to your network. Most wireless routers come with configuration utilities that let you easily activate this type of wireless security, typically during the router's installation/setup process. In addition, you can use Windows' built-in wireless security function, which adds the same encryption via the operating system.

Configuring Your Home Network for Wireless Security

To set the wireless security for your network and assign network keys, you can use the setup utility that came with your wireless router. Alternately, you can configure Windows to manually assign network keys to each computer on your network.

In Windows Vista, you enable wireless security via the Set Up a Wireless Router or Access Point Wizard. To get to the wizard, open the Control Panel and select Network and Internet, Network and Sharing Center, and then Set Up a Connection or Network. In the next window, select Set Up a Wireless Router or Access Point. This launches the wizard.

Click the Next button until Windows automatically detects your network hardware and settings. From here you can give your network an SSID name (different from the name assigned in the Network Setup Wizard), and then either automatically assign or manually enter a network key or passphrase, as shown in Figure 23.2. The type and length of the key you choose depends on the type of encryption you choose, of course.

After the key is assigned, write it down. That's because you need to run this wizard on all the other PCs on the network and manually enter this same key for each computer. (Alternately, Windows lets you save the key to a USB drive, which you can then transfer to your other PCs.) After all the work is done, only those PCs that have been assigned this specific key can connect to your wireless network—which means no more neighbors leeching off your wireless connection.

> > > N O T E

Believe it or not, more than half of all wireless networks don't have wireless security enabled. You can verify this yourself by using a WiFi-equipped notebook to look for all available wireless networks in your neighborhood; any network labeled "unsecured" has no wireless security to protect it. Without wireless security, anyone within range can access the system with nothing more than a notebook PC—assuming that he knows the wireless network exists, that is. To that end, crackers have access to several programs that sniff out wireless networks, that they use on drive-by "war runs" to look for wireless networks to break into.

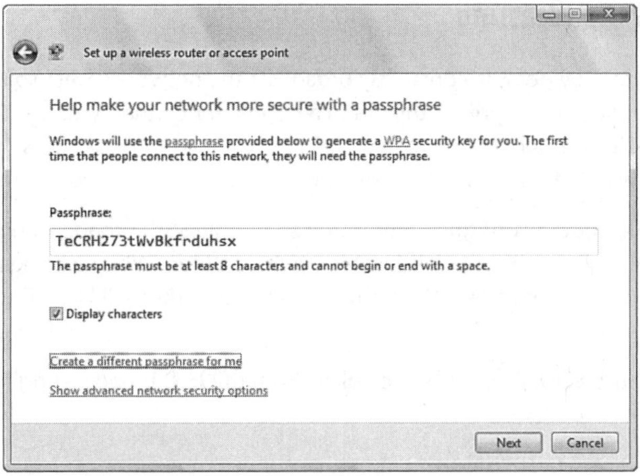

Figure 23.2
Assigning a network key in Windows Vista.

Changing Your Network's SSID and Password

Every wireless network has a name, otherwise known as its SSID (Service Set Identifier). The SSID is assigned by your wireless router.

Many router companies use their company names as the default SSID. For example, a Linksys router might have an SSID labeled "LINKSYS." This type of common SSID could give your network the same name as other wireless networks in your neighborhood, which makes it easy for hackers to locate and gain access to your network.

> > > **NOTE**

> Sometimes the router adds a unique number to this name, such as "LINKSYS123." This type of unique numbering is more secure than generic naming but still is easily hacked.

For this reason, you should override your router's default SSID and assign a more unique name to your wireless network. It's going to be tougher for a hacker to guess that your network is named "MIKE_NETWORK_1007" than if it was generically named "LINKSYS." You should be able to change the SSID from your router's configuration utility.

Along the same lines, you should also change the default password for your router. Most routers come from the factory with a simple password assigned; often, the password is "PASSWORD." As you might suspect, it's relatively easy for a hacker to access a network if the default password is still in use. So when you go to change the router's SSID, change the password, too. (And the longer and more complex the password you create, the more difficult it will be to hack.)

Disabling SSID Broadcasting

Most wireless routers, by default, constantly broadcast the network's SSID, so that all nearby computers know that the network is there and available for connection. The downside of this is that when an SSID is broadcast, anyone with a laptop PC or wireless access point receives notice of your network's name—which makes your network a more obvious target for hackers.

For this reason, you should configure your router to disable SSID broadcasting. If the SSID is not broadcast, your wireless network is less visible to outsiders. When a hacker doesn't immediately see your network on his list of nearby wireless networks, he'll likely find another network to tap into.

As with changing the SSID, you should be able to turn off SSID broadcasting from your router's configuration utility.

> > > **N O T E**

When you disable SSID broadcasting, your own wireless computers can't see your network either. This means you have to enter the SSID manually when you go to connect.

Is It Safe?

How safe are your personal computer and home network? If you follow the advice presented in this chapter, pretty safe. When you employ a combination of firewall and wireless security, you put up enough of a barrier to keep out all but the most dedicated crackers. And, unless a cracker really wants into your specific system (and why would he?), he'll quickly move on to another computer or network with lower security barriers.

This is one instance where a good defense works wonders. Make your home network difficult to attack, and attackers will leave you alone. You're simply not worth their trouble—which is a good thing.

Defending Your Company Network from Attack

In Chapter 23, "Defending Your Home Network from Attack," we discussed how to protect a typical home computer network from an Internet-based attack. The good news, if you're responsible for a larger company network, is that everything discussed in that chapter applies to your network—that is, you use many of the same methods to defend a large network as you do a smaller one.

Of course, you need to augment these basic security measures with enterprise-specific defenses, assuming that the attacks your business will face will be larger and more devastating than the typically smaller-scale attacks facing home computer users. In addition, you have more at stake when you're defending a large corporate network, so it makes sense to employ additional security measures. And, not surprisingly, the bigger your network, the more security you'll need.

Preparing for an Attack

The key to defending against and recovering from an attack on your company's network is to prepare for the eventuality of that attack ahead of time. We're not talking about the obvious technological defenses you need to enact; we get to those soon enough. No, we're talking about creating an incident response policy (IRP) so that the company's employees have clear guidance on what to do if the network is attacked.

Your company's preparation should be based on the assumption that the worst that can happen will happen; this worst case scenario drives all the elements of the IRP. If the worst happens and you're hit with a major attack, you'll know how to respond. If, on the other hand, good fortune blesses you and your company is hit with a less devastating attack, then that attack will be more easily handled.

Your IRP should be prepared by those individuals who will be directly dealing with any future attack, as well as management from key areas of your organization. It needs to be succinct, practical, and easy to implement. The plan should be based on input from all relevant departments in your organization, and address issues of importance to each department. In addition, the plan should be dynamic; it should be constantly revised as your organization changes over time and as new threats develop.

Now let's take a look at the key sections of an effective incident response policy.

Background and Objectives

It's important to lead off your plan with a section that explains the motivation and purpose behind the plan. For most companies, the objective is obvious: To effectively respond to attacks on the organization's digital infrastructure. This objective should be supported by a summary of that infrastructure and why it is vital to the organization's continuing operations.

Response Team Structure

Next, your plan should detail the composition of the company's Computer Emergency Response Team (CERT)—those individuals responsible to responding to said attacks. The purpose of the team should be explained, as well as its goals and responsibilities. Finally, the individuals or positions included in the team should be defined, as well as the responsibilities of each individual.

Incident Classification

In this section, you need to detail the types of incidents for which you're preparing. This may include computer fraud, computer abuse, Internet-based attacks, data theft, and the like. Each type of incident should be accompanied with an example of how it applies to your organization, and how major that type of incident is—that is, what type of response an incident of that type would warrant.

For each type of incident, you should include an escalation list. This list designates the individual responsibilities as an incident progresses and the degree of urgency increases. That is, some incidents get more important as they progress, and require additional attention from individuals higher up the escalation list.

Reporting

This section of the plan details the various types of data that should be gathered before, during, and after every incident. It should also address how this data will be processed and analyzed, and to whom the results will be presented. We're talking about log data, progress reports, incident documentation, and the like.

Business Continuity

One of the most crucial elements of the IRP is that of business continuity. In the event that a serious incident occurs, a decision to halt certain operations may need to be made. (For example, during a denial of service attack you may need to initiate a service outage to minimize the damage from the attack.) Who makes this decision, and under what circumstances? Who determines to bring the operations back online, and on what basis? All this needs to be clear, or you may end up with a situation with no one in charge.

Process Flow

Finally, your incident response policy needs to address what happens in the event of an attack—in excruciating detail. You should outline the steps that will occur from the first notice of an attack all the way through cleanup and recovery operations. Each step in the process should include not only what should be done, but who will be responsible for doing it.

< < < TIP

You may want to present your process flow in both text and diagram formats.

Defending Against a Network Attack

After you have your incident response policy in place, you need to start actively defending your network against the types of attack identified in the plan. The key to an effective defense is to create as many obstacles as possible for a potential attacker. No network can be 100% secure, but the more effort an attacker has to expend, the more likely he'll give up and try a network that's easier to break into.

This concept of multiple defenses is referred to as a Layered Security Architecture (LSA). With this approach, you should employ several different layers of protective software and hardware to protect your valuable network resources. These defenses might include some or all of the following:

- Firewall software
- Firewall hardware

- Proxy server

- Demilitarized zone

- Email gateway

- Intrusion detection system

In addition, you need a clear and comprehensive security policy, complete with restrictions about who can log on where (and how); requirements for strong, constantly changing passwords; and frequent backups of critical data. You have to assume that somewhere, sometime, someone will try to break into your network—and you have to be prepared.

Read on to learn more about these different network security solutions.

Employing a Firewall

As you learned in Chapter 23, a firewall is a piece of software or hardware that acts as a barrier between your network and the Internet. An effective firewall blocks unauthorized Internet traffic from accessing your network, thus cutting off most potential attacks before they ever reach your network's users.

Many different firewall programs are on the market today, from freeware personal firewalls to corporate-sized firewalls costing $5,000 or more. And although we tend to think of firewalls as software programs (especially in the home and small business areas), not all firewalls are software based. There are also hardware firewalls that create a physical barrier to Internet-based attacks.

> > > **N O T E**

> If you have a main firewall on your network, you don't need to activate individual firewall programs on each PC—although you can, if you want.

For small networks, you can obtain hardware firewall protection by investing in a network router with firewall features. For larger corporate networks, firewall hardware is typically complex and costly (in the thousands of dollars), and requires a working knowledge of network theory and administration to set up and keep running. For all this complexity, you get a very effective guardian; hardware firewalls are probably the best solution to thwarting attacks on corporate networks and websites.

Using Proxy Servers

A *proxy server* is a kind of buffer between the Internet and the individual computers on your network. When you use a proxy server, the PCs on your network don't access the Internet directly; instead they access web pages stored on the proxy server.

The way it works is that when a computer requests a web page, that request is filtered through the proxy server. It's actually the proxy server that makes the final request; the proxy server retrieves the requested page and stores it on its hard disk. The PC that originally requested the web page can now view that page because it resides on the proxy server.

> > > **N O T E**

The process of storing web pages on the proxy server is called *caching*.

When you use a proxy server, you prevent the computers on your network from coming into direct contact with the Internet. Outgoing messages and requests continue to move from the inside network to the outside world, but traffic from outside stops at the proxy.

Creating a Demilitarized Zone

If remote users—people not part of your network—need access to resources on your network, consider setting up a *demilitarized zone* (DMZ). In the network world, a DMZ is a part of your network that exists outside the firewall. Because it's on the other side of the barrier, any resources residing there can be accessed by computers outside your network.

You may want to create a DMZ if you're running a website or blog that accepts feedback from (or serves information to) the general user population. A DMZ is also useful if you're running an online business.

Setting up a DMZ is as easy as placing a computer between your Internet connection and your firewall. The DMZ computer remains part of your network, yet it's publicly accessible— and no one accessing the DMZ computer can gain further access to the rest of your network.

Activating an Email Gateway

An email gateway is like a proxy server for your network's Internet email. At its most basic, the gateway computer functions as an email server, handling the typical email storage and routing. In addition, the email gateway manages a variety of security functions—including virus scanning, attachment stripping, content filtering, spam blocking, and attack prevention.

With an email gateway installed, all outgoing email is filtered through the gateway and all incoming messages stop at and are processed by the gateway. No email comes directly from the outside world to your network's users; all messages are first processed by the gateway.

Employing a Network Intrusion Detection System

An intrusion detection system (IDS) monitors various system resources and activities, looking for signs of an outside intrusion or attack. The network version of this software is called, no surprise, a network intrusion detection system (NIDS), and is used to alert you to any intrusions to the network itself. When you're running a big network, or a real-time website with lots of traffic, installing NIDS software is must.

What does an IDS look for? Some of the activities that a good IDS monitors include IP protocol violations or anomalies, IP half scans, password attacks, and other unusual activities. Many IDS programs also use signature-based detection, which compares incoming traffic to the signatures of known intrusion techniques. (This is similar to the signature scanning technique used by most anti-virus programs.)

Some of the most popular NIDS programs include

- Dragon IDS (www.intrusion-detection-system-group.co.uk)

- CA Host-Based Intrustion Prevention System (www.ca.com)

- Check Point IPS-1 (www.checkpoint.com)

- IBM Proventia Network Intrusion Prevention System (www.ibm.com)

- Snort (www.snort.org)

- Symantec Endpoint Protection (www.symantec.com)

< < < **T I P**

If you run a large or medium-sized network, it's probably smart to install NIDS software. It's probably the most effective—and fastest way—to become aware of intrusions and attacks, as they're happening.

Defending Against Internal Security Breaches

Not all computer attacks come from outside the network. Some of the most serious threats are actually internal—from your own employees. According to one survey, 90% of security breaches come from within a company—with almost half of them perpetrated by the company's own network administrators. These internal security problems have many causes: human error, slipshod password protection, and the ever-reliable maliciousness of disgruntled employees.

Protection against internal error and attacks takes many forms. Security analysts recommend that every big company take the following preventive measures:

- Don't let any single person control your entire network—but also don't assign supervisory rights to more than a few individuals.

- Require that every single employee logging in to the network use a password—and that they change their passwords at least once a month.

- Back up the complete network on a weekly basis—and key data daily.

- Establish a strict sign-in/sign-out system for backup media—and make sure that the person in charge of the backup is not the same person in charge of the system.

- Store one copy of your backup media in a remote location.

- Keep the network servers in a physically secured area.

- Be aware of and install the latest security patches for the networking, server, and operating system software.

- Install intrusion detection software to alert administrators when the system is under attack.

- Install network monitoring software to alert administrators if a person is working on a different part of the network, or at a different time, than is usual.

- Have all IT personnel bonded.

- Be aware of any especially troubled or disgruntled employees, especially in the IT department, and especially if they have direct access to the network.

- For even larger networks, create an information security (IS) department, separate from the information technology (IT) department, reporting to the company's chief information officer (CIO) or chief technology officer (CTO).

- Allocate at least 5% of the company's overall IT budget to information security.

- If your network administrator leaves the company, change all the passwords on the system, confirm the existence of the current backup media, perform a new complete-system backup, and have the new network administrator do a complete check of system security—including scanning for the presence of backdoor programs.

In other words, trust no one—not even your own network administrators! Or, to be more politic, trust but verify; don't put any one person in a position where he or she can act unilaterally without some sort of supervision or safeguards. Whether out of maliciousness or carelessness, internal security breaches do occur, and you need to prevent against them.

Recognizing an In-Process Attack

You've prepared an incident response policy and put together a Computer Emergency Response Team. You've put all the necessary security measures in place, and installed firewalls, proxy servers, DMZs, and the like. But none of these things, unfortunately, prevents a cracker from trying to attack your system.

How do you know if your system is experiencing a real-time attack? A good network intrusion detection system helps alert you to an attack, but you should also be aware of any of the following network activities:

- **Unusual amount of hard disk activity on the network servers**—Although there are benign causes for unidentified hard disk activity (normal hard disk maintenance and cleanup, disk defragmenting, and so on), you need to be concerned if the servers' hard disks are operating at full bore for extended periods of time.

- **Unusual amount of Internet traffic**—If your company's Internet connection shows an unusually large amount of incoming or outgoing traffic, *something* is causing those bits and bytes to move back and forth. That something could be an attacker coming in or zombie activity going out—or the beginnings of a potentially devastating denial of service attack.

- **Unusual number of email messages**—If you notice that the company's incoming email server is being inundated with an unusually large number of messages in a short period of time, you could be the target of an email bomb attack—meaning some attacker is bombing the company's email servers.

- **Unusual amount of network traffic**—Just as an extreme amount of Internet activity can signal the presence of an intrusion, so can an unusually high amount of traffic over your company's internal network. Although there are normal causes for high traffic, the situation can also be caused by a backdoor intruder using a compromised PC to access computers across the entire network.

- **Unusual amount of website traffic**—If your company hosts its own website, a huge influx of traffic—far above your normal traffic levels—could be the tip-off that you're on the receiving end of a denial of service attack.

- **Changed or missing pages on your company's website**—If your company's website or blog suddenly sprouts graffiti on the home page, or links that don't go where you want them to go, then you could be the victim of website defacement.

- **Missing or changed files on your server**—If your data has been compromised in any way, it could be the result of an Internet attack or a virus attack.

- **Large number of port scans**—One surefire sign of an Internet attack is the presence of a large number of port scans. A port scan occurs when a potential intruder searches your computer for unprotected ports through which to enter your system; a successful port scan is often followed by the insertion of a backdoor file or other malicious code. Fortunately, most firewall programs monitor port scans, and alert you of unusual activity in this area. You can also install a separate port scan monitor, which monitors all the port activity on your system, looking for port scans from the outside. Although a certain number of port scans is to be expected anytime you're connected to the Internet, an undue number of scans, as well as scans of certain types, are indicative of a current or upcoming attack.

- **Presence of a sniffer program**—Another sign of attack is the unauthorized use of packet sniffer programs on the network. These are network monitoring programs commonly used to steal account and password information. Some intruders surreptitiously install sniffer software on your system, where it works in the background recording your user activity. The intruder can then reenter your system, retrieve the sniffer's log file, and have all your keystrokes and other activity right there, in black and white.

- **Unusual log file activity**—Most network servers come with utilities that create log files that capture all network activity. Many times you can discover an intrusion by examining these log files—which typically show all sorts of unexpected activity.

- **Firewall alerts**—Most firewall software and hardware not only defend against attacks, but also alert you when an attack is taking place. In addition, your firewall's log file is a terrific tool for identifying all sorts of attacks.

Realizing that an attack is in progress is more difficult than you might think, as only certain types of attacks actually shut down your system. Most attacks are of the backdoor type, and are typically discovered in retrospect.

As noted, one sure sign that your system is being attacked is the presence of unusual system activity—lots of server access or Internet traffic. You can also rely on your firewall or NIDS software to alert you of an attack. In short, you should always be on the lookout for signs of unusual activity. Most intrusions require your system to work harder than it typically does when idle, so this type of unexpected activity is a good sign that something untoward is afoot.

Dealing with and Recovering from a Serious Attack

You've done your best to ward off unwanted attacks, but your best wasn't good enough; your network intrusion detection system has just alerted you that a large-scale attack is in progress.

Now what do you do?

If you discover that your network is the victim of an ongoing Internet-based attack, the first thing you want to do is stop the attack; then you can repair any damage done and bring your network back online. Follow these steps:

1. Disconnect your system or network from the Internet, which should break off the attack.

2. After you're offline, run a round of system diagnostics. You should also run a virus scan, particularly looking for backdoor Trojan programs that might have been installed during the attack. In addition, look for evidence of any sniffer software that the attacker may have installed.

3. Examine your network's log files, or use backtracing software, to try to identify the source of the attack.

4. Repair any damage to affected PCs—and remove any backdoor software found. (This is also the time to restore any deleted or damaged data from your backup copies.)

CAUTION!!!

Be cautious about restoring operating system data from backups. The backup could contain the same backdoor program that enabled the attack in the first place.

5. Examine all other PCs on your network—and any PCs that connect to your network via remote access or VPN. After an attacker is inside your network, all machines are at risk—and could be used to hold more backdoors for future use.

6. Change all passwords used to access the network and individual PCs. This keeps the intruder from reentering your system, if he happens to have access to a previous password.

7. Report the attack to proper authorities, such as the CERT Coordination Center (irf.cc.cert.org). You may also want to report the attack to your local authorities.

8. Reconnect the network to the Internet.

9. Closely monitor all Internet traffic to determine whether the attack is still ongoing; if so, you may need to go offline again for the duration.

After you're back online, you may find that you're still being attacked. (This is likely if you're the victim of a denial of service attack.) If you have the proper software, you can block access to your site from specific domains, which the software should be able to identify; this blocks the heaviest attackers. If this is beyond your capabilities, go back offline and then contact your ISP or website hosting service and alert them of the attack. They'll take things from there.

By the way, some experts recommend a more extreme response to an attack, especially an attack on a large network or website. They recommend, while your network is offline, that you install a clean version of your operating system, and then do a program-by-program security check, downloading and installing all relevant security patches. The thinking behind this approach is that an attacker could delete or modify virtually every file on your system, and thus the only way to trust that your system is free from sleeper and backdoor programs is to reinstall the entire operating system from scratch.

Is It Safe?

Here's the disheartening news: You can never completely protect your organization's network from attack. If someone wants to attack your system, there's nothing you can do to stop them.

Sorry.

That said, you can make it more difficult for that attack to succeed. You can also plan an effective response to any attack that might take place.

So, although your company's network may never be completely safe, you can minimize the potential damage from any outside attack. It takes a lot of hard work to harden your system, but it can and should be done. Just remember how much damage can result from a successful attack—the damaged or destroyed files, the downtime, the lost productivity, the bad PR—and you'll see why it's worth investing the time and money in attack prevention and recovery.

Defending Your Website from Attack

If you have your own website or blog, you're at special risk of attack. Any website—no matter how small or large—can be attacked and hacked, in a number of different and disquieting ways.

Some of the biggest sites on the web have been attacked, as have some of the smallest. You need to know what types of attacks are most common, and how to reduce your site's risk of attack.

How Can Your Website Be Attacked?

You've spent the time and money to create a first-class website, easy on the eye and full of useful content. The last thing you want to hear is that some hacker or cracker has targeted your site for attack, and that the site has been forced offline.

To be fair, many so-called website attacks are actually website *hacks*—attempts, successful or not, to alter the site's content. In this scenario, you wake up one morning to find your site's home page replaced by a page full of pay-per-click advertisements, or discover that clicking a link on your site downloads a spyware program to the visitor's computer. It may be a hack, but it feels like you've been attacked.

Let's spend a little time examining the most common types of website hacks and attacks. It pays to know what the enemy might have planned.

Cross Site Scripting

Cross site scripting, or XSS, is a form of website hack that enables an attacker to embed malicious code into a dynamic webpage on your site. This code is used to fool site visitors into entering personal data—which is then transmitted back to the hacker, to be used for identity theft and other disreputable purposes. Some experts say that a quarter or more of all website hacks involve cross site scripting—which makes it one of the biggest problems for websites today.

There are two kinds of pages on the web. A web page you design in advance and that always looks the same is called a *static page*; a page that is generated on the fly based on user input or other factors is called a *dynamic page*. It's these dynamic pages that are vulnerable to cross site scripting.

> > > **NOTE**

Static web pages are not vulnerable to cross site scripting.

As you probably know, a web page contains both text content and HTML code that defines the look and feel of the page. Cross site scripting works by embedding malicious JavaScript, VBScript, ActiveX, HTML, or Flash code into the dynamically generated HTML. This malicious code is typically used to generate a misleading link in the page's content; a visitor clicking this link is taken to a separate web page and phished for personal information, or perhaps has malware of some sort automatically downloaded to his computer.

Any website that has dynamic pages based on parameters passed to a database can be vulnerable to this technique. This means any form-based page can be at risk, including login pages, "forgot your password?" pages, guestbook pages, data input pages, and the like.

The risk of XSS hacks is big; any site that serves up personalized pages is vulnerable. That means profile pages on MySpace and Facebook, account management pages on eBay and Amazon, personalized home pages on Yahoo! and Google, you name it. In fact, all these websites and more—including the CNN.com, Apple Computer, Microsoft, and FBI.gov sites—are potentially vulnerable. Every month one to two dozen XSS holes are found in large websites, and as the number of dynamic pages increases, the problem will just get worse.

SQL Injection

Another popular form of website hack is called *SQL injection*. This type of attack takes advantage of improper coding of web applications to inject SQL commands into a web page form to gain access to the data held in the underlying database.

> > > **NOTE**

SQL stands for Structured Query Language, and is used to retrieve and manage data in many relational database management systems.

SQL injection takes advantage of the fact that fields designed for user input also allow SQL statements to pass through and query the database directly. A clever hacker can enter an SQL query into a form that asks for username or other data; that query then passes to the database and returns the asked-for information. In essence, this lets the hacker pull just about any data out of the website's database, which could include usernames, passwords, and all manner of personal data.

You see, most large websites use behind-the-scenes databases to store all sorts of visitor data. A site that requires password login uses the database to store usernames and passwords. Other sites might store other data entered by visitors, including real names, addresses, credit card numbers, and the like.

Normally this database is isolated behind several different layers of firewalls; the end user never sees it. But if a hacker can surreptitiously pass a command or query to the database, he can retrieve any or all data stored there.

Let's look at the example of a typical login page, where a legitimate user would enter his username and password to gain access to the site. When a user submits this information, an SQL query is generated from this data and submitted to the database for verification. If the data is valid, the user is allowed access.

A hacker using SQL injection, however, doesn't enter the expected information when faced with this login page. Instead, he enters a specific SQL query; the query is passed to the database as if it were username and password data. But the database doesn't know the difference, and treats the injected query the same way it would the normally generated query: It processes it. So whatever the hacker asks via the query, the database returns.

The sheer simplicity of the SQL injection technique has fueled its popularity. It can be applied to any poorly designed input form on a web page—including search forms—and used to pull any sensitive data stored in the database. (Yes, we're talking more identity theft and the like.)

> > > **N O T E**

A properly designed input form includes security measures that block queries to the database submitted in this sort of unexpected fashion.

Authentication Hacking

As you learned in Chapter 22, "Computer Attacks: How Big a Problem?," website hijacking is a major problem. The problem arises when a hacker gains access to the site's underlying HTML code and somehow alters it. The result is a web page or site that has been defaced or altered to the hacker's pleasure.

The question, then, is how does one hijack a website? After all, the site administrator has to enter a username and password to access the site's code, and site administrators don't readily hand out their passwords. How does the hacker gain access?

The key to gaining administrator access to a website is to somehow steal or guess or otherwise obtain the administrator's authentication information—his username and password. Then the hacker can log in as the administrator and make any changes to the site he so desires.

CAUTION

Computers don't recognize people, only usernames and passwords. A web server grants control of a website to whomever enters the correct authentication—even if that person is only pretending to be the administrator. The server doesn't know any different.

How can a hacker gain control of an administrator's username and password? The most common method is simple password cracking, using special cracking software to automatically guess the password. Such software typically utilizes a combination of dictionary cracking (applying a long list—or dictionary—of common words) and brute force cracking (where the software applies all possible combinations of numbers, letters, and symbols). One way or another, the password is guessed—although, to be fair, the longer and more sophisticated the password, the longer it takes to guess it.

After the hacker has entered the correct username and password, he's inside the website— and can do just about anything he wants. (Or anything the administrator is allowed to do, at any rate.) That might mean deleting web pages, uploading new pages, altering existing pages, you name it. If he's smart, the hacker can even change the administrator password, so that the real administrator can't get in to undo the damage!

Directory Traversal Attacks

Here's a neat little hack that takes advantage of poorly designed websites. In these sites, a user can gain unauthorized access to a closed part of the site by entering through an open page— kind of like going in through a backdoor.

A *directory traversal* attack takes advantage of an HTTP exploit that enables attackers to access restricted directories outside the web server's root directory. Normally, users are confined to the root directory on the website's server, and can't access anything above this root. For example, the default root directory of Microsoft's Internet Information Services (IIS) server is c:\Inetpub\wwwroot\; under normal conditions, a user has access to only this directory and any subdirectories underneath. The user cannot access c:\Inetpub\ or any other same-level directories on the c:\ drive.

To perform a directory traversal attack, the attacker uses his web browser to directly access a directory above the website's root by manually entering the path into the browser's address bar. Of course, he also needs to know the name of the directory he wants to access, but this information is easily enough obtained.

When the attacker enters the server above the root directory, he has access to all manner of system files and commands. He can, theoretically, use these system commands to delete individual web pages, copy new files on top of existing ones, and otherwise compromise the website and the hosting system.

> > > **NOTE**

Fortunately, properly designed servers and sites require password access above the root directory. It's only those systems that don't restrict access in this fashion that are vulnerable to directory traversal attacks.

Denial of Service Attacks

Finally, we have our old friend, the denial of service (DoS) attack. As you recall, a DoS attack occurs when an attacker utilizes hundreds of hijacked computers to effectively "bomb" a website with information requests. The huge increase in incoming traffic overloads the site's server, effectively forcing the site offline.

There's no need to go into additional detail on DoS attacks here. To refresh your memory, turn to that section in Chapter 22 for more information.

Defending Against Website Hacks and Attacks

Now that you know the many ways your site can be hacked and attacked, how do you defend against such threats? As you might suspect, it's a combination of technological defense and common sense—and, as in most cases, common sense is perhaps the most important component.

Defending Against a General Attack

You can do a few general things to reduce your risk of most types of website attack. Again, it's mostly common sense—or, in this case, routine maintenance.

For example, you should always keep your website software updated to the latest version. The latest version includes patches to fix known security holes, and it's these holes that make your site more vulnerable. That means, of course, updating all the software you use, including the HTML editor, content management system, and all third-party add-ins and modules—especially modules for web forms and user input.

You should also do everything you can to "harden" your site's publishing platform. Limit access to the site's code and software, and plug all known outside holes. Make sure your site's server is free of viruses, spyware, and other malware. And if your site uses a database, make sure that database is fully secure.

Finally, don't let an attacker take your site completely offline. Make a daily (or hourly) backup of the entire site code, so you can use that backup to get your site up and running again in the event of a catastrophic hack or attack.

Employing a Web Vulnerability Scanner

It's also a good idea to use a web vulnerability scanner. This is a software utility that crawls all the pages on your website and then reports which URLs and scripts are vulnerable to attack, so you can fix the problem.

Some of the most popular Web vulnerability scanners include the following:

- Acunetix Web Vulnerability Scanner (www.acunetix.com)
- Nikto (www.cirt.net/nikto2/)
- N-Stalker (www.nstalker.com)
- Paros Proxy (www.parosproxy.org)
- Watchfire AppScan (www.watchfire.com)
- Wikto (www.sensepost.com/research/wikto/)

Defending Against Cross Site Scripting

It's actually quite simple to defend against cross site scripting. One of the keys is to use a web vulnerability scanner to crawl your entire website and check for XSS vulnerabilities. You also need to apply filters to all web-based input forms. In particular, you need to filter out all metacharacters by converting them to their hex equivalents during the query submission process. Table 25.1 shows the most common metacharacters and their hex equivalents.

Table 25.1 Hex Equivalents of Metacharacters

Metacharacter	Hex equivalent
"	&#34
'	&#39
#	&#35
&	&#38
(	&#40
)	&#41
<	&lt
>	&gt

Defending Against SQL Injection

You can defend against SQL injection by specifying valid types of input for all the user input forms on your site's web pages. Specify, for example, that a valid input for a password field has to include eight alphanumeric characters, and the longer input necessary for successful SQL injection will be rejected as invalid.

You can supplement this whitelist strategy by also employing blacklists of specifically disallowed inputs. Create a blacklist of sample SQL query patterns, and make sure they're blocked from reaching your database.

> > > **NOTE**

A *whitelist* is a list of allowable items. A *blacklist* is a list of items that aren't allowed.

Finally, it's always a good idea to encrypt the data in all your databases. This way, if a hacker does initiate a successful SQL injection attack, the data he retrieves is encrypted—and thus unusable.

Defending Against Authentication Hacking

The best defense against authentication hacking involves employing longer and more secure passwords. To stop brute-force cracking, you can also add some form of random content on the page presented to the authenticating browser. This is typically in the form of a *captcha*—a randomly generated sequence of characters presented as a graphics file, like the one in Figure 25.1. The administrator is required to read the captcha and manually enter it into an authentication form; even if the administrator's password is cracked, the cracking program can't read and enter the captcha code.

Figure 25.1
Add an additional layer of authentication with a graphic captcha code.

> > > **NOTE**

Because the captcha is a graphic image, it's not readable by software programs that can otherwise capture regular text strings.

Defending Against Directory Traversal Attacks

Protection against a directory traversal attack is similar to that used against cross site scripting: You need to filter metacharacters from user input. This ensures that unauthorized commands can't get submitted to your server.

In addition, make sure you've installed the latest version of your web server software, with all appropriate patches applied. Most current web servers should have this potential exploit corrected.

Defending Against Denial of Service Attacks

As you've learned elsewhere in this book, denial of service attacks are particularly harmful; they can take your entire system offline in a matter of minutes. Unfortunately, there's little you can do to defend against or prevent such an attack; if an attacker wants to target you with hundreds of thousands of data requests, there's nothing stopping him from doing so.

That said, if you find your site victim to a DoS attack, you can take your system offline for a brief period of time, determine which computers on the Internet are launching the attacks, and block access from those computers.

Recovering from a Website Attack

What do you do if your website is hacked or attacked? The specific instructions vary by type of attack, but the general sequence of actions mirror those discussed in Chapter 24, "Defending Your Company Network from Attack," with a few slight differences.

Here's what you need to do:

1. Disconnect your website from the Internet, which should break off the attack. If you lease server space from a web hosting service, you may want to give them a call and alert them to your attack—they may be able to block the attack from their end.

2. After you're offline, run a round of system diagnostics. You should also run a virus scan, particularly looking for backdoor Trojan programs that might have been installed during the attack.

3. Examine your site's log files, or use backtracing software, to try to identify the source of the attack. If you're experiencing a DoS attack, block access to the offending IP addresses or domains, at least for a short period of time.

4. Repair any damage to affected server—and remove any backdoor software found.

5. Examine all the pages and related files on your site for any changes—no matter how subtle. Replace or restore any missing or vandalized files, make any necessary system repairs, then prepare to go back online.

< < < **TIP**

If your system was compromised at the root level, you may need to fully reinstall the system because it will be difficult if not impossible to remove all the hidden files the attacker has placed on your system.

6. Examine your site's underlying database(s); assume the worst, and look for data deletion, data diddling, and the like. If necessary, restore the database from a backup copy.

7. Change all passwords used to access the server. This keeps the intruder from reentering your system with a cracked password.

8.   Report the attack to proper authorities, such as the CERT Coordination Center (irf.cc.cert.org). You may also want to report the attack to your local authorities.

9.   Reconnect the server to the Internet.

10. Closely monitor all Internet traffic to determine whether the attack is still ongoing; if so, you may need to go offline again for the duration.

The appropriate response is one of calm, deliberate action. Don't panic, work quickly, but take the time you need to fully understand the nature and extent of the attack. It will probably take you longer to fix a hack or attack than the attack took in the first place. That's to be expected, especially if you have a large site with many pages. (And dynamic pages make your task even more difficult.)

Just remember, determine what happened, repair the damage, and then work hard to prevent a similar type of attack in the future.

Is It Safe?

Large or small, no website can be completely safe from hack or attack. If an attacker wants to take down your site, he can probably do so—for a brief period of time. And although you can guard against most forms of site hacks and hijacks, a determined hacker can make you work hard to defend your site.

Is your website safe? It's certainly safer if you keep all your underlying software and services up to date, if you install all the latest patches and security fixes, and if you take particular precautions against the most common types of hacks—cross site scripting and SQL injection. But, as you've learned throughout this book, there's no such thing as being 100% risk-free.

To that end, make sure you know what to do if your site *is* attacked. Quite often, a detailed disaster response policy is more important than a seemingly bullet-proof defense.

J - K - L

M

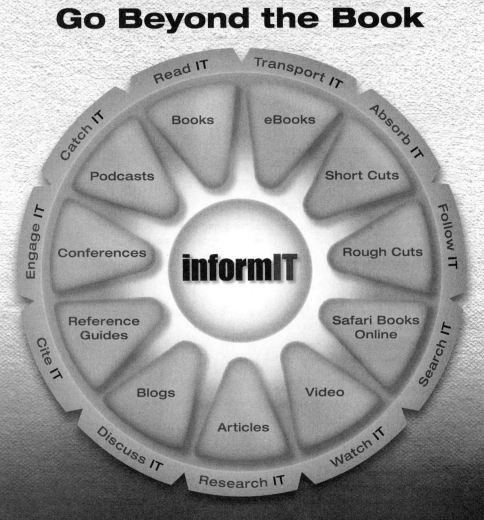